BIOGRAPHICAL QUESTIONNAIRES OF 150 PROMINENT TENNESSEANS

Compiled by
John Trotwood Moore

Colleen Morse Elliott
Editor

SOUTHERN HISTORICAL PRESS
%The Rev. S. Emmett Lucas, Jr.
P. O. Box 738
Easley, South Carolina 29640

ISBN 0-89308-222-8

PREFACE

This collection consists of 150 biographical questionnaires sent to prominent Tennesseans around 1920 by the State Librarian and Archivist, John Trotwood Moore. These questionnaires were returned by 1922 either by the person contacted, or in case of death, by a member of their family. They contain information on place and date of birth, names of the parents and ancestry, education, profession, official positions, their political and religious affiliations, organizational memberships, books or other types of publications written, names of spouses and children and their marriages when applicable, and military service.

There are a number of newspaper articles included with the material, photographs and many additional pages written by the persons returning the questionnaires. The photographs are not included in this book, but the newspaper articles were abstracted in order to benefit the text.

The reader should be aware that not all these persons were always in the state of Tennessee. There are many states represented here and the ancestry records cover a large area of Europe. There are several women included who answered the questionnaire - Saraphina Shannon Baxter, Mrs. John C. Brown, Hulda Jerusha (Woodmansee) Easterley, an old-time midwife, Zilpha Wyatt Flynn, Marion Scudder Griffin, who practiced Law when it was finally permitted in 1907, Rachel Jackson Lawrence, a descendant of Andrew Jackson, Sophia Key Malone, Paralee Matilda (Robertson) Musgrove, Clara L. White and Jennie Williamson. There is a questionnaire returned by a one-time slave, A. H. Officer. Letters written from other persons regarding the personal acquaintance of some of the people concerned with the questionnaires.

Several types of questionnaire forms were used - both the original sent by Mr. Moore and several used when he sent the Civil War Veterans forms, which were two different forms, and one used for the females to sign. This last was not included in full on the microfilm, therefore we have tried to form their answers into a format to supplement this lack.

The questionnaires are placed at the beginning of the text for easy perusal with any additional questions included. The microfilm used here may be found in the Manuscripts Section, Tennessee State Library and Archives and was revised by them on November 15, 1974.

Some were well educated, some were not; many were Pioneers into the state of Tennessee. Some were Legislators, Senators and other persons of important position. Many more were well known for their family connections, others were simple citizens who had lived to a very old age. Little editing has been done to the original material, only where deemed necessary to make reading easier.

Colleen Morse Elliott
Fort Worth, Texas 1981

Form used on Biographical Memoranda Questionnaire:

1. Full name: (do not use initials)
2. Present P. O.: (give last address, with date of death, if dead)
3. Exact date and place of birth: on_______at_____in the county of_____ State of_____:
4. Full name of your father:__________born at_____in the county of_____ State of_____; He lived at___________.
   Give also any particulars concerning him, as official position, war service, etc.; books written by, etc.______.
   He was the son of_____(full name)___and his wife_____(full name)____ who lived at_______.
5. Maiden name in full of your mother:_____. She was the daughter of _____(full name)_____ and his wife _____(full name)_____, who lived at __________.
6. Remarks on ancestry. Give here any and all facts possible in reference to your parents, grand-parents, great-grand-parents, etc., not included in the foregoing, as to where they lived, offices held, Revolutionary or other war service; what country the family came from to America, where first settled, county and State; always giving full names (if possible) and never referring to an ancestor simply as such without giving the name. It is desirable to include every fact possible, and to that end the full and exact record from old Bibles should be appended on seperate sheets of this size, thus preserving the facts from loss:_______________.
7. Early education - where obtained, incidents, names of teachers:_____
8. College education - where attended, and year of graduation, with college honors and degrees:__________
9. Professional education, if any - where obtained, date of graduation, with degrees:__________
10. Profession or occupation - date entered upon, where practiced, and incidents of:__________
11. Every civil office held - city, county, state or national, with the exact dates as far as possible. If ever a member of the Legislature, give date of session:__________
12. Miscellaneous: Reform movements, influence on affairs, etc.:_______
13. Political party - official position, committee work, etc.:________
14. Church connection - with official position, if any:______________
15. If a member of the Masons, Odd Fellows, or other secret order, give names, with official position, if any:____________
16. Titles of books written or edited. Give exact copy of title page, with the number of pages the book contains:__________
17. Maiden name in full of your wife, with date and place of marriage: _______.
    She was the daughter of ____(full name)____ and his wife____(full name)_____, who lived at __________. Give also other and full particulars of wife's ancestry, as far as possible:______________
18. Military Record: (1) Exact rank:____(2) Name of command and commanders:____;(3) Date and places of service:____(4) Heroic or trying incidents personal to your service, all as full as possible, and if necessary on seperate sheets of paper:____.
19. Full list of children (if any) of the subject of this sketch, with full names of husbands or wives of each, in case of marriage, with present place of residence and P. O., numbering them in regular order, viz: 1.________
    ____
    ____

The foregoing data was prepared by________________________

name

Date:__________

____

address

Form #1-Veteran's Questionnaire:

1. State your full name and present Postoffice address:_______________
2. State your age now:__________
3. In what State and County were you born?__________
4. In what State and County were you living when you enlisted in the service of the Confederacy, or of the Federal Government?__________
5. What was your occupation before the war?__________
6. What was the occupation of your father?__________
7. If you owned land or other property at the opening of the war, state what kind of property you owned, and state the value of your property as near as you can__________
8. Did you or your parents own slaves? If so, how many?__________
9. If your parents owned land, state about how many acres__________
10. State as near as you can the value of all the property owned by your parents, including land, when the war opened__________
11. What kind of a house did your parents occupy? State whether it was a log house or frame house or built of other material, and state the number of rooms it had__________
12. As a boy and young man, state what kind of work you did. If you worked on a farm, state to what extent you plowed, worked with a hoe and did other kinds of similar work. (Certain historians claim that white men wouldn't do work of this sort before the war.)__________
13. State clearly what kind of work your father did, and what the duties of your mother were. State all the kinds of work done in the house as well as you can remember - that is, cooking, spinning, weaving, etc.__________
14. Did your parents keep any servants? If so, how many?__________
15. How was honest toil - as plowing, hauling and other sorts of honest work of this class - regarded in your community? Was such work considered respectable and honorable?__________
16. Did the white men in your community generally engage in such work?__
17. To what extent were there white men in your community leading lives of idleness and having others do their work for them?__________
18. Did the men who owned slaves mingle freely with those who did not own slaves, or did slaveholders in any way show by their actions that they felt themselves better than respectable, honorable men who did not own slaves?__________
19. At the churches, at the schools, at public gatherings in general, did the slaveholders and non-slaveholders mingle on a footing of equality?__________
20. Was there a friendly feeling between slaveholders and non-slaveholders in your community, or were they antagonistic to each other?_____
21. In a political contest in which one candidate owned slaves and the other did not, did the fact that one candidate owned slaves help him any in winning the contest?__________
22. Were the opportunities good in your community for a poor young man, honest and industrious, to save up enough to buy a small farm or go in business for himself?__________
23. Were poor, honest, industrious young men, who were ambitious to make something of themselves, encouraged or discouraged by slaveholders?
24. What kind of school or schools did you attend?__________
25. About how long did you go to school altogether?__________
26. How far was it to the nearest school?__________
27. What school or schools were in operation in your neighborhood?_____
28. Was the school in your community private or public?__________
29. About how many months in the year did it run?__________
30. Did the boys and girls of your community attend school pretty regularly?__________
31. Was the teacher of the school you attended a man or a woman?_______
32. In what year and month and at what place did you enlist in the service of the Confederacy or of the Federal government?__________
33. State the name of your regiment, and state the names of as many members of your company as you remember__________
34. After enlistment, where was your company sent?__________
35. How long after your enlistment before your company engaged in battle?
36. What was the first battle you engaged in?__________
37. State in your own way your experience in the war from this time on to the close. State where you went after the first battle - what you did, what other battles you engaged in, how long they lasted,

(Q. #37 - From #1, cont'd):
- what the results were; state how you lived in camp, how you were clothed, how you slept, what you had to eat, how you were exposed to cold, hunger, and disease. If you were in hospital or prison, state your experience here.__________

38. When and where were you discharged?__________
39. Tell something of your trip home__________
40. What kind of work did you take up when you came back home?__________
41. Give a sketch of your life since the close of the Civil War. Stating what kind of business you have engaged in, where you have lived, your church relations, etc. If you have held any office or offices, state what it was. You may state here any other facts connected with your life and experience which has not been brought out by the questions.
42. Give full name of your father__________born at________in the county of________State of__________. He lived at__________. Give also any particulars concerning him, as official position, war services, etc. Books written by, etc.__________.
43. Maiden name in full of your mother______. She was the daughter of______ and his wife______, who lived at__________.
44. Remarks on ancestry. Give here any and all facts possible in reference to your parents, grandparents, great-grandparents, etc. not included in the foregoing, as where they lived, offices held, Revolutionary or other war service; what country the family came from to America; where first settled, county and state; always giving full names (if possible), and never referring to an ancestor simpy as such without giving the name. It is desirable to include every fact possible, and to that end the full and exact record from old Bibles should be appended on separate sheets of this size, thus preserving the facts from loss.__________

Form #2-Veteran's Questionnaire:

1. State your full name and present postoffice address__________
2. State your age now__________
3. In what State and county were you born?__________
4. Were you a Confederate or Federal soldier?__________
5. Name of your Company______(B) Number of Regiment__________
6. What was the occupation of your father?__________
7. Give full name of your father__________born at______in the County of______State of______. He lived at______. Give also any particulars concerning him, as official position, war services, etc. Books written by, etc.______
8. Maiden name in full of your mother______. She was the daughter of______and his wife______. Who lived at__________.
9. Remarks on Ancestry. Give here any and all facts possible in reference to your parents, grandparents, great-grandparents, etc. not included in the foregoing, as where they lived, offices held, Revolutionary or other war services; what country the family came from to America; first settled, county and State; always giving full names (if possible) and never referring to an ancestor simply as such without giving the name; it is desirable to include every fact possible, and to that end the full and exact record from old Bibles should be appended on seperate sheets of this size, thus preserving the facts from loss.__________
10. If you owned land or other property at the opening of the war, state what kind of property you owned, and state the value of your property as near as you can.__________
11. Did you or your parents own slaves? If so, how many?__________
12. If your parents owned land, state about how many acres__________
13. State as near as you can the value of all the property owned by your parents, including land, when the war opened__________
14. What kind of house did your parents occupy? State whether it was a log house or frame house or built of other material, and state the number of rooms it had.__________
15. As a boy and young man, state what kind of work you did. If you worked on a farm, state to what extent you plowed, worked with a hoe and did other kinds of similar work. (Certain historians claim that white men would not do work of this sort before the war.)
16. State clearly what kind of work your father did, and what the duties

(Q. #16-Form #2, cont'd.):
- of your mother were. State all the kinds of work done in the house as well as you can remember - that is, cooking, spinning, weaving, etc.____

17. Did your parents keep any servants? If so, how many?________
18. How was honest toil - such as plowing, hauling and other sorts of honest work of this class - regarded in your community? Was such work considered respectable and honorable?__________
19. Did the white men in your community generally engage in such work?
20. To what extent were there white men in your community leading lives of idleness and having others do their work for them?_________
21. Did the men who owned slaves mingle freely with those who did not own slaves, or did slaveholders in any way show by their actions that they felt themselves better than respectable, honorable men who did not own slaves?_________
22. At the churches, at the schools, at public gatherings in general,did the slaveholders and non-slaveholders mingle on a footing of equality?_________
23. Was there a friendly feeling between slaveholders and non-slaveholders in your community, or were they antagonistic to each other?_____
24. In a political contest in which one candidate owned slaves and the other did not, did the fact that one candidate owned slaves help him any in winning the contest?________
25. Were the opportunities good in your community for a poor young man, honest and industrious, to save up enough to buy a small farm or go in business for himself?________
26. Were poor, honest, industrious young men, who were ambitious to make something of themselves, encouraged or discouraged by slaveholders?
27. What kind of school or schools did you attend?_______
28. About how long did you go to school altogether?______
29. How far was it to the nearest school?_______
30. What school or schools were in operation in your neighborhood?_____
31. Was the school in your community private or public?_______
32. How many months in the year did it run?_______
33. Did the boys and girls in your community attend school pretty regularly?________
34. Was the teacher of the school you attended a man or woman?_______
35. In what year and month and at what place did you enlist in the service of the Confederacy or of the Federal government?________
36. After enlistment, where was your company sent first?_________
37. How long after enlistment before your company engaged in battle?___
38. What was the first battle you engaged in?_______
39. State in your own way your experience in the war from this time to its close. State where you went after the first battle, what you did and what other battles you engaged in, how long they lasted, what the results were; state how you lived in camp, how you were clothed,how you slept, what you had to eat, how you were exposed to cold, hunger and disease. If you were in hospital or prison, state your experience here._______
40. When and where were you discharged?_______
41. Tell something about your trip home_______
42. What kind of work did you take up when you came back home?_______
43. Give a sketch of your life since the close of the Civil War, stating what kind of business you have engaged in, where you have lived,your church relations, etc. If you have held any office or offices, state what it is. You may state here any other facts connected with your life and experiences which has not been brought out by the questions.
44. On a separate sheet give the names of some of the great men you have known or met in your time, and tell some of the circumstances of the meeting or incidents in their lives. Also add any further personal reminiscences. (Use all the space you want.)_____________
45. Give the names of all the members of your company you can remember. (If you know where the Roster is to be had, please make note of this)
46. Give the NAME and POST OFFICE Address of living Veterans of the Civil War, whether members of your company or not, whether Tennesseans or from other States:

NAME	POSTOFFICE	STATE
__________________	________________________	_______________

ALLISON, JULIAN MATT (1877-1948)
Form signed and dated: June 2, 1922 (Biographical)

1. Julian M. Allison
2. Belfast #5
3. Oct. 20, 1877; 19 Dist., Bedford co., Tennessee
4. Dr. Marks W. Allison; 19th Dist., Bedford co., Tenn.; 19th Dist. near Belfast all of his life; he practiced medicine for 45 yrs.; entered war Oct. 15, 1861 and stayed until close. Worked in hospital and as field surgeon; Par.: Thomas H. Allison and Sallie Smith, Bedford co.
5. Margaret Elizabeth (Tucker), dau. of Allen C. Tucker and Elizabeth Bugg, Marshall co.
6. My grand-father was Allen C. Tucker, was borned in Williamson co., who was the son of William Tucker who was of Scotch Irish descent. Was borned in North Carolina. My grandfather Thomas H. Allison the son of James Allison was of Scotch-Irish descent who was born in North Carolina. He married Sallie Smith who was of English descent.
7. -----
8. -----
9. -----
10. farmer
11. I have been Magistrate for 10 years and was a member of the Legislature in 1921.
12. -----
13. Democrat; serve on following committees - charitable institutions, municipal affairs, penitentery, public grounds and bldgs., public roads, railroads, redistricting, retrenchment.
14. Cumberland Presbyterian, Elder and sunday school Superintendent
15. Mason and Odd Fellows. Fill all of the chairs of Odd Fellows and represent the lodge in 1911-12. I am now Senior Warden of Masons.
16. -----
17. not married
18. -----
19. -----

AMIS, JONAS THOMAS (1860-)
Form signed and dated: July 14, 1922 (Biographical)

1. Jonas Thomas Amis
2. Franklin, Tenn.
3. July 12, 1860; Jacksonport, Jefferson co., Arkansas
4. John Erastus Amis; Culleoka, Maury co., Tenn.; Culleoka, Tenn. until some time after his marriage then first moved to Phillips co., Ark., then to Jacksonport, Ark. - returned to Culleoka, Tenn. in fall of 1860 and joined the Confederate Army in spring of 1861 - was captured at the fall of Donelson, carried as a prisoner to St. Louis, Mo., where he died in hospital on Mar. 12, 1862; Par.: Thomas Amis and Hannah Amis, Maury co., Tenn.
5. Miss Rebecca Thomas, dau. of Jonas Erwin Thomas and Martha Collins Thomas; near Bigbyville, Maury co., Tenn.
6. My paternal great grandfather John Amis, came from Granville co. N. C. to Tenn. in the year 1818 or 1819. His wife was Miss Mary Knight. They settled in Fountain Creek about 2 miles S.W. of Culleoka, Tenn. where they lived, died and are buried. The Amis family were French Hugenots and came to America soon after the edict of Nantes was promulgated. My maternal grandfather Col. James Erwin Thomas, came to Tenn. with his father and mother from Virginia. His people on both sides were Scotch-Irish, his mother having the Irish brogue. He was Sheriff of Maury county, represented his district in the State Senate and was a Colonel in the Mexican War. He was a Democrat in politics.
7. All the education I have was gotten under the direction and influence of my mother (of blessed memory) and old man "Sowney" Webb, the greatest teacher of them all - none like him.
8. Attended the East Tenn. University for only a short while, being compelled to leave on account of ill health.
9. none
10. I have been successively a farmer, school teacher, stock dealer, banker, office holder and always a patriotic(!) politician.
11. Served as U. S. Marshall for the middle districts of Tenn. (cont'd:)

AMIS cont'd) - question #11:
for 4 years under appointment of the greatest statesman of the age, Woodrow Wilson. Appointment not sought.

12. Served as Chairman of the State Independent Democratic Executive Committee in contest for Governor between Benn W. Hooper and Robert L. Taylor in 1910.
13. A Democrat by conviction, inheritance and environment, but will not support the organization when undemocratic, that is when controlled by improper influences and not responsive to the masses.
14. -----
15. -----
16. Have never written a book but if I should, old man Nelse Woolard of Maury county will be the chief character.
17. Miss Bettie Fleming, married Nov. 8, 1882 at her father's home 5 mi. south-east of Columbia, Tenn. Rev. J. H. Peoples officiating. Dau. of Alfred Fleming, Esq. and Turza Fleming; between Columbia and Culleoka.
18. -----
19. Mary Porter Amis, now wife of C. H. Kinnard, Franklin, Tenn.
Annie Hearn Amis, Franklin, Tenn.
Reese Thomas Amis, Nashville, Tenn.
John Erastus Amis, Okla. City, Okla., married Miss Josephine Eggleston, Sept. 8, '20.
Lewis Fleming Amis (now dead)
Rebecca Thomas Amis, Franklin, Tenn.
Jonas Thomas Amis, Jr. (now dead)
Jonas Graham Amis, Franklin, Tenn.

BAPTIST, RICHARD BANNISTER (1874-1953)
Form signed and dated: Jan. 31, 1922 (Biographical)

1. Richard Ba_n_ister Baptist
2. -----
3. Nathaniel Wilson Baptist; ....; Mecklenburg co., Va.; Covington,Tenn; was County Clerk of Tipton from 1878-1886; practiced law at Covington, Tenn. from 1886-July 4, 1915 (date of his death); was chairman of the Tenn. Railroad Commission from 1898-1904; served with Picket's Division C. S. A. during Civil War, wounded and captured at Sailor's Creek on Apr. 7, 1865; in prison at Point Lookout, Md.; Par.: Richard Banister Baptist and Mary Wilson Baptist; Boydston, Mecklenburg co., Va.
5. Belle Townes Boyd; dau. of Francis W. Boyd and Isabella Hopkins Boyd, Boydston, Mecklenburg co., Va.
6. Jean Baptiste came to America with Lafayette's troops, served during the Revolution and settled in Mecklenburg co., Va.; from him I am descended on my father's side. Alexander Boyd came to America from Scotland (I am informed) and settled in Mecklenburg co., Va. and founded the town of Boydston, the county site of said county. From him I am descended on my mother's side.
7. Public schools of Tipton co., Tenn.; W. R. Webb's Boys Schoold at Bellbuckle, Tenn.
8. Hampden Sidney College, Va. - no degree
9. Studied law in office of Smitheal & Baptist, Covington, Tenn. and obtained license to practice law April 9, 1895.
10. Lawyer, entered upon practice 1895; in 1905 formed partnership for practice of law with my father N. W. Baptist under firm name of Baptist & Baptist and practiced at Covington, Tenn. under this firm name until date of his death, July 4, 1915; then practiced law alone until election as Judge.
11. Private Secretary to Hon. Edward W. Carmack during his service in the House of Representatives and United States Senate; was elected Judge of the 16th Judicial Circuit of Tenn. and entered upon duties of that office Sept. 1, 1918.
12. -----
13. Democrat; Elector for Tenth Congressional Dist. 1912.
14. First Presbyterian Church, Covington, Tenn.
15. Mason and Elks
16. -----
17. Alice Spencer Hall, married at Covington, Tenn., April 8, 1908;dau. of James Rankin Hall and Mattie Givens Hall, Covington, Tenn.(contd:)

BAPTIST cont'd: -question #17:

James Hall came to America from Ireland at time of Revolution. Lived and died in or near Statesville, N. C. Descended on father's side from him; -----; George Dennis moved from Prince Edward co., Va. to Tenn. and Professor of Mathematics at Cumberland University. Descended from him on mother's side.

18. -----
19. Martha Givens Baptist, b. July 3, 1909
Isabel Boyd Baptist, b. Dec. 12, 1911
Richard Bannister Baptist, Jr., b. July 10, 1913

BASS, WILLIAM JAMES (1853-1923)
Form signed by Mrs. Allen Lupton, 760 Oak St., Chattanooga, Tenn. and dated - Dec. 14, 1922 (Biographical)

1. William James Bass
2. Chattanooga
3. ----; Nashville, Davidson co., Tenn.
4. William James Bass; Nashville, Davidson co., Tenn.; Nashville, Tenn. served as Capt. in Forrest's Cavalry, Confederate Army and was killed at Battle of Nashville; Par.: John Meredith Bass and Malvina Grundy; Nashville, Tenn.
5. Caroline Watkins; dau. of William Eli Watkins and Matilda Shute; Nashville
6. Felix Grundy was the father of my grandmother, Malvina Grundy Bass, you no doubt already have the history of Felix Grundy. The original Bass family came from Holland and the Watkins from Ireland.
7. High schools and Campbell & Anderson private schools of Nashville
8. Kentucky Military Institute of Frankfort, Ky.; left in sophomore year because of gymnasium accident.
9. -----
10. Manufacturer - at one time secretary and part owner of Chattanooga Wagon Co. at Chattanooga - now retired from business.
11. Never sought nor held any office by appointment or election except State Legislature Session 1923.
12. -----
13. Democrat
14. Centenary Methodist Church at Chattanooga
15. 32nd Degree Mason, Knights of Pythias, Knights of Khorasson, Life Member of Elks, United Commercial Travellers.
16. -----
17. Ida Belle Maddin, Nashville, Tenn.; dau. of Dr. Jack Wesley Maddin and Annie Downs; Nashville, Tenn.
18. Became member of Tenn. Nat'l. Guard after leaving college. Helped organize "Troop B", Tenn. State Cavalry; went throught all grades from Pvt. to Major of Squadron, which was the ranking cavalry officer in Tenn.; volunteered in W. W. in 1917; was made Capt. and later Major in Q. M. Corps; served from beginning of war until two years after armistice at Jeffersonville, Indiana, Chicago, New York, Governor's Island, Eastern Dept. and Washington, in Q. M. C. and as Sup't. of Animal Drawn Transportation.
19. Jack Maddin Bass, Caldwell & Co., Nashville, Tenn. (unmarried)
Louise Carolyn Bass, married Thomas Allen Lupton, 760 Oak St., Chattanooga, Tenn.

(NOTE: The following items are found on seperate pages and newspaper articles following the questionnaire)

Dated: Nov. 26, 1922 - Newspaper clippings with story of Rev. Thomas Madden (spelled both Maddin and Madden), D.D. and Mrs. Felix Grundy - with pictures of both persons; others named in the article on Rev. Madden are: Mrs. Ann Grundy Steger, wife of Capt. Thomas Madden Steger of Nashville; P. D. Maddin, Att'y.; Dr. J. W. Maddin; Mrs. J.L. Watkins; Mrs. Alice Tuck (all grand-children of Rev. Madden); others mentioned: Mrs. W. D. F. Sawrie (whose husband was Pastor of McKendree Church(Methodist) in 1839); her son, Charlie Sawrie and daughter, Mrs. L. F. Davis; grandsons: Maddin Sawrie, W. Louise Davis; grand-daughter, Mrs. Tom Parks; E. M. Bond, grandson of Thomas W. Randle, pastor in 1842; and Finley M. Dorris, son of Rev. William G. Dorris , pastor in 1858; Prof.'s J. C. and E. L. Johnson of Vanderbilt and Peabody are grandsons of Rev. John Johnson, McKen-(cont'd)

BASS cont'd.-
dree's first pastor in 1818; Dr. M. M. Cullom, son of Rev. Jere Cullom; Dr. George H. and E. A. Price, sons of D. G. W. F. Price (who was founder and President of Price's College); A. W. Shipp, son of Dr. A. M. Shipp; Dr. B. H. Johnson and J. B. McKee; Henry S. Frazier (gr.-gr.-gr.-grandson of Rev. Green Hill of N. C.and came to Tenn. in 1795, later of Brentwood); other descendants of Hill: Jordon Stokes, Mrs. Laura A. Ross and Miss Mary Hill; F. S. Parker (son of Bishop L_____ Parker); H. H. Ahrens (son of Rev. J. B. A. Ahrens); Mrs. John O. Keener, (dau. of Rev. John Mathews); J. D. Hamilton, son of Mortimer Hamilton; Thomas C. Keel; Walter Keith; W. R. Manier; Thos. Parker; Littel Rust; E. E. French; Dr. H. B. Trimble; E. D. Mouzon.

BATES, SAMUEL OGDEN (1884-1969)
Form signed and dated: 1 Feb. 1922, Court House, Memphis, Tenn.(Biographical)

1. Samuel Ogden Bates
2. Memphis, Tenn.
3. Jan. 4, 1884; Ogden, Little River co; Ark.
4. Wm. Martin Bates; county Kilkenny, Ireland; lived Ogden, Ark. at the time of my birth, later moved to Memphis, Tenn.; was County and Probate Judge of Little River, Ark.; -----
5. Matilda Ogden, dau. of Samuel Ogden and ------; lived at Fulton,Ark.
6. -----
7. Public schools of Little River co., Ark.; St. Joseph's School, Texarkana, Texas; Christian Bro.'s College, Memphis, Tenn.; Catholic University of America, Washington, D. C.
8. Christian Bro's. College, Memphis, Tenn. 1904 A.B. Valedictorian
9. Catholic University of America, Washington, D. C. 1906 L.L.B.
10. Attorney-at-law, 30th June 1906
11. Ass't. Att'y. General of Shelby county 1907-08; member of Lower House General Assembly 1909; State Senator from Shelby county 1917; City Judge 1917; Dist. Att'y. General, 15th Judicial Circuit of Tenn. Aug. 1918
12. -----
13. Democrat
14. Catholic Church
15. Knights of Columbus; Elks
16. -----
17. Rosalia O'Shaughnessy, Sept. 22, 1909, Newport, Ky.; dau. of Peter O'Shaughnessy and Emma Daly O'Shaughnessy; Newport, Ky.
18. none
19. Winona Miriam Bates, Memphis, Tenn.

BAXTER, MRS. JACOB (1828-) (Biographical)

1. Mrs. Sarahphina Shannon Baxter
2. Wash'n. College, Tenn.
3. M'ch. 17, 1828, Cherokee, Washington co., Tenn.
4. Elijah Shannon; Nolachucky, Washington co., Tenn.; lived at Washington College, Tenn.; Par.: John Shannon and Rebecka Erwin Shannon; Nolachucky.
5. Eliza Willett Simpson; dau. of James Simpson and Lettie Willett Simpson; Nolachucky.
6. My grandfather John Shannon was born on the ocean when his parents were crossing from Ireland to America; grandmother Shannon's mother was stolen when a child by the Indians and left with a Stewart family with whom she lived until married; not being found by her parents until after marriage.
7. Attended school near Washington College; Robert Young was teacher; he later became Rev. Robert Young, D.D. of Nashville.
8. Jonesboro Female Academy in 1843; Miss Melvin teacher; boarded at Gen. A. E. Jackson's in Jonesboro; was namesake of Mrs. Sarahphina Taylor Jackson.
9. -----
10. -----
11. -----
12. -----
13. -----

(cont'd)

BAXTER cont'd:
14. Methodist Episcopal Church, South
15. -----
16. -----
17. -----
18. -----
19. Rev. George Washington Baxter, Washington College, Tenn.
Hon. Elbridge Baxter, Jonesboro, Tenn.; wife Mrs. Eleanor Lampson Baxter
Rev. John Franklin Baxter, Pt. Pleasant, W. Va.; wife Mrs. Julia Anna? Curtis Baxter
Rev. William Wheeler Baxter, Bristol, Tenn.; wife Mrs. Minnie Mitchell Baxter
Miss Luler Lee Baxter, Washington College, Tenn.

BENNETT, HUGH TAYLOR (1881-)
Form signed and dated: Mar. 9, 1923, Fruitland, Tenn. (Biographical)

1. Hugh Taylor Bennett
2. Fruitland, Tenn.
3. Mar. 4, 1881, Fruitland, Gibson co., Tenn.
4. Willis Nathaniel Bennett; Humboldt, Gibson co., Tenn.; Humboldt and Fruitland in Gibson co.; he was a farmer and member of County Court of Gibson county for many years; Par.: Willis Bennett and Rebecca Powell Bennet; Humboldt, Tenn.
5. Mattie Frances McLeary; dau. of Andrew McLeary and Martha Hill McLeary; Humboldt, Tenn.
6. Grandfather Willis Bennett came to Tenn. from Halifax co., N. C.; grandfather Andrew McLeary, Scotland - Ireland.
7. High Hill high school in Gibson co.; Mrs. Robt. L. Bennett, Trenton, Tenn.; Prof. W. S. Hess, Humboldt, Tenn.; Prof. G. A. Campbell, Memphis, Tenn.
8. Southern Normal University, Huntingdon, Tenn.; State University, Knoxville, Tenn.
9. -----
10. Farmer, now engaged in farming (fruits, vegetables and live stock)
11. Now serving as member of county court of Gibson county (serving 3rd term now); member of Legislature 1909 Session (notary Public 16 yrs.) Ass't. Clerk of Senate from 1915-1923; Chairman Gibson county Draft Board during Worlds War.
12. -----
13. Democrat - State Senator (1923) session; Sub.-Comm. F. W. & M.; Judiciary? Railroads Banks; public roads; public utilities; agriculture; temperance; charitable institutions.
14. Presbyterian - Fruitland, Tenn. - Elder
15. -----
16. -----
17. Ethel Emel Yandell; dau. of Wilson Yandell and Lou Barton; Rutherford, Tenn.; Wilson Yandell, son of Sam Yandell, Humboldt, Tenn.; Lou Barton Yandell, daughter of T. G. Barton, Rutherford, Tenn.; Mrs. T. G. Barton (Samanthia Jordon), Murfreesboro, Tenn.
18. 1st Lt. State Guards Humboldt, Tenn. (1904); Chairman Gibson County Draft Board, during Worlds War.
19. Hugh Taylor Bennett, Jr., age 15 yrs.
Willis Nathaniel Bennett, age 13 yrs.

BOYLE, WILLIAM GLASS (1859-) (Biographical)

1. William Glass Boyle
2. Nashville, Tenn.
3. Aug. 26, 1859; Knoxville, Blount co., Tenn.
4. Hiram Boyle; Knoxville, Blount co., Tenn.; near Knoxville, Tenn.;---; Hiram Boyle, son of Samuel H. Boyle and J___ Boyle; near Knoxville
5. Martha McCroskey, dau. of James McCroskey and Ann McCroskey;----- Trundler? Cross Roads
6. -----
7. County schools, Montgomery; Bell Academy, Winchester Normal; Prof's. Terrell, Clark, Ble__son?, Yateman? and Garrett
8. ----- (cont'd)

BOYLE cont'd:
9. -----
10. -----
11. -----
12. -----
13. Democrat
14. M. E. Church; Stewart and trustee for 35 years
15. Knight's Pythias
16. -----
17. Sallie Bryan, married at Arling M. E. Church, Apr. 25, 1893; Rev. L. C. Bryan and Sallie; Woodland Cottage; she was the dau. of Esquire Thomas King and Delila King. Esquire King settled on a section 640 acres of land 6 miles from Nashville on Murfreesboro Pike in 1800, as near as can get information.
18. -----
19. -----

BRISTER, JOHN WILLARD (1869-) (Biographical)

1. John Willard Brister
2. Nashville, Tenn.
3. Dec. 28, 1869; Petersburg, Dinwiddie co., Va.
4. Samuel George Brister; Petersburg, Dinwiddie co., Va.; Petersburg, Va. for 79 years; held position in city government; was in confederate service; merchant; -----
5. Mary Ann Prosiee?; -------------
6. -----
7. Public high school, Petersburg, Va.; most famous teacher, Miss Anna P. Bolling, for 40 years principal of the Petersburg, Va. high sch.
8. Peabody College of the University of Nashville; A.B. 1892; A.M. 1893; attended University of Chicago, June 1896-June 1897 and in the summer of 1903.
9. (see above)
10. teaching profession - instructor in Montgomery Bell academy, Nashville, Tenn. 1892-1903; professor of mathematics, Peabody College 1903-1911; State Sup't. of Public Instruction of Tenn. 1911-13; Pres. West Tenn. State Normal School, Memphis, Tenn. 1913-1918; in Europe with YMCA 1918-19; State High School Inspector 1919-
11. -----
12. -----
13. Democrat
14. Methodist; steward for many years; sunday school Sup't.; Bible class teacher, etc.
15. Masons
16. Official publications only - reports of state sup't. of Tenn. 1911-1912; 1912-13, rural school situation in Tenn. publication in 1912, etc.
17. Frances May Brister (nee Taylor), Sept. 1, 1910? (1900?), dau. of Zachary Kenneth Taylor and Mary Frances Croft; Chattanooga, Tenn.
18. Joined Y.M.C.A. for foreign service in 1918, arrived in France in Sept. of that year; spent 4 mo's. at Blois, France; later went with army of occupation to Wittlieb?, Germany, was sup't. of instruction with 7th Army Corps; afterwards became member of Army Educational Corps and was stationed at various places in Germany.
19. Virginia Brister, Nashville, Tenn.
John Willard Brister, Jr., Nashville, Tenn.

BROWN, MRS. JOHN C. (Biographical)

1. Mrs. John C. Brown
2. Nashville, Tenn. March 1, 1919
3. -----; near Murfreesboro, Rutherford co., Tenn.
4. Maj. John W. Childress; Rutherford co., Tenn.; near Murfreesboro;was a planter; owned slaves; entered for war service in Mexican War, but did not go to Mexico; was an influential man - strong southern sympathizer; Joel Childress and Elizabeth Childress; near Murfreesboro, Tenn.
5. Sarah Williams; dau. of Elisha Williams and Mary Phillips Williams; probably in Rutherford co., Tenn.
6. Mrs. Brown's great-grandfather, John Childress and one of (cont'd)

BROWN cont'd: question #6:
her other ancestors,Elisha Williams, served in the Revolutionary Army, the former (Childress) serving at King's Mtn., residing in Surry co., N. C. at date of enlistment. He was in sundry skirmishes. Williams was granted land. See Rev. Military Grants p. 26 Group No.292 State Register.
7. St. Stevens?, Murfreesboro, Tenn.
8. Nashville Female Academy, Nashville, Tenn.; Principal: Prof. C. D. Elliott; graduated with honors.
9. -----
10. a very fine business woman
11. -----
12. ---- was 1st Pres. of United Daughters of the Confederacy; Honorary Regent for Life of Campbell Clafton?; Nashville Daughters of the American Revolution; ardent war worker and generous subscriber in war with Germany; member of many women's protective organizations; traveled abroad.
13. -----
14. Episcopal Church
15. none
16. addresses and articles
17. Wife of Maj. Gen. and Gov. John C. Brown of Tenn.; married in Griffin, Ga. on Feb. 23, 1864; son of Duncan Brown and Margaret Smith Brown; near Bethany, Giles co., Tenn.; Gov. Brown's ancestors served in the Rev. Army and some emigrated from Scotland; he was of Scotch-Irish descent; among his Scotch relatives were the great Duke of Argyle, Mary, Queen of Scots, and Flora McDonald of Waverly, one of Scotland's ________
18. Mrs. Brown before her marriage, witnessed __ Murfreesboro with and at the invitation of Pres. Davis a review of the Confederate Army (in large numbers, perhaps 30,000 troops); her marriage to Gen.Brown was to have been in the evening, but the latter was ordered to report at once to Joe Johnston and the wedding was celebrated (solomized?) at high noon; (see Dr. Wuintard?" by A.? H. Noll); after her marriage she lived much in camp with her husband being exposed to the enemy fire.
19. Marie Brown, married Gov. Benton McMillin of Tenn.; dead
Daisy Brown, unmarried; dead
Elizabeth Brown, married John C. Burch of Tenn.; dead
John C. Brown, Attorney, unmarried; Nashville, Tenn.

BROWN, JOHN CALVIN (1827-1889)
(Gov. and Maj. Gen.) (Biographical)

1. John Calvin Brown
2. Aug. 17, 1889; Nashville, Tenn.
3. Jan. 6, 1827; near Bethany, Giles co., Tenn.
4. Duncan Brown, Oct. 21, 1780, probably Robertson (Robinson?) co., N. C.; in Robertson (Robinson) co., N. C. and emigrated to Giles co., Tenn. probably in the early days of the 19th century; was a farmer; an earnest Elder in the Presbyterian church; Angus Brown and ____ ______ in Scotland and probably America.
5. Margaret Smith ----; Neil Smith and Mary Lytle (Lytele); probably in N. C.
6. One ancestor, Col. Archibald Lytle (Lyttle) of N. C. served in Rev. Army under Washington; granted 7200 acres of land for his services. See State Register Office (Tenn.) p. 2, Grant 1, Military Grants, State Capitol, Nashville, Tenn. Angus Brown was a Rev. soldier, serving under Gen. Francis Marion (see Crew's Hist. of Nashville, p. 592?); Bench & Bar of _______? Cities (p. 416); John C. Brown's ancestors emigrated from Scotland to this country and he was of Scotch-Irish stock (Famous ancestor, etc., etc.-see Mrs. John C. Brown's sketch question #17).
7. County schools in Giles co., Tenn.
8. Jackson College, Columbia, Tenn. ab. 1846(7?)
9. Studied law in office
10. Lawyer about 1848, first at Pulaski, Tenn., where he had a large practice reaching great proportions just after the Civil War; then as Chief Att'y. (or Gen'l. Solicitor) for the Gould So. West Systems of R. R.'s.

BROWN cont'd:

11. Mayor of Pulaski, Tenn. ab. 1851; Elector for State at Large on the Bell & Everett Nat'l. Ticket (Tenn.) ab. 1860; Res. Constitutional Convention (Tenn.) 1870; Governor of Tennessee (1871-1875)
12. Traveled abroad extensively in Europe, Asia, Africa; appointed by Pres. Hayes as only Democrat on Commission to settle the Louisiana trouble right after the Civil War; largely responsible for happy solution to that trouble; in recognition of which Pres. Hayes offered Gov. Brown Post-Master Generalship in his Cabinet which he declined; he founded public school systems of Tenn.
13. First a Whig until its end; Democrat; probably served on committees
14. Member Presbyterian (prob. an Elder or Deacon); in late years of his life financially helped and ___ attended Episcopal church of which his wife was a member.
15. Was Secretary Treasurer J. & S. W. of the Masonic Blue Lodge at Pulaski; was grand master of Masons in Tenn. ab. 1870; was a Clofton(?) Mason and Knights Templar, also a Knight of Pythias
16. Once wrote a novel, also a wonderful account of his European, African and Asiatic travels; descriptions and accounts of Civil War battles, public affairs and matters.
17. Elizabeth Childress; Griffin, Ga.; Feb. 23, 1864; ceremony performed by Dr. Quintard?, Confederate chaplain ___ ___ of Tenn.; Maj. John W. Childress and Sarah Williams Childress, near Murfreesboro, Tenn.; she was descended from Revolutionary stock on the maternal side - (Elisha Williams) and on paternal side (John Childress), the latter enlisting in N. C. and fighting among others, at Kings Mtn.
18. (1) Capt. of Co. A 3rd Tenn. Reg't. C.S.A., Col. of 3rd Tenn. Reg't. Brigidier and Maj. Gen'l.
    (2) Served under Albert Sidney Johnston and Joe Johnson; Gen. Browns command was known as "Brown's Division"
    (3) Enlisted in May 1861; surrendered and paroled with John Johnson's army at Greensboro, N. C. ab. May 1865
    (4) Was wounded 5 times; shot from his horse at Franklin and left for dead on that field of glory; led the charge there; was almost constantly in the fighting during the war except when a prisoner near Boston; after the war was offered a Commission in the Egytian ____? by the Hbedin? but declined
19. Marie Brown
    Daisy Brown
    Elizabeth Brown
    John C. Brown

(NOTE: See biography of Mrs. John C. Brown question #19)

BROWN, JOHN CALVIN, JR. (1874-   ) (Biographical)

1. John Calvin Brown
2. Nashville, Tenn.
3. May 24, 1874; Pulaski, Giles co., Tenn.
4. John Calvin Brown; near Bethany, Giles co., Tenn.; Pulaski and Nashville, Tenn.; was lawyer, Maj. Gen'l. (in Confederate Army)-wounded 5 times in battle; Pres. of Constitutional Convention of 1870; Governor 1871-1875; Grand Master of Masons and head of various organizations; Duncan Brown and Margaret Smith Brown, near Bethany, Giles co., Tenn.
5. Elizabeth Childress; Maj. John W. Childress and Sarah Williams Childress; near Murfreesboro, Tenn.
6. My mother, Mrs. John C. Brown, lived also at Pulaski and Nashville, Tenn.; she was the 1st President of the United Daughters of the Confederacy; a worker in the war with Germany and a member of many religious, civic and patriotic organizations; my maternal ancestors, Elisha Williams and John Childress were in the Revolutionary Army, the former receiving a grant of land for his military services; the latter fought at King's Mtn.; on my paternal side I am of Scotch-Irish descent; my ancestors (paternal), Col. Archibald Lytle(Lyttle) served in the Revolution under Washington and received a grant of 7200 acres for his military services; Angus Brown served under Gen. Francis Marion; Mary, Queen of Scots, the great Duke of Argyle were Scotch relatives of my family.
7. Pulaski, Tenn.; Miss Sallie Shepherd and Miss Mariana Trebna?;Dallas, Texas-Prof. Groves; New Orleans, La.; St. Louis, Smith (cont'd)

BROWN cont'd: question #7-

Academy; Nashville, Tenn., Prof. C. B. Wallace and Prof. W. C. Branham?

8. University of South, Sevier, Tenn.; Vanderbilt University, Nashville, Tenn.; Jennings? Business College about 1904 (Nashville)
9. Vanderbilt University 1896 L.L.B.
10. Oct. 1896, Nashville, Tenn.; admitted to practice before U. S. Supreme Court Feb. 2, 1900 on mention? of Senator Turley?
11. U. S. Appraisor? in Bou_____?, Nashville; Member of Legal Advisory Board (Davidson co., Tenn.); was with Ger_____?
12. Been abroad 3 times; publication - winner of 1st prize "Centennial Dream" (historical contest), Nashville American 1897
13. Democrat
14. Episcopal
15. Mason, Cl_fton ____, Knight Templar and Shriner, Knights of Pythias Delta Tau Delta (college fraternity
16. Articles, stories, sketches and addresses
17. unmarried
18. Pvt. Co. C 1st Tenn. Regt. N.G.S.T.?; 1st Tenn. Regt. N.G.S.T.;Capt. Albert Bayless, Col.; ab. 1890, 1 or 2 (1 yrs. service) we were sent to Coal? Creek and Troy City to quell _____ insurrection; appointed 1st Lt. 4th Tenn. Regt. (war with Spain) by Gov. R. L. Taylor, but did not accept; applied various branches of service in war with Germany but not accepted.
19. -----

BRYAN, EUGENE JACKSON (1888-1958) (Biographical)

1. Eugene Jackson Bryan
2. -----
3. June 25, 1888; Chattanooga, Hamilton co., Tenn.
4. Daniel G. Bryan; Chattanooga, Hamilton co., Tenn.; Chattanooga, Tenn. Par.: J. J. Bryan and ______; Chattanooga
5. Carrie Burg; (no other answers to this question...cme)
6. -----
7. Public schools of Chattanooga; McCollie Prep. School
8. University of Tenn. 1908-(7)
9. University of Chattanooga - Law
10. Attorney 1912
11. Legislature Lower House 1915; Senate 1921-23; Speaker of Senate 1923
12. -----
13. Democrat
14. -----
15. -----
16. -----
17. Mary Ruth Bates, married Chattanooga, Oct. 16, 1912; Par.: Creed F. Bates and _________(no more information)
18. -----
19. Eugene Jackson Bryan, Jr., wife Betty Ann
    William Bates Bryan

BUTLER, JOHN WASHINGTON (1875-1952) (Biographical)
(NOTE: He filled out two forms; information basically the same; the exceptions are listed below his answers...cme)

1. John Washington Butler
2. LaFayette
3. Dec. 17, 1875; Red Boiling Springs, Macon co., Tenn.
4. William Sampson Butler; Defeated (or Difficult), Smith co., Tenn.; Red Boiling Springs until 1881 when he moved near LaFayette where he now resides (until 5 years of age, moving with his parents to Walnut Shade, Macon co., Tenn. in 1859); Par.: Braxton Butler and Polly Ann ___; Walnut Shade, Macon co., Tenn.
5. Eliza Jane Hargis; Par.: Zachariah Hargis and Nancy Susan ___; near LaFayette (who lived at Hillsdale, Macon co., Tenn.)
6. My ancestors came from Virginia; date unknown (on father's side came from Virginia ab. 1774; some who took part in Revolutionary War - supposed to have been at King's Mtn.; my gr.-gr.-gr.-grandfather on my mother's side married a Cherokee maiden, so there is where I derive my Indian blood; on my father's side we were (cont'd)

BUTLER cont'd: question #6-
from Scotch-Irish as tradition has it.
7. In the 3 months rural schools and 10 months in LaFayette Academy; teachers: Profs. Jas. Gerald, J. B. Warren and John C. Price (in country schools and Lafayette college - college in name only)
8. none
9. Taught in rural (Elementary) schools for five years
10. Making a crop and teaching in the fall; have been a farmer and thresherman ever since
11. Have never held any office except for about 10 or 12 years; Election Commissioner which I resigned to make the race for Representative (Member of House of Representatives 1923, 1925; Senate 1927)
12. Have given quite a lot of time, work and some money for good roads (author of the "Tenn. Anti-Evolution Law in 1925" the fame of which was world wide)
13. Democrat
14. Member of Primitive (Testament) Baptist Church since 1908 and clerk of same; also clerk of the Round Lick Association of Primitive Baptists since 1908 to the present time.
15. Belong to nothing except the church
16. Have written nothing except humorous poetry for a county paper (May 5, 1897 at Casey, Macon co.) and a little for campaign purposes and for amusement (No books written yet, have comtemplated writing some; poetry and for newspapers)
17. Magnolia McDonald; Par.: Thomas McDonald and Margaret Smith, Casey, Macon co., Tenn.; of Scotch-Irish descent (from North Carolina)
18. Registered for World War but those of my age were not called for
19. Arta (Butler) and husband, Joel D. Sutton, Red Boiling Springs,Tenn.
Ethel (Butler) and husband, Geanie Jenkins, Scottsville, Ky.
Huber Butler, age 16
Golston Butler, age 14
Kermit Butler, age 12

(NOTE: On seperate pages (2), typewritten and dated April 2, 1927 is the copy of "A Brief History of the Anti-Evolution Law" by J. W. Butler, Author of the Law.)

BYRNS, JOSEPH WELLINGTON (1869-1936) (Biographical)

1. Joseph Wellington Byrns
2. Nashville, Tenn.
3. July 20, 1869, near Cedar Hill, Robertson co., Tenn.
4. James Henry Burns; near Cedar Hill, Robertson co., Tenn.; lived near Cedar Hill, Robertson co., Tenn. where he was engaged in farming for the greater part of his life, afterward moving to Nashville, Tenn. where he died on May 8, 1905; John Byrns and Elizabeth Long Byrns; near Cedar Hill, Tenn.
5. Mary Emily Jackson; dau. of Miles Jackson and Sarah Speer; at or near Cedar Hill, Tenn.
6. My ancestors the Byrns, Longs, Johnsons, Jacksons and Speers came originally from England, Scotland and Ireland, first settling in Pennsylvania, Virginia and North Carolina, finally removing to Robertson co., Tenn. where all were farmers except my great-grandfather Speer who was a Methodist preacher and my great-great-grandfather Byrns who was an M. D. and died of a plague in North Carolina; some of them served in the Revolutionary War as Privates, War of 1812 and the Civil War; my great-grandfather Byrns was at the Battle of New Orleans as a private; my uncle Joseph W. Jackson was killed at the Battle of Atlanta, while serving in the Confederate army and a boy of 18; my grandfather Miles Jackson built the first house in Cedar Hill, Tennessee.
7. First in District schools of Robertson county; a number of years at Cedar Hill; many teachers - most beloved and for longest period, Prof. Joel E. Ruffin, now over 90 years of age and living at Cedar Hill; then at high school in Nashville, Tenn. where I graduated in June 1887.
8. Vanderbilt University, Nashville, Tenn. for 2 years in Academic department and then in law department - L.L.B. June 1890
9. Graduated in law at Vanderbilt University June 1890 L.L.B.
10. Lawyer, Nashville, Tenn.; Sept. 1890; started with nothing & (cont'd)

BYRNS cont'd: question #10-
very limited acquaintanceship; built up a lucrative practice prior to my election to Congress; general practice.

11. Member Tennessee House of Representatives 1895,1897 and 1899; Speaker of the House 1899; Member of State Senate 1901; Democratic Presidential Elector 1904; Member of Congress 6th H___? District, Tenn. from Mar. 4, 1909 (61st Congress) to present time; at present am member Committee on _____?
12. Have always been interested in every movement for moral and material welfare of home, county and state.
13. Democrat - have actively engaged in every campaign since I became 21 years of age.
14. Methodist Episcopal Church, South
15. Mason, Scottish Rite and Knight Templar, Shriner, Odd Fellows,Knights of Pythias, Independent Order of Revolutionary Men, Elks, Past Master of Masonic Order, Past Chancellor of K of P.
16. -----
17. Julia Woodard, Aug. 23, 1898, at country home of her father near Columbia, Tenn.; Par.: Judge John Woodard and Julia E. Pbrter, Nashville, Tenn.; her ancestors finally settled in Robertson co., Tenn. from North Carolina and Virginia; her maternal great-grandfather, Benjamin Porter was one of party of Watauga settlers who first came to Nashville, Tenn.
18. -----
19. Joseph Wellington Byrns, born at Nashville, Tenn., Aug. 15, 1903

CAMPBELL, JOHN CALHOUN (1853-)
Form signed and dated: Feb. 9, 1922 (Biographical)

1. John Calhoun Campbell
2. Johnson City, Tenn.
3. Mar. 16, 1853, Sneedville, Hancock co., Tenn.
4. Robert Campbell; Sneedville, Hancock co., Tenn.; Telford, Washington co., Tenn. where he died; he was a farmer and held no public office except that of Postmaster at Sneedville for a few years; Alexander Campbell and _____ McNeil; Hancock co., Tenn.
5. Elizabeth Stubblefield, dau. of Robert Stubblefield and Polly Rains, near Sneedville, Tenn.
6. My grandfather, Alexander Campbell was raised near Rogersville, Hawkins co., Tenn.; my great-grandfather Robert Campbell was raised near Abington, Virginia; my great-grandfather's foreparents came to Virginia from Ireland in the year 1725; William Campbell of Kings Mtn. fame was said to be related; grandfather Stubblefield was raised at Rockingham, Rockingham co., North Carolina, where my mother was born.
7. Attended schools a few months near Cleveland, Tenn.; Mr. H. B. Burkett was teacher; also 2 years at Buffalo Institute under J. Hopwood in Carter co., Tenn. near Johnson City, Tenn.
8. none
9. none; retail merchandising was my principal business
10. none
11. Trustee of Hancock co., Tenn.; Alderman a few terms of (at) Johnson City; Member of the Board of Education a few terms; also Postmaster at Johnson City from Nov. 1, 1897 to Apr. 15, 1910
12. -----
13. Republican
14. Member Methodist Episcopal Church and have served on official boards from 1885 to present
15. -----
16. -----
17. Harriet J. Nelson, married Sept. 2, 1880; dau. of P. P. C. Nelson & Elizabeth Hoss, Johnson City, Tenn.; P. P. C. Nelson was 3 times elected State Senator and one time Speaker of the Senate, succeeding Gov. Sinter?; he represented the 1st ___? Dist.
18. -----
19. Robert Wilson Campbell, wife Beatrice - Johnson City, Tenn.
Julian H. Campbell, wife Amy - Lebanon, Tenn.
Wm. H. Campbell, Attorney, Baltimore, Md.
James M. Campbell, Dental Surgeon - Constantinople, Turkey; ranks as full Lieutenant in the Navy (cont'd)

CAMPBELL cont'd: question #19-
Dora Campbell Oakes, and husband, L. W. Oakes, Johnson City, Tenn.

CAPEHART, WILLIAM THOMAS (1853-)
Form signed and dated: Feb. 10, 1925 (Biographical)

1. William Thomas Capehart
2. 515 W. 6th St., Chattanooga, Tenn.
3. July 31, 1853, Cass, Bartow co., Georgia
4. Quinton Capehart; Cass, Bartow co., Ga.; Chattanooga, Tenn.; was yard master for N. C. & St. L. R. R. when the Civil war broke out; when Chattanooga was captured by the federals he was placed in prison in Nashville but later released and placed by federal authorities in Stevenson, Alabama, in charge of the N. & C. Ry. terminal there;Par.: Jacob Capehart and Elizabeth Ellis, Chattanooga, Tenn.
5. Susan Freeman Capehart, dau. of William Freeman and Nancy _____; of Cass., Ga. later moving to Chattanooga, Tenn.
6. Great grandfather Jacob Capehart came to this country in 1780 with two sons, Jacob and Leonard and settled in Pickens co., South Carolina; Jacob married Elizabeth Ellis and have 5 children: Jacob, William, Thomas, John and Hugh; Jacob settled in Chattanooga; William in Resaca, Georgia; Thomas in Guntersville, Alabama; John in Pickens co., South Carolina and Hugh in Missouri; no war service is known except the home place of Jacob in Chattanooga was confiscated by the federals during the civil war and used as a hospital; the family refugeeing to Dalton, Georgia.
7. Primary schools in Chattanooga; Miss Mary Fife, teacher and the Masonic School, Chattanooga, Prof. Henry Vanter, teacher.
8. no
9. no
10. Railroad business entirely
11. no
12. Was associated with the law and order league directly after civil war to suppress carpet bagger rule.
13. Democrat - was one of the committee to interview Pres. Roosevelt relative to appointment of Foster V. Brown to Federal Judge of this district but on this committee's recommendation he was appointed Judge to Porto Rico, a judge having been chosen for this district.
14. Methodist Episcopal, South
15. Masons, Knights of Pythias, Order of Railway Conductors, at present hold the position of Grand Outer Guard in the Grand Lodge of Tenn. K. of P.; Past Chief Conductor, O.R.C.
16. -----
17. ~~Wilhemina~~ (this name written over) Cecilia O'Rourke, married at Tuscaloosa, Alabama ___; dau. of Thomas O'Rourke and Mary Boyle, Tuscaloosa, Alabama; wife's parents came from Ireland about 1848, settled in Mobile, Alabama; her father was of the clan O'Rourke of Connaught, which claims descent from Tiernon O'Rourke, Prince of Brefny;Thomas O'Rourke and Mary Boyle were married and lived in Athlone before coming to America; Martin Boyle, uncle, settled in Connecticut; Mary Boyle was descendat of Roger Boyle of Ireland.
18. -----
19. Susan Adline (Capehart) married George Culden: issue- son: Richard George (Culden); George died and she married Frank Knolton Eastman of Cincinnati, Ohio: issue -2 girls: Helen and Dorothy (Eastman); lives 4268 Hamilton Ave., Cincinnati, Ohio.
Florence Caroline (Capehart), married Andrew P. Langford: issue - 1 girl: Marion (Langford) and 1 son: William Langford; lives 523 W.6th St., Chattanooga, Tenn.
Joseph Edward (Capehart), unmarried, lives 515 W. 6th St., Chattanooga.

(NOTE: Following this biography is a typewritten page entitled "William Thomas Capehart", prepared by John Tinker, Grand Keeper of Records and Seals of the Knights of Pythias of Tennessee. Mentions a book of 164 pp. written by Capt. Capehart - memoirs:(i.e.-came to Chattanooga with his parents in 1854 - about 1 year old; Captain Quintain Capehart, charter member of Damon Lodge No. 2; mentions son, J. E. Capehart and grand-son, Richard Gulding (Culden?); good personal sketch....cme)

CAPERTON, JASPER WOODS (1871-)
(Caperton Family) (Biographical)

1. Jasper Woods Caperton
2. Nashville, Tenn. 324 -th Ave. N.
3. Aug. 26, 1871, Spring Hill, Maury co., Tenn.
4. John Hugh Caperton; near Spring Hill, Maury co., Tenn.; Louisville, Miss. until after the war - returning to Spring Hill; served in the Confederate army, discharged after 3 years service at Vicksburg in 1864; was in cavalry; died at the home place Spring Hill in 1879; Jack Caperton and Sallie Haley, on same place at Spring Hill where he owned a section of land.
5. -----
6. My father was a brother of Sam B. Caperton, who married a Miss Childress, who died when I was quite young; to this union were born three children: William B. Caperton, Admiral U. S. Navy; Sam J. Caperton, (who) died in 1905; Mollie J. Caperton, married John F. Wade, died in 1915; William B. Caperton married Miss Georgie Lockwood, daughter of Ex-Senator of Washington, D. C.; they have 1 child: Miss Marguerite Caperton; his present address is Washington City.
7. Attended school at Port Royal, near Spring Hill, taught by Burr Warren and Dave Tisdale
8. -----
9. -----
10. Mercantile business
11. -----
12. -----
13. -----
14. First Presbyterian Church, Nashville
15. -----
16. -----
17. -----
18. -----
19. -----

CHANDLER, WALTER CLIFT (1887-1967) (Biographical)

1. Walter Clift Chandler
2. Memphis, Tenn.
3. Oct. 5, 1887, Jackson, Madison co., Tenn.
4. William Henry Chandler; Enterprise, Clarke co., Miss.; Memphis, Tenn.; is in U. S. Mail Service; educated for dental profession and practiced in New Orleans, La.; Green Collier Chandler and Martha G. Croft, Enterprise, Miss.
5. Mary Knoxie Clift, dau. of James Knox Polk Clift and Mary Jane Campbell, Bolivar, Hardeman co., Tenn.
6. My great-great-grandfather, Shadrack Chandler and his father, Joel Chandler fought in the Revolutionary war from South Carolina; my great-grandfather, William Chandler fought in the War of 1812, was at the Battle of New Orleans and went to Florida with Gen. Andrew Jackson in 1818; my grandfather was Colonel of Mississippi Infantry troops of the Confederate army in the Civil War.
7. Public schools of Jackson, Tenn. and Memphis, Tenn.; University of Tennessee, L.L.B. 1909
8. University of Tennessee, Knoxville, Tenn. 1909 with L.L.B. degree; also Phi Kappa Phi scholarship fraternity.
9. same as above
10. Attorney-at-law, Memphis, Tenn.; began July 3, 1909
11. Ass't. Att'y. General of Shelby co. from Apr. 1, 1916 to Sept. 1, 1916; Representative from Shelby co. in Legislature of Tenn. 1917; Senator from Shelby and Tipton co.'s in Legislature of 1921.
12. -----
13. Democratic
14. Grace Episcopal Church, Memphis, Tenn.
15. Masonic Fraternity, Worshipful Master DeSoto Lodge No. 299 in 1915; S. _?. E. College Fraternity
16. History of the 55th Field Art'ly. Brigade, 30th Div. A.E.F.
17. single
18. -----
19. -----

CHAPPELL, EDWIN BARFIELD (fl 1882 -)
Signed and dated: Jan. 16, 1922 (Biographical)

1. Edwin Barfield Chappell
2. Nashville, Tennessee
3. ---
4. William B. Chappell; Lincoln co., Tennessee; Columbia in early life later at Fletwoods (Flatwoods ?), Tennessee; a farmer and never held any other offices except Justice of the Peace and County Surveyer; William Chappell and Sallie Palmer Chappell; near Columbia.
5. Elizabeth Whitaker; James Whitaker and Delphia Lyons Whitaker;first in Edgecomb co., N. C. and later in Flatwoods (?), Tennessee.
6. My father's family were Virginians; my mother was a North Carolinian; both were of old Colonial stock; my earliest American ancestor (Chappell) having settled on James River in 1636.
7.Ręcieved my preparatory training under W. R. and J. M. Webb.
8. Graduated with BA degree from Vanderbilt University; received the Honorary degree of D.O. from Hunts Central College, Fayette, Mo.
9. Received theological training in Vanderbilt University
10. Was a pastor at Laugrange (probably La Grange...cme), San Antonio & Austin, Texas; in St. Louis, Missouri and in Nashville, Tennessee; in 1906 was elected by the General Conference of the Methodist Episcopal Church, South sunday school editor, still hold this position.
11. ---
12. ---
13. ---
14. sunday school editor and general sunday school secretary, M.E.C.S.
15. have 32nd degree Scottish Rite Masons
16. The Building of the Kingdom, Studies in the Life of Wesley and The Church and its Sacraments are the books I have written; have edited so many that I cannot undertake to enumerate them.
17. Jennie D. Headler, married at Caledonia, Missouri in 1882; Rev. John H. Headler and Carrie Dean Headler; Caledonia, Missouri; my wife's father was a native of Dickson co., Tennessee but went to Missouri when a boy of 16 and became a leader among the pioneer preachers of that state.
18. ---
19. Frank W. Chappell, Civil Engineer, Dallas, Texas; married Pearl Wallace - 2 children
Ethel Chappell Smart, wife of Dr. W. A. Smart of Emory University, Atlanta, Georgia - 1 child
Helen (?) Chappell White, wife of Prof. G. C. White of Emory University, Atlanta, Georgia - 2 children
E. B. Chappell, Editor, Nashville, Tennessee, married Miss Jeanne Legard, Paris, Tenn.(?) (smeared)

CHOATE, GEORGE NEWTON (1881 - 1938) (Biographical)

1. George Newton Choate
2. Trenton, Tennessee
3. Mar. 21, 1881; Brazil, Gibson co., Tennessee
4. Patrick Henry Choate; Williamsport, Maury co., Tennessee; in Maury county for 25 years and the rest of his life in Gibson co.; Joseph Choate and Martha Kirkham Choate; in Maury county.
5. Callie Balsora Harris; Adolphus Harris and Cassandra Wade; Brazil, Gibson co., Tennessee.
6. Descended from John Wade, maternal ancestor who fought in the Revolutionary war as private in Capt. Joseph Magruder's Co. 29th Battalion, Montgomery co., Md. (Scharff's History of Western Md., Vol. 1, p. 141); the Choate family came to America from England .
7. public schools of Gibson co., Tennessee
8. ---
9. ---
10. Real estate, insurance and loans and farmer.
11. Tennessee Legislature 1922-23
12. ---
13. Penal committee, charitable institutions, redistricting committees, claims committees, forestry, fish and game committees, and military affairs committees.
14. Presbyterian Church in U.S. - Deacon. (cont'd next page)

Choate - cont'd:
15. Elks
16. ---
17. Jessie Killough, Trenton, Tennessee, 2 May 1911; Algernon Killough and Louise Lamb; Trenton, Tennessee; maternal grand-parents were Martha Frazier and Benjamin Franklin Lamb who fought in Mexican War; paternal grand-parents Sarah Watson and William Killough, fought in Civil War, whose mother was Mary Woods, whose father was Samuel Woods, whose father was Samuel Woods who fought in the Revolutionary War.
18. ---
19. George Newton Choate, Jr., Trenton, Tennessee
    Algernon Killough Choate, Trenton, Tennessee

(On seperate page - typed):
Squire Choate came to Maury county from Rockingham county, North Carolina; his wife was an Owen; he was born Sept. 9, 1770 and died May 5, 1852; Joseph Choate was a son of Squire Choate; he was born Apr. 7, 1807; he was married to Martha Kirkham who was born May 27, 1814; of this pair were born the following: Squire Choate, Nov. 19, 1836; Redmon P. Choate, Mar. 31, 1738 (should be 1838...cme); Walter C. Choate, Nov. 15, 1839; Edward L. Choate, Nov. 24, 1841; Rebecca P. Choate, Mar. 12, 1843; Joseph P. Choate, Nov. 12, 1846; P. Henry Choate, Nov. 1, 1884; Helen H. Choate, Oct. 17, 1850 and Richard C. Choate, July 31, 1852; Joseph Choate and Martha Kirkham were married Dec. 25, 1835; Joseph Choate died May 5, 1852; Martha K. Choate died Aug. 14, 1865.

(On seperate page - handwritten):
Charlie Sowell and wife Priscilla from Ireland came to Maury county 1818 (?); their daughrer Priscilla married Kirkham (died in Nashville); their daughter Martha Kirkham married Joseph Choate in Maury county; their son Henry Choate married Callie B. Harris.

(On seperate page - handwritten):
Squire Choate, born 1770 in Rockingham co., N. C. and his Miss Owen; their son Joseph Choate b. 1807 and died ____ 1850 (?), Maury co., Williamsport, Tenn. and wife Martha Kirkham; their son Henry Choate, b. Nov. 1, 1884, died Nov. 22, 1922; their son Newt Choate, b. Mar. 21, 1881.

CLARK, WILLIAM C. (1869 -) (Biographical)

1. William C. Clark
2. ---
3. July 12, 1869, Nashville, Davidson co., Tennessee
4. Patrick F. Clark (Ireland); 727 Main St.; served in Union Army.
5. Mary McHugh
6. ---
7. St. Columbia School; old Main St. school
8. ---
9. ---
10. painter
11. ---
12. ---
13. ---
14. none for past 20 years
15. Red Men
16. ---
17. Batchelor (should be bachelor)
18. ---
19. ---

CLARKE, WILLIAM HENRY (1892 -) (Biographical)

1. William Henry Clarke
2. Jonesboro
3. Apr. 2, 1892, Telford, Washington co., Tennessee
4. Jesse D. Clarke; Giles co., Virginia; Giles, Virginia until 1866, when he and his father and the remainder of the family moved to Washington co., Tenn.; John Randolph Clarke and Sarah Jane ______;

Clarke cont'd:
Giles co., Virginia.
5. Eliza Ann Fox; Samuel D. Fox and Elizabeth _____; Jerroldstown, Green co., Tennessee
6. ---
7. in the grammar schools of Washington co., Tennessee; high school education in preparatory department of Carson-Newman College
8. Carson-Newman for 1 yr of college work; Daleville (?) College (Va.), 1 yr; graduation work with A.B. degree from Milligan (?) College in 1919 with the honor of Summa Cum Laude
9. ---
10. Teacher; teaching experience began in 1911 at little country school at Cabel (?) Springs in Washington co., Tenn.; since then until 1919 I would go to school 2 years and teach 1 year; since 1919 have been a teacher; have taught in 2 grammar schools and spent 4 yrs. in superintending high schools.
11. member-elect of 63rd Session of General Assembly from Washington co. - session to convene Jan. 1, 1923.
12. ---
13. Republican
14. Baptist
15. Modern Woodmen of America
16. ---
17. Juda Edith Huddleston, married at Livingston, Tennessee, Dec. 22, 1920; Thomas B. Huddleston and Sophronia Zachary; Birdstown, Tenn.
18. ---
19. "little daughter", Louise, born Oct. 17, 1921

CLAYTON, WILLIAM MARVIN (1886 - 1963) (Biographical)

1. William Marvin Clayton
2. Lewis burg, Tenn.
3. Dec. 4, 1886 at Cornersville, Marshall co., Tennessee
4. Daniel Bachman Clayton; Cornersville, Marshall co., Tennessee; he lived in county all his life; William G. Clayton and Jane Bachman; Cornersville, Tennessee
5. Cora Ann McCord; Cowden McCord and Sarah Elizabeth Williams; Chappell Hill, Tennessee
6. Daniel Bachman, a great-grandfather came from Holland and settled in Jersey (?) and moved to Tennessee in 1801
7. 1 year at Morgan School, Fayetteville, Tenn.; 2 years at Massey school, Cornersville, Tenn.
8. Vanderbilt University, class of '10, A.B. degree; varsity track team, glee club and commadore club.
9. ---
10. taught Latin and Greek 2 years in Massey school, Pulaski, Tenn. 1911-1912; since 1912 in lumber and building materials business
11. Senator elect from Marshall and Lincoln counties for the 1923 General Assembly.
12. teach a sunday school class; member of the Rotary Club; treasurer.
13. Democrat
14. Methodist Episcopal Church, South; member of the board of stewards
15. ΠΚΑ fraternity
16. ---
17. Rachel Hughes Witt; married June 21, 1916 at Lynnville, Tennessee; George Bugg Witt and Mattie Webb Wilkinson; Lynnville, Tennessee.
18. Supply Sgt. 6th Battalion, 20th Engineers (forestry), Mar. 4, 1918 to Apr. 8, 1919 was stationed at Chateauroux, France.
19. Ann Witt - 5 years old

COOPER, WILLIAM DANIEL (1869 -) (Biographical)

1. William Daniel Cooper
2. Paris, Tennessee
3. Dec. 3, 1869; Big Sandy, Benton co., Tennessee
4. Thomas D. Cooper; Clarksville, Montgomery co., Tennessee; near Big Sandy, Benton co., Tennessee having moved from Montgomery county at an early age in his childhood on a farm which he owned and operated to a few years before his death in May 1910; John Cooper and Mary Fain Cooper; near Clarksville, Montgomery co., Tenn. before marriage.

Cooper cont'd:

5. Lucinda J. DeBruce; Prof. Robert DeBruce and Marguerite Buchannan; North Carolina in early life, came to Tennessee with his parents.
6. My grandfather Robert DeBruce was born and raised in Pennsylvania; he was a schollar, being the Master of several languages finishing his literary education at a College in England; he came to Tennessee as a pioneer school teacher where he taught at various places - among them the town of Clarksville, D____?, Trenton and Camden; in 1844 (?) he married Marguerite Buchanan; my grandfather John Cooper on my paternal side came to Tennessee with his people from North Carolina in his youth and settled in Montgomery county, Tennessee in early manhood - he married Mary Fain and soon they moved to Benton county, Tennessee where they lived on a farm till about the year 1858 when they went to Howell county, Missouri as comprised by six children, leaving my father and our sister in Tennessee.
7. My early education was obtained in the county schools of Benton co., Tennessee - at the age of 22 I entered high school, in seccondary school at Big Sandy where I attended 3 sessions and completed ____? in the year 1893 under Prof. John F. (?) Hill; later 1894 I attended a part of an session at Murray Institute.
8. Student in the Southern Normal University under J. A. Bab___? for 2 years and in 1898 received the degree of B.S.
9. Made appraisal study of Pedagogy in high school and university and taught during the summer and fall months the year that I was going to school; I also studied law and am a member of the bar.
10. Began teaching in county schools in the year 1892 in Benton county, Tennessee; taught in Henry county and also in Calloway county, Kentucky, these were usually 3 to 5 months and I attended school in the remainder of these years to 1898; I was elected principal of the city school at Camden (?), Tennessee and held this position 4 years going out in 1902 into the office of County Clerk of Benton county.
11. County Clerk of Benton county, Tennessee 3 times 1902-1914; Secretary City Board of Education Dec.-Jan. 1904 to 1910; Member of City Board of Education at Paris, Tennessee 1916 to 1920 (next line difficult to read...cme) Member of State Board of Education 1918-1931; Member of the State Legislature in the Senate representing the 24th _____?.
12. It has always been my purpose to support such men and such principles in public affairs as would result in the greatest good to my community, to my state and to the nation and during the 1921 (?) session of the Legislature as chairman of the Senate Committee on Education I did all in my power to promote the education in terest in the state
13. Democrat; served as chairman of the County Democratic Executive Committee in 1912 to 1915, when I moved to Paris, am now a member of the Henry county Democratic Executive Committee.
14. Member of the official board of Stewarts in the M. E. Church, South at the 1st Methodist Church at Paris, Tennessee.
15. Mason, Odd Fellow, W.O.W., M.W.A. and of the W.O.W. Circle; have served as Vice (?) grand Noble, Grand and Dist. Deputy in the I.O.O.F.
16. Have never written a book nor edited a paper.
17. Lizzie McCullough, married at Camden, Tennessee, Dec. 18, 1902; Wm. B. McCullough and Martha (Bomar - possibly Boman or Bowan); Manleyville, Tennessee; Wm. B. McCullough, my wifes father was raised in Overton co., Tennessee where his people now reside; her mother - Martha Bowan(?), was the daughter of Rueben and Mary Ann Bowan(?); the Bowan (?) family and connections is one of the largest and best known in Henry county, Tennessee.
18. I have no record in the military, never having served in the army nor navy; I served as one of the Legal Advisory Board in Henry co. during the World War; also as a member of the Committee in the Sale of Government Bonds and war saving certificates.
19. William Fain Cooper, age 17 (18?) years
Bonnie (?) May Cooper, age 15 years
Mattie Lou Cooper, age 11 (12?) years
All reside with me at Paris, Tennessee; the eldest, William Fain is at present in Logan College at Russellville, Kentucky.

COOPER, WILLIAM PRENTICE, JR. (1896-1969)
Oct. 29, 1924 Shelbyville, Tenn.

1. William Prentice Cooper, Jr.
2. Shelbyville, Tenn.
3. Sept. 28, 1895, Shelbyville, Bedford Co., Tenn.
4. William Prentice Cooper; Smith Mills, Henderson Co., Ky.; Henderson, Ky. and Shelbyville, Tenn. and was Speaker of the House of Representatives of Tennessee in 1915, and is one of the Trustees of the University of Tennessee; Dr. James William Cooper and Eliza Ann Royster, Smith Mill,Ky.
5. Argentine Shofner; Jacob Morton Shofner and Melissa Landis, Shelbyville, Tenn.
6. ....
7. Butler's Creek School, Miss Cooper teacher, no relation, but a very excellent lady; Hanna's Private School, Mrs. C. Clinton Hanna, my most beloved teacher the Tate School; Webb School of Bell Buckle, Tenn., Mr. John Webb the greatest scholar who ever taught me and his brother "Sawnie Webb", the greatest lecturer; in the Hanna's School I won two gold medals - one for being the best scholar for the year, and one for declamation.
8. Attended Vanderbilt University in 1914 and 1915; was Vice-Pres. of the freshman class, freshman debater, member of Phi Delta Theta Fraternity and Secretary of the Y.M.C.A.; in 1916 and 1917. I attended Princeton University and graduated in 1917 with a B.A. Degree; while at Princeton I was on the Intercollegiate Debating Team; was the winner of the French Medal Debate, and won one of the Junior Orator Medals; I was a member of the Key and Seal Club.
9.Professional education obtained at Harvard University in 1919, 1920, and 1921, graduating in the latter year from Harvard Law School with the degree of LL.B., was a member of the Beal Law Club & of Lincoln's Inn.
10. My profession is that of a lawyer and I have practiced law in Shelbyville, Tenn. since my admission to the Bar in Feb. 1922.
11. I represented Bedford county in the State Legislature of 1923. On August 3, 1924 I was elected Attorney General, 8th Circuit-term expires Sept. 1, 1926.
12. In the legislature of 1923, as Chairman of the Committee on Uniforms laws, I secured the passage in the House of a number of laws reforming procedure in our courts of law, the most notable of which was the Uniform Declaratory Judgements Act, which is now law.
13. Democrat - at present I am chairman of the Democratic Victory Club-an organization formed in Bedford county by the Democratic National Committee to get out the vote for J. W. Davis for President of the U. S.
14. Lutheran - at present I am teacher of a sunday school of the Methodist Church South of Shelbyville, Tenn.
15. Phi Delta Theta fraternity.
16. ..
17. ..
18. On Jan. 5, 1918 I volunteered as private in the Field Artillary at Princeton, N.J., I subsequently trained at Camp Dix, N. J.; was later transferred to Fort Monroe?, Va. where I was appointed Master Gunner, warrant officer, by Gen. Coe.-chief of Coast Artillery; in the fall of 1918 I was selected to attend the Officers Training School at Fort Monroe, Va. and successfully completed the course and was given a commission as 2nd Lieut. Heavy Artillery and latter part of Jan. 1919;I was given an honorable discharge from the military service Jan. 23, 1919.

CRESWELL, EDWARD EVERETT (1881-)

Jan. 31, 1922 Sevierville, Tenn.

1. Edward Everett Creswell
2. Sevierville
3. Nov. 9, 1881; Skyland, Buncombe co., N. C.
4. Adam Hugh? Creswell; Boyds Creek, Sevier co., Tenn.; White Pine, Jefferson co., M. E. minister; Rufus Creswell and Anne Randles?; Boyds Creek, Sevier co., Tenn.
5. Ella Sumner?;____ Sumner? and Rosella Hallman; Skyland, N. C.
6. The Creswell family located in Sevier county where he engaged in many Indian battles in pioneer days.

7. Common schools education received in Jefferson county, Tenn.
8. Graduated from Maury Academy, Dandridge, Tenn.
9. Graduate in law-Grant? University, Chattanooga, Tenn. 1907
10. Att'y at law 1908 Sevierville, Tenn.
11. Member of Lower House Tenn. Legislature 2 terms 1913-1915; State Senate one term 1917; Att'y Gen. Second Circuit elected Aug. 1918.
12.---
13. Republican - member of the State Executive Committee, Chairman 1st Dist.; Congressman Executive Committee
14. M. E. steward
15. W.O.W.-Modern Woodman
16.---
17. Polly Molla (Moela?) Ogle, Sevier co., Tenn. May 17, 1895; Levi Evans Ogle and Nancy Ann King, Barnes?, Tenn.; descendants of Oglethorp who settled in Ga. 17__.
18. Captain in State Militia 1914-15.
19. 1. Beulah Estel Creswell
    2. Annie Eleanor Creswell
    3. Edna Everette Creswell
       (Evrette?)

CROSKERY, ROBERT HARRISON (1889-)

Dec. 16, 1922 Bethel Springs, Tenn.

1. Robert Harrison Croskery
2. Bethel Springs, Tenn.
3. Nov. 24, 1889, Bethel Springs, McNairy co., Tenn.
4. Thomas Croskery; Belfast, county Down, Ireland; in Ireland until he was 5 or 6 years of age; he lived in McNairy county, Tenn. about 10 years, then a few years in Kentucky; he came back to McNairy county and spent the remainder of his life; John Croskery and Eliza Croskery; Bethel Springs, McNairy co., Tenn.
5. Louisa D. Lain; Thomas Lain; Jane A, Lain; McNairy county, Tenn.
6. My grandparents on my father's side came to America from Ireland; my grandparents on my mother's side came to McNairy county from North Carolina.
7. In the public schools of McNairy county, Tenn.; teachers were C. Hamm, Wilber Hester, Mrs. Eliza Croos, Mrs. Mamie Lipford, Mrs. Vina Hodges, P. E. Cheshier, J. B. Graham, B. C. Dodds, J. H. Etheridge, H. G. Hodges, J. C. Brooks, J. R. Swain, A. H. Grantham.
8.---
9.---
10. Did work on a farm; taught public schools of McNairy co., Tenn. 45 months.
11. no
12.---
13. Republican
14. (religious preference) Presbyterian
15. member of American Legion
16. none
17. not married
18. Private in 9th Div. Co. "L" 45th Infantry, Commanded by Gen. Holbrook, Camp Sheridan, Ala. I was inducted into the service at Selmer, Tenn. July 5, 1918, Honorably discharged Dec. 19, 1918 at Camp Pike, Ark.

CUNNINGHAM, JOHN (1859-)

Dec. 11, 1922 Arlington and Gallaway, Tenn.

1. John Cunningham
2. Arlington, Shelby co., Tenn.
3. July 31, 1859, near Wentworth?, Rockingham co., N.C.
4. Alexander Cunningham; Milton, Person co., N. C.; Dauville? Va.; farmer and tobacco manufacturer; Alexander Cunningham and Martha Wilson Cunningham; Milton, Person co., N.C.
5. Mary Laura Galloway; Thomas Spraggins Gallaway and Lucinda Chalmers Gallaway; near Wentworth, Rockingham co., N.C.
6. My grandfather, Alexander Cunningham came to U. S. from Scotland and married Miss Martha Wilson of Person co., N. C. she was the daughter of

Col. Wilson who was a Col. in the Revolutionary War; my great granfather Charles Gallaway also came to U. S. from Scotland and settled in Rockingham co., N. C.; he owned a large landed estate both in North Carolina and Tennessee.
7. educated at home until 1876 went to Culleoka Tenn. at that time to Webb Bros. 5 mos. at University North Carolina 10 mos. and University Tenn. 10 mos.
8. graduated Leddin? Business College Aug. 1881
9. ---
10. was drug clerk at Mason, Tenn. and Covington, Tenn until Jany. 1882 came here and managed farm and saw mills for my uncle until 1888 going into business for myself then and have been in mercantile business at Gallaway continously since that date now operating store at Gallaway and Arlington.
11....
12....
13. Have always been a Democrat casting my first vote in 1880 for Hancock and English Democratic nominees for President and Vice President.
14. Have always been an Episcopalion - brought up in that church; baptised in infancy was confirmed by Bishop Gailor (Gailon?) in 1901.
15. Mason and am at present 1. M. of Arlington Lodge 604 also Chapter at Somerville? Tenn. also Knight Templar, St. Elmo Commandary, Memphis, Tenn.
16. none
17. Bell Battle; Jan 6, 1886, Gallaway, Tenn; Lucius Lucullus Battle, M.D. and Martha Chester Battle; Arlington, Tenn.; Bell Battle's grandfather (maternal) was Col. Robt. I. Chester of Jackson, Tenn.; grandfather (paternal) was Wm. Battle of North Carolina who moved to Tennessee in early life, reared 13 children the youngest is still living at Arlington, Tenn. 81 years old.
18....
19. 1. Alexander Marvin Cunningham, 34, unmarried, Arlington, Tenn
    2. Mary Laura Cunningham,wife of M. Gerald Benson?, Tunica, Miss.
    3. William Battle Cunningham, 21, unmarried, Arlington, Tenn.
    4. Bell Cunningham, 17, now a student of Gulf Port College, Gulf Port, Miss.

DAVIS, EWIN LAMAR (1876-1949)
Tullahoma, Tenn. July 25, 1922

1. Ewin Lamar Davis
2. Tullahoma, Tenn.
3. Feb. 5, 1876, 5 miles S. of Shelbyville, Bedford co., Tenn.
4. Maclin Hezekiah Davis; near Flat Creek, Bedford co., Tenn; on the farm where he was born until young man , when he moved to Normandy, Tenn. until 1880, after which he lived most of his time at Tullahoma, Tenn., until his death in 1898. He was a business man.; Maclin Davis and Martha Jane Ray, near Flat Creek in Bedford co., Tenn.
5. Christina Lee Shoffner; Michael Shoffner and Sophronia E.Morton; five miles South of Shelbyville, Tenn.
6. (see attached memoranda.)
7. (see attached memoranda)
8. (see attached memoranda)
9. Attended the Law department of Columbian University (now George Washington University), Washington, D. C. 1897-99, receiving degree LL.B.
10. Began active practice of law in summer of 1899 at Chattanooga, Tenn., but in January, 1900, returned to Tullahoma, Tenn. and engaged in active practice there and in surrounding counties until he assumed his duties as Circuit Judge Sept. 1, 1910.
11. (see attached memoranda)
12. (see attached memoranda)
13. Democrat. Chairman Democratic Executive Committee of Coffee county, repeatedly delegated to the State Conventions, alternate delegate from the State-At-Large to Democratic National Convention to San Francisco in 1920. Presidential Elector in 1904.
14. Member of First Baptist Church, Tullahoma, Tenn. Deacon in said church, and one of the Trustees thereof for many years.
15. 32nd Degree Mason, and was elected President of the largest Scottish Rite Masonic Class ever initiated by Trinity Consistory No. 2 Nashville, Tenn.; a Knight of Pythias M.W. of A Jr. O.U. and A/M. Alpha Tau Omega

and Phi Delta Phi Fraternities.
16. Editor of Annual Year Book, Columbian University, 1899, wrote legal essay on "Equity Jurisprudence", which won first prize at Columbian University.
17. Carolyn Windsor, married Dec. 28, 1898 at Americus, Ga.; John Windsor and Emily Lester, Americus, Ga. (on separate sheet)....... Ancestry of Carolyn Windsor Davis. John Windsor was born in Webster co., Ga. in 1847; when 16 yrs. old enlisted in the Confederate Army and served until the close of the war, being Commissary Sergeant during the last six months of his service. He is now living at Winter Haven, Fla. He was the son of Alexander Windsor, who was born in South Carolina in 1815. and who, when a young man, moved to Georgia, where he resided until his death in 1894; he was in the Seminole Indian War. The mother of said John Windsor whom Alexander Windsor married in 1836, was Harriet Terry, born in Ga., in 1821, where she resided until her death in 1899. She was the daughter of Richard (Dick) Terry, born about 1794, presumably in Virginia, who moved to Georgia where he resided until his death in 1856; he was in the Seminole Indian War and in the War of 1812. He was the son of Robert Terry, who lived and died in Virginia, and of Jane Taylor. The mother of Harriet Terry was Isabella Armstrong Powell, who died in Ga. in 1871.The wife of the said John Windsor and mother of Carolyn Windsor Davis was Emily Lester, born near Americus, Ga., in 1855. and now residing with her husband at Winter Haven, Fla. She was the daughter of Alfred Jefferson Lester, born in 1808, and who lived in Ga., until his death in 1874. The said Alfred Jefferson Lester was the son of Nixon Lester; the mother of Emily Lester, whom Alfred Jefferson Lester married in 1834, was Amelia B. Barlow, born in Georgia in 1813, and who died in 1898 in Americus, Ga. She was the daughter of James J. Barlow, who died in Dublin, Ga. about 1860.
18. I have had no military service, but was Chairman of the Dist. Exemption Board for Middle Tennessee 1917-19. My son, John Windsor Davis, enlisted in the 136 Field Artillery about two weeks after his eighteenth birthday and in about two months was sent overseas and saw active service at the front, in the Marbache Sector and in the Meuse-Argonne offensive, being on the battleline when the armistice was signed. Subsequently he was transferred to Paris and assigned for duty as an orderly at the Peace conference.
19. 1. John Windsor Davis, Tullahoma, Tenn.
    2. Margaret Davis, " "
    3. Ewin Davis (daughter) " "
    4. Latham Shoffner Davis," "
    5. Carolyn Davis, " "

(Note -following is a letter written to John Trotwood Moore on 24 July 1922, from Washington, D. C. by Ewin Lamar Davis, regarding the letter and form asking for data on both Davis men-Ewin and his brother, Norman. Mentions he is sending ancestral data on both and is of considerable length) Page 1 - includes much of same material on form. Also mentions service as Circuit Judge, and campaign booklets attached. Ewin L. Davis is a brother of Norman H. Davis, a sketch of whose life appears in this work. He is also a brother of Paul M. Davis, First Vice President of the American National Bank, Nashville, Tenn.; Chairman of the Board of Director of the Tenn. Central Railway; Chairman of the Executive Board of the Nashville Industrial Corporation, and a Director of the Nashville Branch of the Federal Reserve Bank.

These Davis boys are sons of Maclin Hezekiah Davis and Christina Shoffner-Davis. Their ancestors in every line settled in the colonies of Virginia, North Carolina, South Carolina and Pennsylvania prior to the Revolutionary War. They are likewise descendants of John Morten, who was a member of the Continental Congress and who signed the Declaration of Independence.

Maclin Hezekiah Davis was born Sept. 12, 1852 in Bedford co., Tenn. He grew to manhood on the farm where he was born, and was later actively engaged in business 'till the time of his death, April 1, 1898. He was a Mason and Knight of Honor, and a prominent citizen. The said Maclin H Davis was married on Dec. 5, 1872, to Christina L. Shoffner, who was born May 3, 1854, in Bedford co., Tenn. and is now residing at Tullahoma, Tenn.

There were born to this union the following children: (page 2)

1. Ewin Lamar Davis, born Feb. 5, 1876
2. Norman H. Davis, born Aug. 9, 1878

3. Paul Maclin Davis, born June 3, 1882
4. Auga Lee Davis, born Apr. 17, 1884; died Nov. 25, 1889
5. Thurman Jefferson Davis, born Nov. 20, 1890
6. Christine Davis, born June 14, 1893
7. Lamont Davis, born June 14, 1893

The said Maclin H. Davis was a son of Maclin Davis, who was born in Lewis co., Tenn. in 1826, later moved to Bedford co., Tenn., served in the Confederate Army, was a Bedford county farmer until his declining years, when he retired and moved to Tullahoma, Tenn., where he died in 1910; the sd Maclin Davis was the son of Maclin Davis, who was born in Wilkes co., N. C., moved to Livingston co., Ky. where he married Matilda Greenwell; later moved to Lewis co., Tenn and still later to Wayne co., Tenn., where he died at the age of 95 years. The last named Maclin Davis was a son of Snead Davis, who was born Aug. 1, 1752, and who served in the North Carolina line throughout the Revolutionary War, participating in numerous battles including the Battle of Kings Mountain, and being twice wounded in action. After the Revolutionary War, he moved to Livingston co., Ky. He died in 1838, at the age of 86 years. The sd Snead Davis has a brother Nocolas Davis, who served with distinction in the Rev. Army, his heroism being mentioned in Ridpath's History of the Revolutionary War.

The mother of the sd Maclin H. Davis was Martha Jane Ray, born in 1832, in Bedford co., Tenn. where she married Maclin Davis in 1846. She died in Bedford county in 1867. She was a daughter of Hezekiah Ray,born at Cross Keys, S.C. in 1780; moved to and settled in Bedford co., Tenn. in 1818, where he died in 1870, age 90 years. The father of the sd. Hezekiah Ray, who resided in S. C. fought through the entire Rev. War under Gen. Francis Marion.

The mother of the sd. Martha Jane Ray was Patsy Jones, born in 1793, in South Carolina, and who moved with her husband, Hezekiah Ray, to Bedford co., Tenn. in 1818, where she died in 1863.

Their ancestors in six different lines settled in Bedford co., Tenn., in the early part of the nineteenth century, being amoung the earliest settlers in that territory, some of them settling prior to the year 1800, one of them, John Shoffner, went to Bedford county in 1803 with Newton Cannon, who afterwards became Governor of the State. The sd John Shoffner assisted Newton Cannon, who was a surveyor, in surveying out the greater portion of Bedford county, which was established in 1807.
(page 3)

The sd. Christine Lee Shoffner-Davis, the mother of Ewin L. Davis and brothers, is a descendant of Michael Shoffner, who was born near Frankfort-on-the-Main, Germany, in 1721. When a young man he came to America, landing in Philadelphia, but he soon removed to what is now Orange co., N.C, where he permanently located and where he died in 1810. He had four sons: Michael, George, Martin and Peter. The first three named served in the Continental Army during the war of the Revolution, and were in many of the hardest battles of that struggle. For the most part they served under the command of Gen. Greene, but at times they were with Steuben and DeKalb, and the records show that each of them served faithfully and were honorably discharged. Martin was a cavalryman and a noted athelete, and Michael was an infantryman. It is thought that Peter likewise fought for American independence.

The sd. Michael Shoffner, the younger, was born in 1752, and lived in North Carolina until his death in 1820. The sd. Martin Shoffner was born in 1758, and in 1780 married Katherine Roundtree, who was born in 1760, and died in 1823. The sd. Martin Shoffner and family moved to and settled in what is now Bedford County in 1808, where he lived until his death in 1838. The fifth son of Martin Shoffner was named John, who was born in Orange county, N. C. in 1787. In 1803, in company with Newton Cannon and a surveying party, he crossed the mountains and penetrated the wilderness into what is now Bedford county; and they surveyed what was later established as Bedford county, and John returned to his parents in North Carolina in about two years. In 1810 he married Amelia Shoffner a daughter of his uncle, Michael Shoffner. He returned with his family to Bedford county, Tenn. in 1815, where he resided until his death in 1857, his wife having died in 1849. The fourth son of sd. John and Amelia Shoffner was Michael Shoffner, who was born in Bedford co., Tenn. in 1818, and who died in the same county in 1892. In 1839, he married Sophronia E. Morton, who was born in Bedford co., Tenn. in 1819, and who died in the same co. in 1875. Their tenth child was the aforesaid

Christina L. Shoffner, who married Maclin H. Davis, as before stated.

The sd. wife of Michael Shoffner, Sophronia Eglentine Morton, was a daughter of Jacob Morton, who was born in Caswell co., N.C. in 1787. At the age of 21 he left N.C. with the tide of emigration that was flowing west, and stopped in Bedford county for about three years, then he moved to Nashville, Tenn., where he lived for several years, and then returned to Bedford county, where he married Anne Fisher, in 1815.

The sd. Jacob Morton was the oldest son of Mesheck Morton, who was born in Virginia in 1766, and who in 1785 married Nancy Asburn, and soon afterwards moved to Caswell co., N.C. near Yanceyville. Mesheck Morton was a son of George Morton, who was born in Pennsylvania in 1745, and after an early marriage settled in Virginia and reared a large family. George Morton was a son of John Morton, who was born in 1724 near Philadelphia, Penn. and who died Apr. 20, 1777. John Morton was a member of the Continental Congress from Penn. and was one of the signers of the Declaration of Independence. His father was named John, and was of Swedish descent.

The sd. Anne Fisher, who married Jacob Morton, was born in N.C. in 1798, but about the year 1802 or 1803 moved with her father to Bedford co., Tenn., married Jacob Morton in 1815 and resided in Bedford co., Tenn. until the time of her death. Anne Fisher was a daughter of Michael Fisher, who was born in Penn. in 1756, and moved to N. C. soon after the Rev. War, where he married Christina Earnhart in 1786. As before stated, Michael Fisher and family, including Anne, moved to Bedford co, in 1802 or 03 where he resided until his death in 1833. His sd. wife, Christina Earnhart, was born in 1764 and died in Bedford co. Tenn. in 1830. At the age of 16 years Michael Fisher enlisted and served Capt. Heinrich Nach's Company, Berke county, Penn. Militia, fighting in behalf of American Independence.

(page 5)

Article on Ewin L. Davis, written by Savoyard (Eugene W. Newman) dated 26 June 1922.

(page 6) More published articles from various newspapers.

(page 7) more of same

(page 8) letter written to Hon. E. L. Davis by John Skelton Williams, June 1922 re Ship Subsidy Bill.

(page 9) photograph of Ewin L. Davis (Candidate for Congress)

(page 10) Political endorsement, etc.

(page 11) more of same (page 12, 13,14,15,16,17,18,19,)

(page 20) Includes index from previous book pages: i-e-letter from Ewin L. Davis to Voters; comments by State Papers: Nashville Press, Memphis Press, Chattanooga Press, and other state papers ;Endorsements and newspaper comments: in the Fifth Congressional Dist.:Bedford, Cannon, Coffee, Dekalb, Lincoln, Marshall, Moore and Rutherford counties; Correspondence and comments on Joint Discussions; Replies to Mr. Bean and Lynchburg Banner relative to work of Judge Davis on District Board; Further Replies to Charges and Insinuations of Mr. Bean and Lynchburg Banner. (Note: this material covers from pages 3-31 of this book included in the material sent in by E. L. Davis....cme)

On page 7 of this book (not entitled): mentions Judge W. C. Houston; page 9: Frank S. Washburn; page 9; W. C. Houston; Fletcher S. Brockman; page 10; page 10: Mr. Ewell; Judge J. C. Higgins and Andrew Todd; page 11 Edward Albright, Editor of Sumner County News; page 11: Geo. L. Diemer of Fayetteville and J. J. Bean of Lynchburg; same page: Judge M. D. Smallman and R. W. Smartt, Joe Gessler; page 13: mentions sister of Christina Shoffner, Mrs. Margan Webb and Jno. E. Shoffner; page 14: H.T. Stewart; page 15: names - James D. Richardson, W. C. Houston,; Lawyers:James J. Finley, Goodloe Warden, Jr., J. L. Ewell, A. L. Davidson, R. W. Green, C.N. Townsend, J. K. P. Pearson (73years old), J. H.Ashley, J. H. McKenzie, John A. Chumbley.

County Officials: H. S. Lowery, Trustee; J. Q. Davidson, Cir.Crt.Clk; W. H. McBride, Dep. Co. Clk;H. R. Summers, Clk. & Master; J. A. Gibson, Co.Crt.Clk.; W. J. Gullett, Sheriff; T. R. Holmes, Dty. Sher'f; Geo. W. Nobles, Register; J. H.Leming, Co. Sup't.; Wm. Rodes, Ranger; LeRoy McFerrin, Co. Surv.-also names Hugh J. Doak, Sec'ty Democratic Ex. Comm. of Coffee County and J. P. McGregor, T. G. Powell, B. Ashley, J. W. Leek, G. H. Sherrill, S.R. Henley, W. R. Marshall, Doak Aydelott,, Henry Warren, J.K. Farris, R.M. Stepp, Wm. Rodes, W. C. Throneberry, C.M.H. Farrar,J. H. McCrary, J.R. Bailey, E. C. Carroll, Hence Winton, W. B. Lyon, W. A. McMichael, J. P. Shelton,L. B. Simmons, F.M. Jarrell, J. N.Tipps, J.N.

Chitwood, and A. E. Ray. (Page 18). Dekalb county - Dr. James T. Bell and Brown Davis, J. E. Hobson, F. M. Love, J. E. Hobson, D. B. Wilson, W. H. C. Lasiter and Tom Squires; Guy Davis, R. L. McGinnis, and Henry Puckett; (Page 20) - ..... Fairbanks and Lawson Myers, mentions also- the State vs Roy Grandstaff for the murder of Charlie Smith near Alexandria. (Page 23) James J. Bean; (Page 24) - W. J. Bryan, also Bean and Houston; (Page 25) - J. W. Ross; (Page 26) -..... McAdoo, Geo. Harvey, J. J. Bean; (Pages 31-32) - much more on Mr. J. J. Bean. (Note: Most of this is political material only.)

(Separate page entitled: "Congressional Record" 67th Congress, 2nd Session - The Ship Subsidy Bill - speech by Hon. Ewin L. Davis, June 13, 1922; mentions Harold Phelps Stokes, a member of the staff of the New York Evening Post; also includes about 8 pages of this bill named above).

(Separate page) - titled: Norman H. Davis - Norman H. Davis, was born in Bedford co., Tenn., Aug. 9, 1878; son of McLin (Maclin) H. and Tina Lee (Shoffner) Davis; student at Webb School, Vanderbilt University, and Leland-Stanford University. The degree of Doctor of Civil Laws was conferred on him by the University of the South in June 1921. He is a member of the Board of Trustees of Vanderbilt University. Married Mackie Paschall of Atlanta, Ga., in Oct. 1898, and has eight children: Macklin, a graduate of Harvard University and now residing in Nashville, Tenn.; Norman P., a student at Harvard; Martha, a student at Vassar; Christine, Goode, Paschall, May and Sarah. He is a brother of Ewin L. Davis, formerly ....also a brother of Paul M. Davis.......Mr. Davis went to Havana, Cuba in 1902, where he successfully engaged in various enterprises....banking, construction, sugar mills, etc. Organized the Trust Company of Cuba, and was president of same;...when U. S. entered World War, Mr. Davis volunteered.....was associated with the Treasury Department in Washington as adviser on loans to the Allied Governments; was special delegate from the U. S. to Spain; sent to Paris as Special Representative of the U. S. Treasury;...names many more positions held; Mentions Herbert C. Hoover and Bernard M. Baruch, Edward N. Hurley,Vance McCormick and Thos. W. Lamont...was offered post of Under Secretary of State on resignation of Frank L. Polk, but declined; and later accepted in the spring of 1920; he was appointed by Pres. Wilson as a member of the International Communications Conference, and was elected Chairman, continued in that capacity until latter part of April 1921 and resigned. He was decorated by the Belgian Government and also was elected to the French Legion of Honor.
(Some typed pages of press releases)...Norman H. Davis for Democratic candidate for president in 1924; followed by several pages of political notes, etc. and a write-up by the noted political writer, Mark Sullivan; "Woodrow Wilson and The World War" by Charles Seymore and "The War, The World and Wilson" by George Creel, mention Norman H. Davis at the Paris Peace Conference; page following ..mentions Ex-Sec'y of Navy, Josephus Daniels and Norman Davis, 1921.

DAVIS, NORMAN HEZEKIAH (1878-1944)

First part of film is address delivered before the Council on Foreign Relations, Feb. 17, 1922, by Hon. Norman H. Davis - includes about 12 pages of the address. See Ewin Lamar Davis for further material on Norman Hezekiah Davis.

DE LA VERGNE, GEORGE HARRISON (1868-)
2332 Andrews Ave., New York, Apr. 24, 1922

1. George Harrison De La Vergne
2. New York, N. Y.
3. Dec. 5, 1868, Clinton, Henry co., Missouri
4. George De La Vergne; Marietta, Ohio, Marietta, Ohio also in the Cumberland Mts., Tenn., Clinton, Mo., Colorado Springs, Colo., Honolulu,the Hawaiian Islands and Los Angeles, Cal.; Lt. Col. 8th Tenn. Vol.; George Washington De Le Vergne and Mary Yates; n. Poughkeepsie, N. Y.
5. Emily Dole Rice; William Harrison Rice and Sophia Hyde Rice; Honolulu, Hawaiian Islands.
6. Maternal grandfather and mother went as missionairies to Hawaii under American Board in 1840. My grandmother........Sophia Hyde Rice.........

(maiden name was Hyde), the family came from England about 1633, finally settled in Norwich, Connecticut. My father's family came from France five or six generations ago and settled near Poughkeepsie, N.Y. They were Hugenots.
7. Public school Clinton, Mo. and Colorado Springs, Miss Anna Packs? my first teacher, and Miss E. E. Wadleigh in Colorado Springs, I recall distinctly.
8. Colorado College, '91, PH.B Post graduate course Princeton 91-92 attended lectures Woodrow Wilson, Cornell University Law School '94 LIB Chas. E. Hughes, in contracts.
9. see above
10. Law, Honolulu, Hawaiian Islands 1894-98; in Attorney General's Office, assistant Prosecutor District Magistrate of Honolulu, Jan. 11, 1896-June 97.
11....
12....
13. Republican
14. Protestant Episcopal Church; member of the Vestrey St. James, Fordham in the Bronx.
15....
16."Hawaiian Sketches" 1898, San Francisco, Cal. book now extinct, Crocker Co.; "The Pines and Other Poems", Los Angeles, Cal. B.R. Baumgardts co. 1902 61 pages "The Wilderness and Battle Picture", The Knickerbocker Press, N.Y. 1926; these all published by the Author.
17. Bertha Henderson Smith, Apr. 30, 1907, Newtown, Connecticut; Walter Smith and Melissa Henderson; Paterson, New Jersey; New England families Hawley, Henderson, Sears, Castle and Olmstead. Daniel Webster and Lorenzo Dow appear in the line of my wife's ancestry.
18....
19. 1. George Harrison De La Vergne
2. M'liss Aline De La Vergne

DEPEW, JOHN DULANEY (1879-)
Johnson City, Tenn. Jan. 30, 1922

1. John Dulaney Depew
2. Johnson City, Tenn.
3. 23 Apr. 1879, Jonesboro, RFD 12, Sullivan co., Tenn.
4. Elbert Sevier Depew, Jonesboro, RFD 12 Sullivan co., Tenn.; Jonesboro, RFD #12, all his life; he was a physician; he was also a teacher; had 4 years in Civil War, serving with 8th Tenn. Cavalry, Co.K, and he was hospital steward; John Depew and Mary Boyd Depew; Jonesboro, RFD #12, Sullivan co., Tenn.
5. Maria Caroline Willard; Dulaney Willard and Caroline Clark Willard; Fordtown, RFD # 1, Tennessee.
6. The Willards came from the old New England Willard family, evidently, but I have never been able to locate the first one to settle in Tenn. The Clarks, my grandmother Willard, belongs to the East Tennessee Clark family. The Depews first came to Tenn. from New Jersey. There was one in the Battle of King's Mountain. They have been in every war since then.The Boyd's my paternal grandmother, came to Tenn. early and there was one of them in the Battle of King's Mtn. and there have been in all other wars. They came from Virginia.
7. Rock Springs Seminary, Sullivan co., Tenn. H. F. Ketron and John Daugherty, teachers; Church Hill High School, William E Henson, teacher; Paine's Business College, New York City.
8. none - but had hard home study and taught several years.
9. LL.B from Law Dept. of the Unv. of Chattanooga, Tenn. class 1910.
10. Lawyer, 1910 Johnson City, Tenn.
11. Justice of Peace for Sullivan co. 1912-15, member Board of Education for Washington co. Tenn. 1919-20; member Tennessee Legislature 1921-22.
12....
13. Republican
14. Methodist Episcopal; board of trustees; member of board of stewards; asst. sunday school supt. and sunday school teacher for years.
15. Masons
16. none
17. Mary Alice Boyd, married Dec. 31, 1901, George Washington Boyd and Mary Elizabeth Boyd; Fordtown, RFD #1, Tenn.; same as mine on her father's

side, as our fathers were double first cousins; her mother was Mary Elizabeth Iric; have been here a long time, but do not know where they came from; very small number in the Iric family.
18. none
19. none

DE WITT, SAM M. (1851-)
"Pioneer"
(Veterans Form #2)

1. Sam M. DeWitt, Nashville, Tennessee
2. 71
3. Jackson county, Tennessee
4. none
5. ...
6. Lawyer
7. Allen DeWitt; Red Boiling Springs, Macon Co., Tenn., was serving as Judge of the Circuit Court.
8. Ellen Davis; Zacrion(?) Davis; ___; Red Boiling Springs
9. My grandfather, Sam DeWitt was a minister of the Church of Christ; my bro.(?), Wm. DeWitt, served 4 yrs. in the Conf. Army, was in Col. Dibrell's Reg., his Capt. was Mourie(?) Gare(Gore?); was wounded at Chickamauga, again in Va.; my uncle, W. H. DeWitt was a member of the Southern Congress, was also in Pres. Davis cabinet.
10. ...
11. my father owned 3 slaves
12. two farms, house in town
13. $10,000
14. log and frame
15. the white men did the same kind of work as the slaves in field and woods; I grew up on the farm - did all kinds of work the year around.
16. my father worked on the farm at night he studied law by the light of a grease lamp and board light in the fire place my mother the house work - spun and weaving cloth to clothe the family - we taned our own leather to make our shoues.
17. ...
18. in my community yes - every man worked at all kinds of labor, no idlers no ____ of ____.
19. yes
20. no
21. yes
22. absolutely
23. just a few discontented ones
24. I dont think so
25. yes
26. I never heard of any ____ (blurred)
27. I attended what was known as subscription school about 3 months each year
28. one and half year
29. close by
30. yes
31. public
32. 3 months
33. not very
34. my teachers was both men and woman
35. ...
36. ...
37. ...
38. ...
39. ...
40. ...
41. ...
42. ...
43. ...
44. ...
45. ...
46. ...

DORSEY, ALBERT LEE (1879-1949)
Springfield, Tenn. June 26, 1922

1. Albert Lee Dorsey
2. Springfield, Tenn.
3. Nov. 29, 1879, Lovelaceville, Ballard co., Kentucky
4. Andrew Walker Dorsey; Shelbyville, Shelby co., Kentucky; in Shelbyville county until fourteen years of age, enlisted in the Confederate Army at that age, after that settled in Western Kentucky and was a contractor and builder.; Richard Merriwether Dorsey and Martha Glass; Shelby co., Ky.
5. Winnie Cathern Burrow; Green Berry Burrow and Matilda Cathern Morgan; Ballard county (now Carlisle) in the state of Kentucky.
6. (typed sheet added but appears to have been microfilmed and cut off lower section) Mr. Dorsey is a descendant of the Maryland Dorseys. He can trace his ancestry without a break to Edward Dorsey, the first settler, in 1857. The Dorsey line running back is as follows; Albert Lee Dorsey, son of Andrew Walker Dorsey (m. Winnie Cather Burrow), he the son of Richard Merriwether Dorsey (m Martha Glass), he the son of Corban Nicholas Dorsey (m.Martha Daniels), he the son of William Dorsey (m. Rachael Hobbs), he the son of Vachael Dorsey (m. Ruth Dorisey), he the son of John Dorsey (m. Honor Elder), he the son of Edward Dorsey (m. Ruth Todd), he the son of John Dorsey (m. Pleasant Ely), he the son of Edward Dorsey, first settler, who was of the Dorseys of Kiltulla Castle, Ireland, established by the Dorsey who was Governor General sent there by William the Conqueror from England,and the Dorseys came with William in the Conquest and were of the line of D'Arcie near Paris; Martha Glass-Dorsey, grandmother of A.L. Dorsey was the daughter (here the microfilm is redone and complete ancestry continues:) of Robert Glass (m. Sarah Owen), born in Ireland, son of Joseph Glass (m. Eliza Wilson),born, lived and died in Ireland, son of Samuel Glass (m. Mary Gamble). Samuel brought his grandson, said Robert, to U. S. A. L. Dorsey's mother, Winnie Cathern Burrow-Dorsey, was the daughter of Greenberry Burrow (m. Matilda Cathern Morgan-Burrow),he the son of Russell Burrow (m Obedience Horn) born in Tennessee, he the son of James Burrow (m. Miss Weathero), came from Scotland or was of Scotch descent; lived at or near Greensboro,N.C. and from there went to East Tennessee. Was in Revolution. Matilda Cathern Morgan Burrow was daughter of Thomas Morgan who was born and reared in Wales, and married Cathern Jones in London,England, and came to this country.
7. educated at public schools at Lovelaceville, Folsomdale, Mayfield in Ky.; business course at Draughon's Nashville, Tenn.
8. none
9. studied law at Springfield, Tenn., admitted to bar at Springfield, Tenn., March, 1903.
10. practice of law at Springfield, Tenn. Mar. 1903, and ever since.
11.none, except chairman of election commissions, chairman of Democratic executive committee, member of important committees in county during World War.
12.never a reformer, believe in old time Democracy; that country is best governed which is least governed, and that we need a reform against reformers.
13.Democrat; often times chairman of Co. Democratic Ex. Comm.; chairman of election commissions, etc.
14.Baptist; teacher of young men's class in S.S. with the largest membership of any S.S. class in county.
15.member of Blue Lodge Masons, Scottish Rite, 32 degree Masons,Odd Fellow; Knights of Pythias, Modern Woodmen of American, etc. Held principal offices in most of them
16. none
17.Lennie Sue Sprouse-Dorsey, married at Springfield, Aug. 25, 1920.; Elisha B. Sprouse; Mary Frances McMurry-Sprouse; Springfield, Tenn.; the McMurry's were descendant of the first settlers in Middle Tennessee. The Sprouse are old stock in Middle Tenn.
18. none
19. none.

DRINNON, ALFRED TAYLOR (1884-1944)
Ruthledge, Tenn. Dec. 20, 1922

1. Alfred Taylor Drinnon
2. Rutledge, Tenn.

3. Dec. 20, 1884, Sneedville, Hancock, Tenn.
4. James Douglas Drinnon; Sneedville, Hancock co., Tenn.; Sneedville, farmer, merchant and stock trader; W. B. Drinnon and Mary E. Drinnon, Sneedville, Tenn.
5. Mary E. Greene; Alfred Greene and Mary E. Greene; Sneedville, Tenn.
6. Alfred Greene, Captain in Civil War killed in Service.
7. Sneedville High School and Lincoln Memorial University, Harrogate?,Tenn.
8. none
9 Law school, Lebanon, Tenn. graduated June 1912.
10.Lawyer and banker, admitted to bar in 1912, engaged in banking business 1903 continued to this date.
11.Clerk Master Chancery Court Sneedville 12 years; member of Legislature 1921-22; re-elected for 1923-24.
12....
13.Republican; nominated for Speaker 62nd Gen. Assembly;_____? for Republicans in Legislature 1921.
14. Baptist
5. Masons-Shriner
16....
17.Gertrude Jorris; Lewis Coss? Jorris; Dord?Jorris, Sneedville.
18....
19.1. Hugh Kyle Drinnon, a son
2. Coss Jorris Drinnon, a son
3. Mattie Peal Drinnon, daughter

DRINNON, JAMES LLOYD (1873-)
Morristown, Tenn. Apr. 7, 1922

1. James Lloyd Drinnon
2. Morristown, Tenn.
3. May 26, 1873, Sneedville, Tenn., Hancock co., Tenn.
4. Burton Jefferson Drinnon; Sneedville, Hancock co. Tenn.; Sneedville, Tenn.; Sheriff four years; County Court Clerk eight years; Richard Drinnon and Sarah Housely, Sneedville, Tenn.
5. Sarah Elizabeth Drinnon; James Drinnon and Eliza (Walker),Sneedville, Tenn.
6. James Drinnon, my father's grandfather came from Ireland, his wife, Polley came from Scotland, some of her folks came from Holland. Came into this state from Virginia. My grandmother on my mother's side came from S. Carolina, her father was J. P.in Hancock co., Tenn. when first established.
7. A. A. Campbell, S. E. Jones, Prof. Carson.
8. Carson & Newman, Jefferson City, Tenn. 1896, President of graduating class; Bachelor of Science.
9. Preparatory law course, Princeton, N. J.; W.W. Wilson, teacher.
10. Law, 1898, Sneedville, and later at Morristown.
11. Internal Revenue service, 1901-1906.
12....
13. Republican delegate to various conventions, gubnatorial, Senatorial, Floterial.
14. member of Baptist church since 1892
15. Shrine, Kerbela Temple, Knoxville
16. ..
17. Nora Alice (Goodson) Feb. 12, 1902, Morristown, Tenn.; Milton Anderson Goodson and Matilda Jane (Hill); Morristown, Tenn.; her father came from N. Carolina; was in the Confederate army.
18. none
19. none

DURHAM, JOHN BRECKENRIDGE (1875-1944)
Gallatin, Tenn. Dec. 7, 1922

1. John Breckenridge Durham
2. Gallatin, Tenn.
3. Feb. 13, 1875, Angle, Sumner co., Tenn.
4. James Henry Durham, Sumner co., Tenn.; all his life in Sumner co., was a confederate soldier from 61 to 65; was 1st Lt. under Col Battle? 20 Tenn. Reg. Com. H. Breckenridges command; William Goolsberry Durham and Caroline Durham; all his life in Sumner co., Tenn.

5. Caroline Brizendine; Jas. Wright Brizendine and Lucinda Brizendine; a greater portion of lives in Sumner co., Tenn.
6. My father's grand parents come from Ireland to N.C. and then to Sumner co., Tenn.; my mother's grandparents come from England to Virginia and from there to Sumner co., Tenn.; my father was a farmer and stock raiser; owned his farm and lived on it all his life.
7. have a high school education obtained in the common schools of Sumner county.
8. never attended college.
9. had non
10. taught in the public schools of Sumner county for 15 years; elected Co. Trustee of Sumner co. in 1910; served 2 terms; merchant 3 years.
11. Trustee of Co. 1910-1914; Deputy Circuit Court Clerk 1917-1922; Legislature Nov. 7, 1922.
12....
13. Democrat
14. Presbyterian
15. Mason, Odd Fellows, Lawyal Order Moose.
16. none
17. Myrtle A. Campbell, 1903, Sumner co., Tenn.;Calvin H. Campbell and Sarah Brown, in Sumner county; my wife's father, C. H. Campbell came to Sumner county from Cannon county, Tenn.; my wife's mother daughter of Robt. Brown and raised in Sumner county.
18. none
19. 1.Arlene Durham, unmarried 18 years of age, lives in Gallatin, Tenn.

EASTERLEY, HULDA JERUSHA (WOODMANSEE) (1825-)
Crab Orchard, Tenn. Dec. 2, 1925

1. Huldah Jerusha Easterley
2. Crab Orchard (Tully)(Onondaga)
3. Jan. 21, 1825, town of Tulby Onondagua co., New York
4. Varnum Woodmansee; Charleston, S.C. Rhode Island, Cattaraugus co.,New York; school commissioner, Justice of Peace, Doctor, Revolutionary soldier, fought in battle Bunker Hill; David Maxum Woodmansee and ______
5. Polly Ann Christian; John Christian and Huldah Christian; Onondagua co., New York.
6. My grandparents on my fathers side came frong (sic) England. I was so small I don't remember anything about my grandmother except that her given name was Elizeabeth. My grandfather Christian came to Onondagua co., from the Susquehanna River, bought five hundred acres of land at .50 per acre and paid for it by killing wild game such as bears, wolves, panthers, etc. He owned this land long before I was barn still I can remeber being there at times till I was eleven years old, can remember all kinds of fruits It has been about 95 years ago.
7. My first school was in Onondagua co and teacher, Miss Polly Ann Irish, Amelia Palmer, Mr. Ransom Palmer
8....
9. Nurse, encouchest woman, I have waited on hundred and have never lost one. The last one I waited on was about two months before I was 100 yrs. old (written in space for question 10) It was a hard, dangerous case, but I brought both the woman and child through alright, but I am laid up now with a sprained wrist cause by waiting on the woman.
11...
12...
13...
14. I was twenty four years old when I joined the Christian Church in New York and have still continued to be a member.
15...
16...
17...
18...
19. 1. Alice Dette Easterley, married Filander Lafferty, New York
    2. LaFrancis Price Easterley, married Mary Tingue, New York
    3. Henry Denison Easterley, married Bertha Steadman, New York
    4. Lillian Rose (Rase?) Easterley, married John Rigsby, Cumberland co, Tenn.

Form followed by: 5 pages of handwritten notes:

(1) I was born in Onondagua co, in earstern New York and stayed untill

about five years old until my father moved to Cattarraugus co., New York and we lived there about one and one half year then my mother went back to Onondagua I was about seven years old. My grandmother died and my mother left me here with my cousin and lived with her until I was eleven years old. At that time I could milk cows, wash, cook and do most any kind of work. My brother then came and took me home. A year after this these people that I lived with came to Cattarraugus co. I made home with them the most of the time until I was married.
(2) My husband and I lived together until we had four children. the oldest one was married. At that time he and I parted as my health being very poor and my children also. At this time I came to tennessee and my children with me. When the oldes boy was twenty one he went back to New York. When there he married and is till living there. the next boy was sixteen and he went back to New York and he married there and then came back to me in Tennessee. They lived here until they had one child. ther mother left for New York leaving the baby with me and I had her to raise. I took care of her until she married. She is still living and is the (3) mother of six children. When I first came to tennessee I took up doctring wemen. I went through storm and all kinds of weather then I would go home and go to work on the farm making a crop, getting w...? and all kinds of farm wark I lived a long ways from market and I raised everything that is raised on a farm I had to take my produce sixteen miles to market one year I sold $1.50 worth that I and my two younger children made We worked on and had cows, horses, hogs, chickens, and etc. Now my children are all dead and I am alone. I have lived alone about 13 yrs. until I was 99 yrs old. The last year I lived alone I had (4) as fine a garden as any one living around me. The last year my neighbor is (was.) afraid for me to live alone and I was not able to make a living any longer and my means were all exaused and I had nothing to live on(e)? I have always been mindful of my health I have always practed my selft with pleanty of clothse. I have ridden 21 miles the coldest weather in feb. that has ever been since I have lived in this country. to wait on a man that was sich that the Doctar had given up to die and said he couldent be cured and I brought him out alright in two weeks time he was able to be walking about I also waited on his wife aftr that who died with a cancer of the stomache. I am not feeling very well now and cant get around very well. If you want to know any more write me again as it takes me some time to think up things and if I can tell you any more I will be glad to do so. Their was ten in my fathers family and I am the only one living. I was the seventh one in the family and I have got no one to inquire of to find out my folk on my mothers side are also gone. If you think of any other question you want to ask I will try to answer you as best I can.

Mrs. Huldah Easterley

EASTERLY, OSCAR WILLIS (1881-)
Parrottsville, Tenn. Dec. 8, 1922

1. Oscar Willis Easterly
2. Parrottsville, Tenn.
3. Jan. 23, 1881, Parrottsville, Cocke co., Tenn.
4. John Calvin Easterly; or near Warrensburg, Greene co., Tenn.; place of birth until nearly grown also lived a few years in Illinois moving back near Tullahoma Tenn. from there to Parrottsville; was trustee of Cocke county for 6 years and was tax assessor for 8 years; Isaac Easterly and Emiline Easterly; places mentioned above.
5. Margeret Elizebeth Smith; Joseph Smith and Martha Smith; Parrottsville, Tenn.
6. Joseph Smith served in Civil War and died at Port Hudson, La. while in Confederate prison. He was of erman descent. Easterlys came to Tenn. from New York do not know of what country they emigrated from.
7. was educated at Parrottsville Seminary, Teacher: Henry F. Ketron, M. H. Monroe, R. P. Driskill
8. Commercial courses Knoxville, Business college, 1900-1901.
9.
10. Farmer up until 1913, appointed pension clerk in Treasurer's Office N. H.D.U.S. at Johnson City. served 1½ years resigned -became traveling salesman until death of mother in 1915 have been farmer since that time.
11. Have never held office before, but have worked as Deputy Trustee in Cocke co.

12. ...
13. Republican
14. Methodist Episcopal. member board trustees on church property Parrotsville, Tenn.
15. G.? O.? V.A.M.
16...
17. Jennie? Eliza Kelley, married May 15, 1901; Oliver Madison Kelley and Emma Camilla Kelley, Parrottsville, Tenn.; Father was Scotch-Irish.
18...
19. J.(G.?) C. Easterly Parrottsville, Tenn. born Oct. 5, 1903; Mildred Kelley Easterly, Parrottsville, Tenn. born Jan. 12, 1910.

EDWARDS, JAMES BUCHANAN (1857-)
Cornersville, Tenn. Dec. 9, 1922

1. James Buchannan Edwards
2. Cornersville, Tenn.
3, Mar. 6, 1857 on farm, Marshall co., Tenn.
4. William Russell Edwards; home, Marshall co., Tenn.; Jessie Loves place in south fort (part?) Marshall county, Tenn. -ran a water mill on Richland creek, he was a Mexican Soldier under Capt. William Chambliss also Confederate soldier; Johnie Edwards/ dont know/dont know.
5. Mary Louisie Ragain; Thomas Ragain and Peggy (Brawley) Ragain; Cornerville, Marshall co., Tenn.
6. All I Know of my ancesters I have heard my father speak of his Grand father coming to Tennessee from North Carolina near the South Carolina line.
7. Log school house - old first Dis. Marshall county, Tenn. "Ebineazer" Miss Puss Fields, Mrs. Lon Devins, Parson Childres (teachers)
8. none
9. none
10. Farmed first part of my life - sold nursey stock good part of time and have been in the real estate business of late years.
11. none of this
12. Voted for the Constitunial Amendment of 1887 so we could commence to get shut of the "Saloons"
13. have always been Democrat never voted any other ticket in my life never scratched one.
14. Christian or Church of Christ.
.5. Masons have been worshipfull master diferent times.
16...
17. Susan Jane Braden Feb. 16, 1887 at Ostella, Marshall co., Tenn.; John W. Braden and Sarah Avlin (Taylor) Braden, in Lincoln and Marshall counties, Tenn. do not know.
18. have none
19. Three, one son Julius Tillman Edwards, P. O. Cornersville, Tenn. (2) Daughters - Selma May, wife of Wiley Allen Bridges, P. O. Martin, Tenn., Vera Louisie, wife of Kenneth Lane Clark, P. O. Cornersville, Tenn.

ELLIS, GEORGE ROBERT, JR. (1889-)
Mumford, Tenn. 12-11-1922

1. George Robert Ellis, Jr.
2. Mumford, Tenn.
3. Jan. 9, 1889 Bantin?, Shelby co., Tenn.
4. Geo. Rush Ellis; Brunswick, Shelby co., Tenn.; Memphis, Mumford, Randolph and Kerrville, Tenn.; George W. Ellis and Martha Goodwin; Memphis, Tenn.
5. Emma Cross Cato; Robt. Cato and Puss Cross; Mississippe & Tenn.
6...
7. public schools of Randolph and High school at Mumford. Business course at Nelson Business College of Memphis.
8. did not attend college
9....
10. bookkeeper in the years 1908,9, 10,11,12,13,14; merchandising and farming since 1914. asst. cashier of the Citizens Bank and Trust Co. Mumford, Tenn. for the last 5 years.
11. Justice of Peace since 1912, member of County School Board of Educa-

tion for the last 2 years; member of the county election board for the last 6 years; recorder of my town for 4 years. member of the board of alderman of Mumford at present.
12..
13. Democratic member of the Democratic District Committee of my district for the last 10 yrs.
14. Methodist
15. W.O.W., Odd Fellows, have been clerk of the W.O.W. Camp for 13 yrs.
16...
17. Lillie Rookah? Burkhardt, Dec. 21, 1910, at Mumford, Tenn.; Frank L. Burkhardt and Callie D. Burkhardt, Mumford, Tenn.
18. No military record
19. 1. George Burkhardt Ellis, age 11 yrs.
    2. Udolphus (Adolphus?) Cato Ellis, age 9 yrs.
    3. Robert Littleton Ellis, age 7 yrs.

ENGLISH, THOMAS YOUNG, JR.(1882-1932)
Mt. Pleasant, Tenn. Dec. 8, 1922

1. Thomas Young English, Jr.
2. Mt. Pleasant, Tenn.
3. Aug. 8, 1882 Mt. Pleasant, Maury co., Tenn.
4. Thomas Young English; Lynnville? Giles co., Tenn.;Lynnville, Giles co. ,Tenn and Mt. Pleasant, Maury co., Tenn. was confederate soldier, badly wounded at Ft. Donnelson, member of the 3rd Tenn. Inf.; John Willoughby English and Sarah ... Lynnville, Tenn.
5. Elisha Agnes Spain, Neville Spain and Sarah Spain; Mt. Pleasant,Tenn.
6...
7. Howard Institute? Mt. Pleasant, Tenn. J. A. Butrick?, McPaines Academy, R. L. Harris, Principal.
8. Cumberland Univ. completing Junior year only '99
9. Farming, school of life, not graduated yet
10. Farming since 1905, struggling up hill at present time.
11. Justice of Peace, Maury co. since 1912; member of House of Representatives 1917, Supervisor of census 1920.
12...
13. Democrat...Secretary County Executive Committee 1914-1916
14. M. E. South, Steward, District Steward since 1912
15. J.O.V.A.M. Mason 32nd degree Post master Mt. Pleasant Lodge 610
16...
17. Elizabeth Nelson, Mt. Pleasant, Tenn. Nov.?16, 1907; Willoughby Howard Nelson and Laura Nelson; Mt. Pleasant, Tenn.; W. H. Nelson wifes father was Representative in House for Maury co. also county judge; W.H. Nelson, Jr. a brother of wifes, warden at Petros? for 20 years. H.B.Nelson another brother is Colonel 6th U.S. Inf.; Jr. E. Nelson another is former Justice of Peace and Representative in Legislature.
18. P...Cpl _8_?Co. G. 10th U.S. Inf. July 1901-1904; Cadet Inf. and cav. school Ft. Leavenworth, Kansas Feb. 1904-July 1904; resigned serious illness of father; 1st Lt. 2nd Tenn. Inf. July 17-20, 1917 Capt. Co. B 113 M. G. Bn. July 25 1917 to Dec. 25, 1918; Capt. Co. B. 115 M.G. Bn Xmas-'18 - Apr. 3,'19, mustered out wounded Selle? River Frances Det? 17-1918 113th M.G. Bn. Divisional Unit commanded by I.H. H de; 30th Div. in action commanded by _? C. Lewis Major General, at different times by Gen's Morrison, Townsend?,Reed, Fai__?
19. 1. Naomi Claire English
    2. Laurie Agnes English
    3. Margaret Elizabeth English
    4. Francis Dickey English
    5. Thomas Young III English
    6. John Nelson English
    7. Grover Cleveland English

ESKRIDGE, WILLIE B. (1850-)
(form for veterans-headed "Pioneer") Veterans Form #1

1. Willie B. Eskridge; Antioch, Tennessee
2. 72
3. Tennessee - Davison
4. Tennessee - Davison
5. farming

6. farming
7...
8. yes, about 7
9. yes, 175 acres
10. $3,000
11. it was made of logs and had 4 rooms
12. I plowed and howed most all time
13. my father worked on the farm, my mother cooked, spined and weaved and cleaned the house allso.
14. no
15. all kinds of people worked all together excep two family close, they were to good.
16. yes
17. there were a few that did not work but the most of them worked hard.
18. not many a few though themselves better
19. equality most of the time
20. friendly, except a few was beter than others they thought
21. do not know did not take part in politicks
22. yes, but thoes kind were few then
23. encouraged
24. two or three terms to a free school, and a part of a term to a pay school
25. about three years
26. a mile are so over bad road
27. little pay schools here and there, but one free school finely come
28. public
29. sometimes three mo. and some time six, owin to how many
30. not fery regularly
31. sometimes a man but most of the time a woman
32. did not enlist liked a few yrs. being old enufe.
33...
34...35...36...
37. Douring the war I went with my mother after some fee s(?) and a rebel come up on a horse and ask if any yankeys were around, we said we didnt know so he drove off. I told my mother to come on and lets go to house we started and ___ ___ rebels come up and shot a yaneky and then ran back. just as I clime over the fence a yanke shot at me, the bullet hit a log at the side of my hand. we then went behind a tree and anouther bullet hit the tree at the side of my head we ran and ran into a lot of yankes and they called my mother all sort of names and told us to get for home as quick as possible. When we got here we could not find my father, the yankes had shot him throw(through?) the leg and he had run ___cane?in the night the shot was not bad it got well in about two weeks.the next week, (single page hadwritten) General Joe Wheeler attacked the yanks. in front of our house he arded the calvery to the quickline and then retreat he orded enfrantry to take aroand the road and come to thr__ back and they messunderstood and wated in the road. We were hid unde the river bank we come back the yanks were using the house as hospital some were dead and some all most dead.Coalonel of the yanks was in the frount room on the bed dead. a boy 14 years of age shot him threw the hart this meant well for the boy. They took all our beds and corn, hay, and set fire to the barn we had som mules stolen but do not know weather they got ther are not
39. (above written in this space)
40. I did not go in service. I stade at home and farmed
41. I have farmed all my life till I became too old, but I still live on a farm. I go to church every Sunday. I am a member of the Church Christ
42. William Birdit Eskridge; on farm near Antioch, Rutherford co., Tenn. Lavergne? firs and then moved back nere Antioch.
43, Ceynthia Ann Neal; Ceth Neal; Frances Hinber? Neal; do not know
44. my parents were poor people; my grandparents came North Carolina on my fathers side-my great-grandparents came from Ireland and are proud of it. (I am enclosing a small picture of myself and favorite saddle horse (Rockie B) which you may use in book and then return when through with it. W.B. Eskridge, Antioch (picture follows that page...good clear photograph ...cme)

FARRELL, LOUIS (1878-)
Fort Leavenworth, Kansas 10 Oct. 1924
1. Louis Farrell

2. Adjutant General U. S. Army
3. 17 Dec. 1878 Nashville, Davison Co., Tenn.
4. Norman Farrell; Nashville, Davidson co., Tenn.; Nashville. Tenn.Served in Confederate Artillery and Cavalry. Paroled at Pond Springs Alabama while a member of Co I-11th Ala. Cavalry, May 17, 1865.; Dr. John Farrell and Jane Barbara Kirkman Farrell; New Orleans, La.
5. Josephine Elliston; William Robert Elliston and Elizabeth Blackman Boddie Elliston; Nashville, Tenn. "Burlington Place"
6. Dr. John Farrell was born county Down, Ireland, Jane Barbara Kirkman born Nashville, Tenn. 7th child of Thomas Kirkman and Eleanora Jackson. William Robert Elliston born Nashville, Tenn. Son Joseph Thorpe Elliston and Louisa Mullen (see history Early Methodism in Tennessee") Elizabeth Boddie born Sumner county, Tenn. Daughter of Elijah Boddie & Maria Platt Elliott. (see History of the Boddie Family). KIRKMAN ANCESTRY WILL BE FURNISHED SEPARATELY.
7. University School, Nashville, Tenn. C. B. Wallace, Principal. Webb School, Bell Buckle, Tenn. W. R. and J. M. Webb, principals; Vanderbilt University, Nashville, Tenn. Dr. J. H. Birkland, Chancellor.
8. Vanderbilt University, Entered 1895 - ended 1898. Accumulated no honor or degrees. played on football eleven member;Phi Delta Theta Fraternity.
9. none
10. entered United States Army March 23, 1903
11. none
12. none
13. none; nominally a Democrat though due to being in Military Service rarely eligible to vote.
14. Presbyterian
15. Phi Delta Theta fraternity
16. none
17. Mallie Gaines Wilson, married at Pulaski, Tenn., Mar. 29, 1910 Dr. M. S. Kennedy officiating minister; Dr. William Edwin Wilson and Malvina Gaines Winchester Wilson; Pulaski, Tenn.; Her great-grandfather was Boone Wilson, who came from N.C. Her grandfather Andrew Madison Wilson married Xantippe Little McCallum; (she was a first cousin of Gov. John C. Brown) on maternal side her great-grandfather was Gen. James Winchester.
18. Enlisted as Private in U. S. Army Mar. 23, 1903. Commissioned 2d. Lt. Oct. 9, 1913, 1st Lieut. 1910, Capt. 1917?, Major 1920. Served during the World War with temporary rank of Major and Lieutenant Colonel of Infantry Served in campaign against Moros in 1902-1903. Mexican Border 1917. Commanded 3d Battalion 59th Infantry in action 1918. On July 18-20, 1918 Battalion was reduced by casualties from 23 officers 900 enlisted to 1 officer 300 enlisted. Was personally wounded by sharpshooter and evacuated. Unable, on account of to return to front prior to armistice. Reported"Dead" on War Department Casualty list of July 31, 1918. Report apparently in error.
19. 1. Louis Farrell, Jr. born Manila, P.I. Jan. 29, 1911
    2. Elizabeth Elliston Farrell, born Nashville, Tenn. Oct. 19,1912
    3. Jean Farrell, born Fort Logan, H. Roots, Ark. Jan. 1914
    4. William Edwin Wilson Farrell, born Monteagle, Tenn. Aug. 1915
    5. Norman Farrell, born Ft. McPherson, Georgia July 9, 1917

FINNEY, JAMES I.

1. James Imboden Finney
2. Columbia, Tennessee
3. May 31, 1877, Kilbourne, West Carroll Parish, Louisiana
4. Samuel Greenway Finney; Guilford, county of Surrey. England; lived in Louisiana,Tennessee, Florida. Served in Union army war between the states. Came to this country during civil war and served with Union forces then settled in West Carroll Pa., La. son of Samuel Greenway Finney and Annie (Douglas) Finney; Guilford, co. Surrey, England.
5. Cornelia Jane Imboden; David Imboden and Nancy (Dunklin) Imboden; near Kilbourne, Carroll Par., La.
6...
7. Attended school at Crossville and Pomona, Tenn. from 1884 to 1889. Then attended public school McMinnville, Tenn. to 1892; never attended a school after 15 yrs. of age
8. Never attended one
9. Studied law in court house at McMinnville and under lawyers and was

licensed to practice in 1898, but never practiced.
10. Commenced newspaper work with the McMinnville New Era in 1900 and has been engaged in that profession since. In January of 1904, accepted place as political reporter on the Nashville American and was with that paper until Tennessean started in 1907, when he became the city editor of that paper. In September of 1907, moved to Columbia to be the editor of the Daily Herald and has since been continously engaged as the editor of the Daily Herald.
11. Served as deputy clerk of the county court of Warren county, Tenn. from January 1897 to January 1904; served as the register of Warren Co. from January 1, 1902 to September 1, 1902. Was journal clerk, house of Representatives, Tennessee session of 1905. Served from 1900 to 1904 as secretary to Democratic county committee of Warren county, Tennessee and from 1908 to 1910 in the same capacity in Maury county.
12. The Daily Herald, the first Democratic daily in the state to espouse the cause of Governor Hooper in 1910 in the great prohibition and law and order fight. Served from 1912 to 1913 as the president of the Tennessee Press Association. In addition to newspaper work he is actively engaged in farming, spending a considerable portion of his time at his farm "Sleepy Hollow" near Culleoka, Maury county, Tennessee.
13. This question is already answered - Independent Democratic in politics and newspaper independent democratic.
14. Member of the Methodist Episcopal Church, South. Has served as steward and repeatedly been a lay delegate to the annual and district conferences.
15. Member of Jr. O. U. Am. and Royal Arcanum.
16. Never wrote a book.
17. Herminie Jeanmaire. Married at McMinnville, Tennessee on September 12, 1899 by Rev. Wycliffe Waekley, pastor of the Methodist church. She was daughter of Louis F. Jeanmaire and Heloise (Desporte) Jeanmaire; McMinnville, Tenn.; her father was born in Canton Berne, Switzerland, was French Swiss. Her mother was born in Montpellier, France. Both emigrated to this country in the fifties and were married in Nashville in 1854 and moved to McMinnville where their daughter, Herminie, was born.
18. Volunteer, April 1898, in war with Spain and served in the First Tennessee Vol. Infantry until his honorable discharge in November 1898. In August 1917, volunteered and was appointed to second officers training camp, Fort Oglethorpe, Ga. and was assigned to infantry company for training, but was honorably discharged because of physical disabilities. Immediately after discharge, he was drafted by H. A. Morgan Federal Food Administration for Tennessee and served (as Federal Food Administrator) until after the armistice as assistant food administrator for the state. Took part in every liberty loan, Red Cross, Y. M. C. A. food drive and campaign of the war, speaking in all parts of the state and devoting his entire time for seventeen months to war work.
19. John Wesley Finney, born June 8, 1900; volunteered and joined the U. S. Navy, April 19, 1917 and served to January 3, 1919, when honorably discharged. Graduated County High School, Columbia, Tenn. 1919(?) and entered University of Tennessee from which he expects to graduate in 1923.

James Imboden Finney, Jr., born July 5, 1906 at Nashville, Tenn.

Louis Jeanmaire Finney, born Nov. 11, 1912 at "Sleepy Hollow" farm of his parents near Culleoka, Tenn.

Feby. 8, 1922, James I. Finney
Columbia, Tenn.

FLYNN, MRS. RICHARD

1. Zilpha Flynn
2. Lantana(?), Tenn.
3. July 7th, 1825, near Ashville, N. C.; Buncombe county; North Carolina
4. John Wyatt; Buncombe county, N. C.; lived in North Carolina for a number of years. In 1826, he moved to Tennessee, locating in what was known as Hiwasseu Purchase and about 1831, moved to Crossville, Tenn. John Wyatt was born March 29, 1772; son of James Wyatt and ___________.
5. .....
6. .....
7. limited

8...
9...
10. Wife, mother and as good housekeeper
11...
12...
13. Republican
14. Church of Christ
15...
16...
17. Zilpha Wyatt married Richard L. Flynn in 1845 in Bledsoe co. Richard Flynn died Oct. 17, 1905.
18. "This is imperfectly done as there is many things I cant call to mind, Resp...T.S.F."
19. Richard and Zilpha Flynn were the parents of nine children, two of whom are now living.
John died at the age of eight years
Elsie at the age of eight years
Ruth died at the age of five years
William L. Flynn married Eliza (?) Martin of Crossville, Tenn. Cumberland co. and lived his entire life in that county,(father?) of a large family and died April 13, 1923 at the age of 75 years.
A. L. born April 13, 1862, married Frances Martin; died Oct 17, 1917
Elizabeth married P. H. Norris, died June (Jan.?) 1, 1891 at the age of 40
T. S. Flynn married Miss Flora Brown, lives Castleford, Idaho.
P.S. (ditto under T.S. Flynn, but not sure what he meant) youngest son still lives with his mother Lantana, Tenn.
April 27, 1925, T.S. Flynn, Castleford, Idaho

FORT, JOEL BATTLE (1854-1934)
(Veterans questionnaire) Veterans Form #1

1. Joel Battle Fort, Springfield, Robertson county
2. 67
3. Robertson co., Tenn
4. I was not old enough
5. Riding stick horses
6. Farmer
7...
8. My father lived with my grand father and they farmed together and owned about 60 slaves.
9. about 1800 acres
10. something like $15000.00
11. Two story frame old colonial style 8 rooms
12. During the war, and after my father and I worked along side the negroes at all sorts of farm work. Before the war my father was the manager of the farm and directed the negroes in their work.
13. Superintending farm and did all sorts of work My mother and grandmother were the busiest women I ever saw, they did all the sewing and cutting out for all the negroes, some of the negro women helped to sew, and they did all the spinning and weaving, all the clothes worn by whites and blacks were spun and woven on the place except the sunday wear.
14. Two cooks and two house maids
15. A hustling worker was considered the best man and honest labor was at all times lauded by all
16. By a large majority
17. There were not as many idlers by a large percent as now
18. Yes, the ownership of slaves had nothing to do with the mingling, it was the char-(acter?) and intelligence that mated the different classes.
19. Slave holders and slaves belonged to and attended the same church, the slaves had a separate part alloted to them, and when they got to shouting they got closer together, for both master and servant shouted in those days.
20. Yes, the negroes did not like the non slave holders, and were eager to speak of them as "poor white trash".
21. I dont think it did to any appreciable extent the capacity and intellectuality counted and not money at the election.
22. The finest ever on this continent, and they did.
23. Yes and helped financially, and every way.
24. The teacher was employed by certain prominent citizens, and the price

of tuition fixed by them, and everyone could send, both slave holder and the hired white man.
25. from 8 years to 20, Graduated at Cumberland University, Lebanon, Tenn. in 1874.
26. Between 2 and 3 miles.
27. Old Field schools.
28. Public but supported by private subscription, I never went to a free school.
29. 10 months
30. Yes, they were better educated and had better thinkers than now.
31. Both men and women
32. 7 years old when the war commenced
33...
34.35,36,37,38,39,40---no answers; also 41.
42. Josiah W. Fort, Adams, Tenn., Robertson co., Tenn.; was Judge of Co. Court and ended his career as Minister.
43. Elyza Penelope Dancy; William Dancy and Nancy Diggs.
44. Came from Edgecomb county, N.C. in 1791 to Robertson co. Elisa Fort-great grandfather of my father was a revolution army soldier. Seven of his grand sons were with Andrew Jackson at New Orleans, William Fort was the member of the first Gen. Assembly of N.C., a member of the 1st Const. Convention of N.C. and a member of the 1st Constitutional Convention of Tennessee.
(On separate sheet of stationary of Joel B. Fort, County Judge, Robertson county, Tenn. addressed to John T. Moore, Apr. 13, 1922...a letter concerning an article written on the "Electric Chair".; following is a lovely letter (or literary work describing Mr. Fort's home and family... a must for reading..cme) Mentions some of the family slaves by name; i.e.-Martha, Uncle Mack, Uncle Austin, Aunt Lyza,(wife of Austin), Nelson, Richard, Jacob; the Metcalfe place; Aunt Rachel, Shed Graves, Aunt Chaney(to be Shed's wife), (this little gem is 3 pages of excellent reading)
Following is a Land Deed; Charles H. Fort ---to---Joe Fort. (Col.) Joe Fort was a servant, the son of Melinda Fort, a slave of Josiah W. Fort. Property lying in the 17th Civil Dist., Robertson co., Tenn.-bounded on north by Monroe Chambers, on east by...and on west by the Talley land, now held by Dr. M. L. Bradley and containing 10 acres. Dated 4 June 1913. Signed: Chas. H. Fort and Jennie P. Fort. S.S. Farmer, Notary Public.

FRAZIER, DAVID JONES (1870-)
Nashville, Tenn. Feb. 1, 1922

1. David Jones Frazier
2. Nashville, Tenn.
3. Dec. 15, 1870, Spivey, Clay co., Tenn.
4. Reuben J. Frazier;-----; lived at Monroe co., Ky.; Co. "H",9th Ky. Infantry, serving 3 years as a volunteer in the Federal army during the Civil War; Joshua Frazier and____.
5. Kittie Ellen Hall; David T. Hall and _____; Monroe co., Ky.
6....
7. public schools of Ky.
8. Tompkinsville Normal School; Glasgow Normal School; Southern Normal School and Business College, Bowling Green, Ky. (no degrees)
9...
10. Teacher in public and high schools in Kentucky 1888 to 1906
11. Inspector Tennessee Food and Drug Dept. 1911 to 1920, Appointed Commissioner of the Dept. by Gov. A. A. Taylor, Jan. 17, 1921.
12. First to enforce pure food law as applied to the sale of eggs. First to enforce Weight and Measure laws as to electric meters.
13. Normally Republican, somewhat inclined to be independent.
14. Ruling elder in Cumberland Presbyterian Church (Edgefield C.P. Church, 10th and Russell)
15...
16...
17. Alice Ellen born March 27, 1869, married Arat, Ky, July 1, 1891; Lewis Allen and Martha Naomi Barron; Cloyds Ldg., Ky. Maternal grandfather, Perry Barron, at one time member of Ky. Legislature. Maternal grandmother Martina Kirkpatrick, daughter of Hugh Kirkpatrick. Paternal grandfather, Norman Allen; paternal grandmother, Amanda Turk.
18...

19. 1. Cecil R. Frazier, and wife Leah Everson, now at El Paso, Tex.
2. Lucile Frazier married Roy Stone now at Nashville, Tenn.
3. Margie Frazier
4. Sarah Leatrice Frazier

GAILOR, FRANK HOYT (1892-1954)
Dec. 6, 1922

1. Frank Hoyt Gailor
2. Memphis, Tenn.
3. May 9, 1892, Sewanee, Tenn., Franklin co., Tenn.
4. Thomas Frank Gailor; Jackson, Miss.; lived at Memphis, Tenn.; son of Frank M. Gailor and Charlotte Moffett; Memphis, Tenn.
5. Ellen Douglas Cunningham; George Cunningham and Nannie Hough; Nashville, Tenn.
6...
7. Memphis University School, Memphis, Tenn.; Racine College, Racine, Wisconsin.
8. University of the South, 1908-12, B. A. Degree; Columbia University N. Y. 1912-13 (Law); Oxford University, England, Rhodes Scholarship,(Law) B.A.
9. cf. supra
10. Lawyer, 1919, Memphis
11. House of Representatives 1921; State Senate, 1923
12...
13. Democratic
14. Protestant Episcopal
15. Master Mason, B.P.O.E., A.T.O.
16...
17. Mary Louise Pennel; Aug. 9, 1922, Memphis; J. W. Pennel and Perce Westmoreland; Memphis ...
18. 2nd Lieutenant, Royal Garrison Artillery, British Ex. Force; 1st. Lt. F.A. U.S.R., A. E. F., 91st Division
19...
Second form on Frank Hoyt Gailor:
states his father was Protestant Episcopal Bishop of the Diocese of Tennessee; President of the Executive Council of the P. E. Church U.S.A.
#5. George W. Cunningham
#15 Alpha Tau Omega fraternity
#18 Hoover's Commission for Relief in Belgium, 1914-15; Field Service American Ambulance, Section 2, 1915-1916; Battles-Verdun, 1916, Messinees, Passchsendsele, Ypres. Kemmel 1917-1918; Ypres-Lys., Audenarde, Scheldt, 1918, Medal: Albert Medal and Elizabeth Medal (Belgium); Reconnaissance Francaise 2e cl (France); various service medals.

GAILOR, THOMAS FRANK (1856-1935)
July 25, 1932 Memphis, Tenn.

1. Thomas Frank Gailor
2. Memphis, Tenn.
3. Sept. 17, 1856, Jackson, Mississippi
4. Frank M. Gailor; Lockport, Niagara co., New York; lived at Jackson, Miss., owned and edited "The True Witness", newpaper; moved to Memphis, 1857; editor of Memphis "Avalanche"; enlisted in Confederate army; Capt., Major and Colonel; killed in action, battle of Perryville, Kentucky,Oct.8, 1862; led the charge of the 33d Mississippi regiment, Wood s Division; son of Amzi_ Hazen Gailor and Lucinda...; Lockport, New York.
5. Charlotte Moffett (Gailor); Charlotte Langston Moffett and William Moffett; Castlebar, Ireland.
6. The Gailor, Gailard, family goes back to Oliver de Gailard, Chancellor of France in the reign of Charles III. My father was a descendant of the Hugenot Gailards, who settled in England at Pittminster, near Taunten in the 16th century. Two of the family came to America in 1630 and settled in Massachusetts. Many of their grandsons served in the American armies in the Revolution. My grandmother's family, the Moffetts were a Scotch-Irish stock. very prominent in educational work. My grandmother's cousin, Sir Thomas Moffett was President of Queen's College, Galway. My gr-mother came to this country with four children, after her husband's death, and bought a place and built a home on Walnut Hills, Cincinnati, Ohio. She

founded the Episcopal Church there and there is a memorial chapel erected in her honor. My mother Charlotte Moffett, made a visit to Jackson, Miss. and married there.
7. Private and public schools, Memphis, Tenn. First boy graduate of Memphis Public Schools, 1872. Two outstanding teachers-Dr. Richd. Hines and Capt. T. C. Anderson. Went to work after graduation and saved money to go to College. Had yellow fever in 1873; and was taken to Wisconsin to recuperate and there entered Racine College, Racine, Wisconsin.
8. Attended Racine College 3 years; graduated, head of class and Valedictorian, 1876; won Greek prize; awarded B.A. and M.A. degrees. Outstanding professors: Dr. J. J. Elmendorf, philosophy, J. A. Converse, Latin; Dr. Jas. DeKoven, Prs. of College.
9. General Theological Seminary, New York City; graduated 1879 S.T.B. degree; won Greek Prize, 1879.
10. Ordained Deacon and Priest, Pulaski, Tenn. 1879-1880. Accepted election as Professor of Ecclestiastical History in University of the South, Sewanee, Tenn. 1882. Secretary of the diocese 1883-1893-Deputy to General Convention 1886, 1889, 1892. Elected Bishop-Coadjutor by unanimous vote, 1893.
11.....
12....
13....
14. Bishop of Tennessee, 1893, Declined Bishopric of Georgia, 1892. Chair man of House of Bishops, 191_-1922. President of National Church Council, 1919-1925 and Presiding Bishop; Honorary degrees; Columbia University, NY S.T.D.; Trinity College, Hartford, D.D.; Gen. Theol. Sem.D.D.; University of the South, D.D.; Oxford Unv. England, D.D; Oglethorpe Unv. Ga. LL.D.
15....
16. Lectures on Education, 100pp. The Church, the Bible and the Creed, 150 pp. Many sermons and lectures.
17. Ellen Douglas Cunningham, Nashville, Tenn. Nov. 11, 1885; Major Cunningham was a descendant of the Scotch family of Cunninghams; George W. Cunningham and Ann Hough Cunningham; Nashville, Tenn. Mrs. Cunningham was a descendant of Judge Dudas Minor, Colonial Judge in Virginia.
18...
19. 1. Nannie Cunningham, married Robt. W. Daniel, both deceased, leaving one son, R. W. Daniel, Jr.

2. Charlotte Moffett, M.A. Vassar College, Sewanee, Tenn. Artist

3. Frank Hoyt, Lawyer and County Trustee, Memphis, Tenn.

4. Ellen Douglas, married Richard F. Cleveland, Baltimore, Md.

(Letter dated July 25, 1932 addressed to Mrs. John Trotwood Moore from T. F. Gailor.; also the newspaper obituaries from the "Nashville Banner" on death of Rev. Thomas F. Gailor, dated Oct. 4, 1935. Names mentioned in the notices: Rev. James F. Maxon;(Also mentions that Rev. Gailor's wife had died 4 years earlier)(at Sewanee); Rev. Moultrie Guerry; Dr.Prentice A. Pugh of Nashville; Dr. William Hassel DuBose; Rev. Henry J. Mikell; Rev. F. A. Juhan(Florida); Rev. Theodore D. Bratton (Mississippi); Z.C. Patten (Chattanooga); B. F. Finney; Rev. James Craik Morris (Louisiana); family: Frank Hoyt Gailor, Charlotte Gailor, Mrs. Richard Cleveland (of Baltimore, a daughter-in-law of the late President Grover Cleveland), Robt. Daniel, grandson; Rev. Henry Wise Hobson;(Ohio); Rev. Edward Denby(colored) (Arkansas); pallbearers: Vernon Tupper, B. H. Wilkins, Otey Walker, Wright Broadbent, William F. Orr, W. H. O'Keefe, Joe Summers, Allen Harris, Frank S. Mead, Clem Jones, Walter A. Sadd, S.J. Shepherd, George M. Darrow, Stenning Coate, C.N. Burch, Arthur Crownover, Will G. Simmons, Charles S. Martin, Robert L. McKinney, James T. Granbery, W. S. Bransford(Honorary pallbearers); Telfair Hodgson, Tudor S. Long, Eugene M. Kayden, Henry M. Gass, Ross Sewell, John Banholzer, Jr.,R. M. Brooks and Dr. Alexander Guerry (active pallbearers)(Following is picture from newspaper of Rev. James M. Maxon and Rev. Theodore Bratton, and more notices from "Nashville Banner, Oct. 4 and 10, 1935. Also picture of Processional at Gailor's funeral. In another article of tribute, "Banner", Oct. 3, 1935: tributes from Rev. H.J. Mikell, Rev. William T. Nanning, Dr. B.F. Finney, Chaplain Moultrie Guerry, Dr. E.P. Dandridge, Dr. Printice A.Pugh and Charles S. Martin, Sr. Newspaper photo showing Rev. Gailor and Rear Adm. Cary T. Grayson in 1933; another column concluding tributes from Rev. John F. McCloud, Rev. A. Donaldson Ellis, Rev. A. Myron Cochran, Rev. Arthur E. Whittle, W. D. Hudson, and Wesley Drane, another column with photo of Bishop Gailor and another obituary; also photo of Rev. James M. Maxon several more articles, obituaries, photo, etc.

GANT, WILLIAM ELISHA(1860-1940)
Shelbyville, Tenn. March 13, 1923

1. William Elisha Gant
2. Shelbyville, Tenn.
3. March 24, 1860, near Shelbyville, Bedford co.. Tenn.
4. William Washington (Gant) near Shelbyville,Bedford co., Tenn.;near Shelbyville most of his life; his father, my grandfather, John Gant, entered a section of land in Bedford co., having come from Abbeville,S.C. John Gant and Sarah (Ashley); Abbeville, S.C.
5. Galaca Conwell; dau. of Thomas Conwell and Elizabeth (Robertson); Flat Creek near Shelbyville.
6. My grandfather, Thomas Conwell, served in the War of 1812, and was with Jackson at the Battle of New Orleans. My grandmother, Elizabeth Conwell, was the daughter of Elisha Robertson. See Robertson genealogy in State Archives.
7. Educated in country school taught by Senator Whit Ewing and James Lipscomb. P.W. Dodo___ and Winchester Normal under Clark and Terrell.
8....
9....
10. Farmer in Bedford county
11. First elected Justice of Peace in 1894 and have held this office ever since, nine years as chairman of County Court; member of State Senate, 63rd Session of Gen. Assembly.
12. A prominent part in prohibition movement; was secretary of Co. Fair Assoc. for five years; enthusiastic advocate of good roads and good schools; worked to secure bond issues for Dixie and Jackson highways.
13. Democrat
14. Church of Christ since 1885; am an elder in the church; also clerk for many years.
15. F & A.M.
16...
17. married twice: (1) Mary Davidson; Dr. J. (I.?) S. Davidson & Martha (Smith); Richmond near Shelbyville; (2) Ethel Parsons, dau. of George and Mollie (Pate) Parsons who lived near Shelbyville.
18...
19. 1. Stella, born Jan. 1885, married E. O. McLean, living near Wartrace, Tenn.
2. Allie, born Dec. 1894, married C.B. Ingle, living at Shelbyville, Tenn.
3. Eugene, born Jan. 1903, chief journal clerk in State Senate.
4. Paul, born Aug. 1914
5. Winston, Born May 9, 1919
6. Terry, born Nov. 17, 1922

The last three by the second wife.
(on separate sheets- typed)
Elisha Robertson was a private in a company...Capt. Fleming's then called Moss' and then Mennis' Co. of the 1st Va. Reg. in the Revolutionary War. Enlisted June 5, (year not given) his name first appears June 9, 1777 up to Apr. 1779 when the 1st and 10th Reg. were incorporated; continues shown on roll to Nov. 1779 of Capt. Mennis's Co. Elisha Robertson was a younger brother of James Robertson-called the founder of Nashville, Gen. James Robertson and his wife Charlotte Reeves Robertson were married in Wake co., N.C. in 1768. She and children came to the site of Nashville on the ship "Adventure" in 1780. The first white child born in the settlement was their child Felix Robertson on Jan. 11, 1781. Mrs. Robertson saved the first settlers of Nashville by turning out a pack of hounds on the Indians in the Battle of the Bluffs. Gen. Robertson died at the Chickasaw Indian Agency on Sept. 1, 1814. His body later removed to Nashville where he and wife are both buried .(their tombs there with an old pair of andirons made from the anchor of the shop "Adventure".) Children of Elisha and Polly (Burrough) Robertson are: Elizabeth (our ancestor) married Thomas Conwell; Nellie married (1) Burrough and(2)Banks Lucey married Rainey; Katie married Rainey; Jennie married Rodgers; Elisha, never married; Burrell was hardly old enough to go to Rev. War, but went and took his father's place for a while during the father's illness. Elisha Robertson was born in Brunswick co., Va. in 1744-married in 1784 and died near Pine Bluff, Ark. in 1830.
Elyzabeth Robertson, dau. of Elisha Robertson was born in 1798-married 1821-Thomas Conwell, a Pvt. in the War of 1812, was in Capt. Giles

Giles Bendette's Co. 2nd Tenn.; began service Sept. 28, 1814 and left service Apr. 27, 1815.
Thomas Conwell first married a Miss King. Their children were:

1. Matilda, married William Rainey
2. Mahaley, married William Bonner
3. Minerva, married Jerome Albright
4. Billie, married Elizabeth Black.

Then he married Elyzabeth Robertson and their children were:

5. Mariva, married Zeek Phelps
6. John Conwell, never married
7. Polly, married Newell Bryant
8. Nancy married Plummer Shofner
9. Jakie, married
   (1) Katherine Shofner
   (2) Miss Black
10. Jane married Elic Gill
11. Galaca (born 1833) married W. Gant 1857;
12. Elisha,married Sue Chandler;
13. Marion, never married

The children of Galaca Conwell Gant and William Washington Gant: John never married; William Elisha married Mary Davidson 1883; Callie, married Albert Stang; Julia, married John Stang; Edna, never married; Mattie, married H. Lee Nease.
The rest of the history I have not filled out - want to get all the dates and places of marriage as accurately as possible. Most of this was given by Aunt Nancy Shofner who lived to be more than 90 years of age.

GARDENHIRE, JOSEPH McMILLIN (1874-1949)
Carthage, Tenn. Jan. 31, 1922

1. Joseph McMillin Gardenhire
2. Carthage, Tenn.
3. May 10, 1874, Sparta, Tenn.; White co.
4. John Halsell Gardenhire; Livingston, Overton co., Tenn.; lived Sparta and Carthage; he was merchant, farmer and for 15 yrs. Clerk & Master at Carthage; Erasmus Lee Gardenhire and Mary McMillin Gardenhire; Livingston, Sparta, Carthage
5. Eliza Snodgrass; Joseph Snodgrass and Mary Leftwich Snodgrass;Sparta, Tenn; Adam Gardenhire, father of Judge E. L. Gardenhire, came from Germany and settled in North Carolina, later moving to Tennessee; Mary McMillin Gardenhire was an aunt of Gov. Benton McMillin.
7. Common school, short course at Geneva Academy, Carthage, under Prof. Jno. A. Reubelt(Renbelt?) noted German professor.
8. none
9. Studied law in office of Judge Jno. A. Fite and Chancellor Jno. R. Aust, at Carthage; admitted to the bar 1896.
10. Lawyer, Judge Criminal Court 5th Cir. Tenn.
11. Justice of Peace, Chm'n County Court, Smith Co. 3 terms 1902-1904; appt'd Judge by Gov. M. R. Patterson 1907 3 times nominated and elected without opposition Term expires 1926.
12. Active in all progressive movements, particularly schools and roads.
13. Uncompromising Democrat - chairman Co. Ex. Comm.
14. Christian Church
15. Knights of Pythias
16. none
17. Lynnie? Blanche Smith, married at Memphis, Tenn. July 9, 1903; Dr. A. S. Smith and Julia Simmons?Smith, Magnolia, Miss.
18. none
19. none.

GARRISON, ABRAHAM LINCOLN (1879-)
Crossville, Tenn. Feb. 3, 1922

1. Abraham Lincoln Garrison
2. Crossville, Tenn.
3. Sept. 15, 1879, Jewett, Cumberland co., Tenn.
4. James Simpson Garrison; Jewett, Cumberland co., Tenn.; he has lived in Cumberland county all his life; Garrett Garrison and Katherine Garrison Jewett, Cumberland co., Tenn.
5. Mary Blanche Monday; Pleasant Monday and Blanche Monche; near Roddy,

Rhea co., Tenn. my great-grandfather came south from New York and was of Irish descent; my great-grandmother was a Tennessean, coming from the state of North Carolina.
7. Public schools of Cumberland county, Tenn. and Grassy Cove Academy.
8. Graduated from Cumberland Normal College, in the class of 1898, with a B.A. degree.
9. Have made a close study of law under private tutors but have never been a practitioner.
10. Business
11. Trustee of Cumberland county from 1902 to 1906; was Mayor and City Judge of the city of Crossville for 4 yrs.; member of Tenn. Legislature 1907 and 1911; Chief Feed, Seed and Fertilizer Inspector for State of Tenn. 1911 to 1915.
12...
13. Republican; candidate for Congress 1907, 4th Congressional Dist. of Tenn.; Sec'y to Gov. A. A. Taylor 1921-19__
14. Congregational; trustee
15. 32nd degree Mason; I.O.O.F. I of P- Red Men; have held most all the higher official positions in these organizations.
16...
17. Effie Wallace, Sparta, Tenn. Aug. 23, 1906; Simon Doyle Wallace and Laura Virginia Wallace, Sparta, Tenn.; Mr. S. D. Wallace was a Capt. in the Confederate Army and was considered one of the State's keenest business men; Mrs. Wallace was Laura Virginia Stephens, one of the oldest families in the State.
18. Registered for military service and waived exemptions but was never called.
19 . Helen; Powell; Agnes Lee; Horace Partridge; Mary Virginia and A. L. Jr.

GILBERT, LEON (1891-)
Nashville, Tenn. Feb. 2, 1922

1. Leon Gilbert
2. Nashville, Tenn.
3. Dec. 17, 1891, Nashville, Davidson co., Tenn.
4. Harris Gilbert; Nowy Dwor, Poland; came to Nashville in the "60's" and resided here continuously until his death in 1917......
5. Pauline Nelkin, Nowy Dwor, Poland...../..........
6.....
7. Public schools of Nashville, Tenn.
8. Vanderbilt Unv. Nashville, Tenn. Bachelor of Science, 1914
9. Vanderbilt Unv. Nashville, Bachelor of Laws, 1916 (Freshman "Scholarship Prize", Callaghan Prize for highest Scholarship in graduating class)
10. Practiced law until entering U.S. Army in May (12), 1917.
11. Member House of Representatives, State of Tenn., 1921 Session
12....
13. Democrat
14. Vine Street Temple, Nashville, Tenn.
15. Cumberland Lodge #8, F & A.M. Scottish Rite Mason, Shriner, American Legion.
16...
17...
18. 1st. Lt. Q.M. Corps, Detached - no foreign service (entered first training camp at Fort Oglethorp, Ga. in May 1917, receiving rand of 2nd Lt. Q.M.C. later being promoted to 1st Lt. serving as such at Camp Jackson S.C. and Schenectady, N.Y. until July 3, 1919, date of discharge.
19...

GINN, ROBERT ELMER (1900-)
Knoxville, Tenn. Dec. 11, 1922

1. Robert Elmer Ginn
2. Knoxville, Tenn.
3. Feb. 19, 1900, Knoxville, Knox co, Tenn.
4. John Bolon Ginn; Knoxville, Knox co., Tenn.; lives at Martel, Loudon co., Tenn.;engaged in general farming; Francis Asbury Ginn and Jane Parker Ginn, Knoxville, Tenn.
5. Agnes Ethel Minge; Peter Minge and Magnolia Minge, Lenoir City, Tenn.

great grandson of Jeptha B. Ginn, who was one of the pioneer Baptist ministers of East Tenn.; grandfather Ginn, Union soldier; grandfather Minge, a Confederate, two uncles, James Ginn and Sam Ginn served through Spanish-American war in Phillipines and Porto Rico; original ancestors on paternal side Scotch-Irish, on maternal side of German origin.
7. Public schools of Loudon county and the Farragut High School of Knox county, graduated at latter. Prof. Adams Phillips, Prin.
8. Unv. of Tenn., Law Dept., winner of second scholarship prize of both first and second year law, Phi Kappa Phi. LL.B.
9. Univ. of Tenn. Law School, LL.B. graduated and degree conferred June 8, 1921.
10. Practicing attorney since July 25, 1921 at Knoxville, Tenn.
11. Member elect of Legislature for 1923 session; notary public.
12. none
13. Republican - member-elect of legislature
14. Baptist, teacher of sunday school class and ass't supt. of sunday school in Loudon county.
15. J.O.U.A.M., Phi Kappa Phi, Phi Delta Phi and other university fraternities.
16. none
17. not married
18. Pvt. in the Student's Army Training Corps, stationed at the Unv. of Tenn. Knoxville; entered service Oct. 2, 1918, discharged Dec. 11, 1918; Commander, Captain Johnson.
19. none

GRIFFIN, MARION SCUDDER (1881-1957) (Female)
#105 South Court Ave., Memphis, Tenn. Apr. 5, 1923

1. Marion Scudder Griffin
2. Memphis, Tenn.
3....;Greensboro, Greene co., Ga.
4. John Alexander Griffin, Greensboro, Greene co., Ga.; Greensboro,Ga.; went to the Confederate Army in 1863, at the age of fourteen years; Pvt. in Co. F.,27th Ga. Battalion; Dr. Walter Griffin and Rosa W. Griffin (he was a surgeon in the Confederate army), Greensboro, Ga.
5. Anna Maria Longstreet Scudder; Samuel Erwin Scudder and Eunice Burr Scudder; Princeton, New Jersey, but moved to Greensboro, Ga.
6. Earliest ancestors in this countr: Thos. Scudder, who came from Kent, England in 1630 or 1632, and died at Salem, Mass. where his will is still on record. Thos. Safford, who came over and settled at Ipswich, Mass., sometime prior to 1641. Descendants of Thomas Scudder moved to Long Island, thence to New Jersey, where they lived during the Revolution and many still remain there. Among my ancestors in the Revolutionary Army, including great-great and great-great-great-grandfathers were: 1. Nathaniel Scudder, a Colonel, at one time on Washington's staff; he was one of the signers of the Articles of Confederation for New Jersey, a member of the Continental Congress, and was killed near Monmouth, N.J.the only member of Congress(so the record says) to be killed in the Revolution. Nathaniel Scudder was also one of the early Trustees of New Jersey College which afterwards became Princeton Unv. 2. Jacob Safford, of Royalton, Vt., a captain in the Rev. Army. 3. Archibald McLean, a colonel in the Rev. Army lived at or near York, Pa. and with his brother was one of the surveyors of the boundary known as Mason and Dixon's Line.
7. small private schools, at Greensboro, Ga. and in South Carolina.
8. Unv. of Michigan, Law Dept. - graduated in 1906 with degree of LL.B
9. Lawyer, since 1906, practiced at Memphis, Tenn. since 1907, when law permitting women to practice law in Tenn. was passed by the legislature.
10. Representative from Shelby Co., in Gen. Assembly of Tenn. 63rd Assembly, 1923-1925
11...
12...
13. Democrat
14,15,16,17...
18. Member of Legal Advisory Board at Memphis, Tenn. 1917 and 1918.Being a woman that was all I could do.
19...

HAKE, WALLACE OTTO (1891-)
Dickson, Tenn. Mar. 12, 1923

1. Wallace Otto Hake
2. Dickson, Tenn.
3. Oct. 30, 1891, Minneapolis, Kansas, Ottawa, co.
4. Wm. C. Hake, Sheboygan, Wisconsin; Minneapolis, Kansas for 30 years up to his death.; ______; par. lived in Wisconsin
5. Anna L Walschlaeger?; par. lived in Wisconsin.
6. My great grand uncle on my fathers side was secretary of War under Bismark during the Franco-Prussian War.
7. Obtained in Rural schools of Ottawa co., Kans.; graduate Minneapolis Kansas high school.
8. Kansas Unv. graduated 1918; won gold "K" by representing the University in Debates against three adjoining states.
9. Rec'd LL.B. at Kansas Unv. in 1918, in all attended the Unv. 6 years.
10. Have taught school, am a member of the Bar of Kansas and Tenn.; Have not practiced law in Tenn.
11. Am Ch. of Co., Education Board of Dickson elected for 6 years.
12. Have constantly given time and labor to improvement of roads and schools in Tenn.
13. Democrat; stumped for party
14 Congregational Church
15. Master Mason, Scottish Rite and Shriner
16.....
17. Lura Berdun? Gilmore, married June 3, 1917; Hedran Gilmore and ____; Minneapolis, Kansas
18. Enlisted Jan. 29, 1918 in the Aviation Dept., but never saw active service.
19. 1. Hamilton. 4 yrs. old
    2. Martha Louise, 2 yrs. old

HAMILTON, JOHN D. (1864-)
Form not filled out:
Question #15: Mason, Post Master Clay Lodge# 386
Newspaper article follows: " For Enforcing Laws Rigidly " John D. Hamilton, Hawkins-Sullivan Representative, a Baptist Moderator (Knoxville Sentinel) Church Hill, Tenn., Dec. 16, (no year)...was born at Church Hill, Tenn. Oct. 9, 1864, son of John S. and Bettie Ott Hamilton; educated in the public schools of the county and Carson College, now Carson-Newman; became active in farming and stock raising when young and still actively engaged; owns a farm on the Holston river; member of the county court at Hawkins co., and an advocate of good roads and better schools; member of the school board and now its chairman; followed the example of his parents & became active in church work; his father was one of the organizers of the Holston Valley Assoc. of Baptists and was its moderator for 7 conescutive years; John D. is now moderator; has been elected sixth time; The McPheters Bend Baptist Ch. of which he is a member, is one of the strongest country churches in East Tenn; he lived in Bristol for several years, becoming associated with his brothers in business, later under the corporation of Hamilton-Bacon-Hamilton Co., wholesale seeds, grain and farm-machinery; his brother, W.R. Hamilton, was Pres. and Mgr. and later gave up this business and became associated with the Anti Saloon League (the subject of this sketch was also involved); he then returned to his farm in Hawkins county; Mr. Hamilton married Miss Mollie Kinchelo of Church Hill, who died while they were living in Bristol; He was then married to Miss Julia Kinchelo, sister of his first wife; Two daughters, one deceased and a son of the first marriage: the daughter now Mrs. Frank Stokley, of Delio, and Maxwell M. Hamilton, the first volunteer fron Hawkins co., to the world war, both graduates of Carson-Newman college; one son, J. D., Jr. by the last marriage, now a pupil in Church Hill High School.; he later organized the Church Hill Supply Co., a corporation made up of a number of the leading farmers and stock dealers of Church Hill; he has been president and manager of the corporation since organization (largest general store in East Tenn.); also vice-president of the Church Hill Bank; Democratic nominee to the Legislature from Hawkins co.
(Article has picture of John D. Hamilton)

HARPER, C. A. (1845 -)
(Veterans form) Veterans form #2

1. C. A. Harper, Joelton, Tenn.
2. 79 years, born March 7, 1845
3. Robertson co., Tennessee
4. Neither
5. (nothing in this space)
6. Clerk in country store; farmer
7. John H. Harper; 5 miles of Halifax, Halifax county, North Carolina; lived in Halifax until 22 years of age, moved to Robertson county;clerk on steamboat, school teacher, after he married in 1836, became a farmer.
8. Elizabeth Hanna Williams; Christopher C. Williams and Lucy King; lived in Robertson Co., Tenn.
9. My grandfather, Ambrose Harper, was a Captain in the Revolutionary War and was in the battle at Gilford Court House; he was also sheriff of Halifax county, North Carolina in 1796; he died in 1816; in his will he gave my father, John Harper, two negroes which he brought to Tennessee - their names were Sandy and Briton.
10. I was only 16 years old when the war began so I did not own any property.
11. My father owned two (slaves).
12. 200 acres when the war began.
13. About $2000 would cover the value of his estate.
14. A hewed log house with four rooms; it had a stone chimney on east and west ends; one fireplace 4 ft. wide and one 3 ft. wide.
15. I worked on the farm; plowed until 40 years old barefoot, hoed corn, made potatoe hill knee high, grubed sprouts, cleaned out fence corners, split rails, chopped and hauled firewood; they did this kind of work before the war between the states.
16. Had a loom in the house; the women folks carded cotton, spun and wove cloth at home; my father worked on the farm, as shoemaker and as schoolteacher.
17. Two negro servants.
18. It was considered respectable and honorable to have honest toil in my community.
19. Yes
20. There were some who fished and idled around and others to do their work, but only a few.
21. The slave holders mingled to some extent with men who did not own slaves; some felt themselves too good to do so.
22. Generally they did.
23. Mostly friendly.
24. I think not.
25. Yes
26. They were discouraged to some extent by some slave holders.
27. Small log cabins, public.
28. About 8 months.
29. Two miles.
30. Primary schools and sunday schools.
31. Public
32. No certain time, made up by subscriptions, generally about 3, 5 or 6 months.
33. Yes
34. I went to both.
35. I was not in either army, but my brother, S. W. Harper, did enlist in the Confederate Army in Company G, 42nd Regiment of Volunteers at the Sulphur Springs on Spring Creek in Cheatham county, June 1861.
36. Sent to Camp Cheatham near Clarksville, Tennessee.
37. 4 months.
38. Ft. Donelson.
39. Sent to Shilo, Atlanta, was killed in the battle at Franklin on Nov. 30, 1864; slept in tents on blankets; was never in hospital or prison.
40. (no answer)
41. (no answer)
42. (no answer)
43. C. A. Harper was born on March the 7th, 1845; was married to Louisa
(cont'd on following page)

(Note: Veterans form with questions at front of this book)

Mcormack, May 10, 1864 and 9 children was born to us 4 boys and 5 girls - all lived to be grown and married and ___ me I worked on a farm all my life but now I have becume too feable to do good manuel labor;served as J. P. 2 terms in Cheatham county i lived in Cheatham county Tenn. until 1910 then i mooved to Davison county to live with my son, J. J. Harper who is a J. P. in Davison county now - when i a boy i like very much to go to shoot matches and shoot a rifle like to run foot races and rassle with my frinds and was good at all such games - there was very few that could throw me down or out run me and i did lo___ to work on the farm and i ___ i could git but oh I am a lover of Liberty Justice honesty and rite which is my Religion.

44. I never met vere many great men i have met Bob Taylor and Alf Taylor - William G. Bryan but think Jo. W. Byns as great as any. C. A. Harper, this May 29, 1924.

45. Ike Walton was Captain; Lieutenant - Rob Weekly; George Pardue, Anderson Morris, George Weekly was ordurly sergant but got to be Captain. Some of the members: S. W. Harper, J. J. Duram, Joe Ally, John Helly(?), Pete Morris, Joe Cannsel(?), Tom Turner, Wily Woodall, Jess Sheran, Zac Sheron, Billy Frazier, Ivanson Frazier, Cal Gupton, Mov_d(?) Page was drummer boys, Bill Qualls was colonel of the regiment but got to be a Brig. General for bravery and was wounded at the battle of Franklin; George Maliry, Ruff Weekly, Pok(?) Weekly, Soney Blankinship, Green Law, Tom Balthrop, Ross Wilson, Shade Wilson.

46. James Everett, Ashland City, Tenn.
J. D. Hirks, Joelton, Tenn.
Will Evans, Joelton, Tenn. R.R. #1

HARRELL, WILLIAM MANLIUS (1840 -)
(Veterans form marked "Pioneer") Veterans form #1

1. William Manlius Harrell, McLemoresville, Tenn.
2. 82
3. Carroll co., Tenn.
4. I was not in the army.
5. Farming
6. Farming
7. I did not own any property at the opening of the war. I bought land in the fall of 1865.
8. My father owned one man, one woman and three small children.
9. My parents owned about 300 acres
10. I suppose $600.00
11. Log house, two rooms, brick chimney
12. I worked with hoe until 12 years of age, after which I was a regular plow boy all my life. Through the winter I got wood, split rails, made boards and did other necessary work.
13. My father did all kinds of farm work, including all wood work on the buildings and farming implements. He made shoes for his family. My mother did all kinds of house work, cooking, sewing, spinning, weaving, mending, etc.
14. No servants in the house.
15. All kinds of work in the community were considered respectable and honorable. There were no big rich slaveholders in my immediate community.
16. Yes
17. There were a few men who did not work themselves, but had it done.
18. Class distinctions between slave holders and non-slave holders was not marked in my neighborhood.
19. Yes
20. They were friendly
21. I had no chance to observe this.
22. Not very good.
23. I can't say.
24. Subscription school.
25. Six months.
26. About one mile.
27. The one above and another one about two miles but at a different time.
28. Private
29. Three to four months; there was a boarding school at Lavinia about 8 miles (cont'd on following page)

and Bethel College at McLemoresville 7 miles from my home

30. no
31. man and one woman
32. I volunteered in a company of Confederates under Sheriff Bryant but the company was not completed
33. The number was two small, so the company failed
34... 35... 36... 37... 38... 39... 40...
41. Bought land 1865, married and settled on it in 1872, one mile east Shiloh Camp ground,seven miles south of McLemoresville, Tenn.
42. Seth Harrell, Gatesville, Gates co., N. C.; moved to West Tenn. in 1833; he did not hold any public office nor was he in the army
43. Cynthia Lenora Algee; Robert Algee and (don't know name), moved to West Tenn. from North Carolina.
44....

(no 45 or 46)

HARRIS, WILLIAM ROBERT (1876-)
Hilham, Tenn. May 22, 1922

1. William Robert Harris
2. Hilham, Tenn.
3. Dec. 24, 1876, Celina, Clay co., Tenn.
4. James Harris, Crossville?, Cumberland co., Tenn.; Celina, Tenn. Son of Benjamin Harris and Rebecca Jane ? Farr, Burksville, Ky,;
5. Rebecca Jane Farr; William Farr and Peony/ Ellen Hom__?; Clinton co Ky.
6...
7. none
8. none
9. none
10. Farming
11.....
12...
13. Democrat
14. none
15. none
16. none
17. Lee Ada White. Hestond. Monroe co. Ky; Reno White and Malissa Slaughter, Monroe Co., Ky.
18. Pvt. in Spanish-American War. 1st Tenn. Reg. Cpt. Rus Richmond, Col. William Smith, saw service nine months discharge at Camp Mariam Percidio San Francisco, Cal.
19. Maggie Florence Harris, Hilham, Tenn.
Clinton Harris, Hilham, Tenn.
Dulcinia Harris, Hilham, Tenn.
Bonnie Harris, Hilham, Tenn.

HARWELL, THOMAS EDWARD (1855-1928)
Prospect, Tenn. Feb, 13, 1922

1. Thomas Edward Harwell
2. Prospect, Tenn.
3. Aug. 18, 1855,at Pisgah, Giles co,Tenn.
4. Herkimer L. Harwell;....;....; lived in the Pisgah Community a few miles east of Pulaski and reared a large family of children there, never lived else where after his marriage; Raleigh and Cisily Lester (don't know middle name); at Pulaski in early life.
5. Cicly Lester; Jas. Lester (I think) and Mary Buford Lester;.......
6. The Harwell family, originally came from England; it is a fact that its history is illustrious for its moral and religious stature....no record of any one of the family of ever having been convicted in the courts of the land for crime or any one becoming an habitual drunkard. My mothers family___ of the ____ ______ of Giles county order of the day. They were people of fine intellect,personal appearance ....My mother died when I was an infant and was said to have been a woman of great

intellectual and religious power.
7. My education was obtained in rural school, though it was my good fortune to finish up under the training of two finely educated men.
8. none.
9. none.
10. I am a retired farmer; read law a couple of years but never finished up
11. Was a member of the 50th General Assembly and am a member of the present Legislature, 62nd
12. Nothing more than to speak make in behalf of political reformers and that that was but for the communities in which I have lived.
13. Democrat by inheritance, affiliation,
14. Methodist; have been a steward, trustee and have participated in Church work in other ways
15. I have been a K of P only-served in all of its official capacities pretty much
16.Author of no books-have written editorials or communications for many papers for many years
17. Viola Elizabeth Blanche Westmorland, married in Pulaski,26 Jan. 30 years ago.; John F. Westmorland and Mary Indiana; who lived in Prospect, Tenn.; my wife's grandfather Westmorland was founder of our city, Prospect; a man of wealth and unbounded influence in his community; I know but little of my wife's people on her mother's side.
18. no military record. I am one of the few generations who has ____through life without war fare.
19. 1. Lillian Oliver Harwell and was married to William A. (R.) Pittard of Pulaski. They live on the farm given by me. Post Office address Pulaski, Tenn., R.R. No. 4. Their residence in the old Pisgah community a few miles east of Pulaski.
2. Thomas Herman Harwell, was married to a Miss Octavia? Walker of Sparta, Tenn. They live in this community Prospect, Tenn. P.O. is Prospect, Tenn., RR 1?

HASTON, ERNEST NATHANIEL (1877-)
Nashville, Tenn..Dec. 1, 1921

1. Ernest Nathaniel Haston
2. Nashville, Tenn.
3. Mar. 26, 1877 Cunningsville, Van Buren co., Tenn.
4. Geo. Washington Haston; Cummingsville?, Van Buren co., Tenn.; the place of his birth all his life; Isaac T. Haston and Sarah Shockley Haston, Cummingsville, Tenn.
5. Sarah Shockley; Phillip Shockley and Bettie Rhodes Shockley; Gillentine, Tenn.
6. A sturdy race of Scotch-Irish descent came from N. C. and settled in Van Buren co., ___ state only the younger descendents ever ask for or held public office of any consequence being devoted farmers and stockmen
7.....
8. graduated Burritt College Spencer, Tenn. May 1900.
9....
10. Lawyer, Admitted to the bar Spencer,Tenn., July 1902
11. Co. Court Clerk, 1906-1914; Co., Supt. Pub. Instruction 1904-1906; Fed. Tax Re_____ Agent 1914-1916; Senator 9th Dist. 1917-1919 and Special Session 1920; Secy. of State Mar. 1, 1921 for 4 yrs.
12. State wide prohibition, 18th Amendment and 19th Amendment
13. Democrat; Nat'l Delegate 1908 to Denver Convention, Woodrow Wilson Elector 1912- member present Stott De_____ Ex-Comm. and Secy. of _____.
14. Church of Christ
15. Mason, W.O.W. ; ________ & Elk
16.....
17. Miss Vollie Sparkman, Nashville, Tenn. Jan. 20, 1904; Ozious Sparkman and Sara Hodge, Angel?, Sevier co., Tenn
18....
19. Miss Evelyn Haston, born Apr. 25, 1905
Ernest Haston Jr.

Note attached; "Under No.4, there is an error: this should read Isaac T. Haston and his wife Elizabeth Sparkman Haston."
D.R. Haston

HAYNIE, JOHN WESLEY (1874-)
Dec. 8, 1922

1. John Wesley Haynie
2. Milan, Tennessee
3. Sept. 8, 1874, Olive Branch, DeSoto co., Mississippi
4. Charles M. Haynie, Memphis, Shelby co., Tenn.; Olive Branch, Miss.; ex-Confederate soldier, joined the Confederate army in April 1861 and served 4 years, surrendering with his company in May 1865; Charles Haynie and Julia Ann Pierce; Memphis, Tenn., having moved there from Culpeper co., Virginia in 1834.
5. Sarah Ann Crutcher; Thomas Crutcher and Ann Crutcher; DeSoto co., Mississippi.
6. Our family came from England and landed at Jamestown in 1607. My great-grandfather was with Washington at Braddock's defeat, fought with him as a captain in the Revolution and was a brother of the "Dear Sallie Haynie" named in Washington's will. My grandfather was born and reared in Virginia.

(Page 2 and 3 of the questionnaire missing from microfilm)

18. ......
19. Marian Haynie
    Charles Pearce Haynie
    Martha Haynie

HEARN, SIMPSON COLUMBUS (1839-1918)
(Form signed: J. M. Foster, Gleason, Tenn., Feb. 1922)

1. Simpson Columbus Hearn
2. McKenzie, Tenn.
3. Mar. 10, 1839, Henry co., Tenn.
4. Cyrus R. Hearn; near Lebanon, Wilson co., Tenn.; near Como, Tenn.; George W. Hearn and Milly Hearn; near Lebanon, Wilson co., Tenn.; died in Weakley co., Tenn.
5. Charlott Alexander; William Alexander and ______; near Como, Tenn., Henry co.
6. William Alexander, father of Charlott Alexander, was a missionary Baptist minister, being instrumental in the organization of Thompson's Creek and other missionary baptist churches.
7, 8, and 9. (no answers)
10. Was licensed to practice law in 1877 and followed that profession 12 years in Paris, Tenn. Gen. J. D. C. Atkins said of him: "...was a lawyer of much eloquence and held his jurors spellbond in every case."
11. 1879-80, made an unsuccessful race for congress some time during his law practice.
12. Was instrumental in bringing about prohibition of sale and use of intoxicating liquors; was always foremost in any and all moral reform and christian movements.
13. Democrat
14. Turkey Creek Baptist Church in Madison co., Tenn. in Aug. 1857(?) and was ordained to preach by the same church in 1858.
15, 16. (no answers)
17. Fannie Carlton, married to her in Campbell co., Ga. She was born on Jan. 1, 1837. (no other answer)
18. S. C. - Hearn joined the fifth Tenn. Reg. C. S. Army in Aug. 1861; served as a Pvt. two years then was app'td Chaplain of his regiment and served to close of civil war. It was said of him that he was a power for good and had a wonderful influence with many of the rough class of soldiers and was very successful in persuading them to accept Christ as their personal savior; he died at the home of his daughter, Mrs. Rosa Carlton Harrison, I think in 1918. William Henry Harrison and his wife, Rosa Carlton Hearn Harrison live at present at Hartford, Connecticutt.
19. His children: Anna Laticia, b. Jan. 13, 1865, married Dr. C. W. Rodgers, Nov. 16, 1886, lives at Como, Tenn.
    2nd child: Effie Judson, b. Aug. 24, 1868, married Wm. Rufus Lasater, Dec. 26(?), 1886, lives at Paris, Tenn.
    3rd child: Mary Ella, b. Nov. 10, 1879, d. Aug. 26, 1872.
    4th child: Rosa Carlton, b. July 18, 1873, married Wm. Henry Harrison, lives at Hartford, Conn.

5th child, Alice Clara, born May 29, 1877, died Sept. 30, 1880
6th child, John Robert born May 20, 1880, lives at Louisville, Ky. married Mary Bundy of Erin, Tenn.

HEWGLEY, CHARLES EDWARD (1853-1927)
Feb. 15, 1922 Lebanon, Tenn.

1. Charles Edward Hewgley
2. Lebanon, Tenn.
3. Oct. 14, 1853, Rural Hill, Wilson co., Tenn.
4. Charles William Hewgley, Virginia; Rural Hill, Wilson co., Tenn.;farmer and live stock dealer; Charles William Hewgley and Mary Hardie; Rural Hill, Wilson co., Tenn.
5. Elizabeth Mills Hooker; Joshua Hooker and Frances (Francis) Wynne; Gladeville, Wilson co., Tenn.
6. My great grandmother Hooker was of Irish decent, died at the age of 103; my grandfather Hooker was a minister of the M. E. Church and served in the war with Mexico; my grandfather Hewgley was of German descent.
7. My early school days were in winter months little log school houses. Teachers Washington Telford, Rev. Hughes Telford, Rev. Joseph Alexander, Dr. Oval Ornwhundro?
8.....
9....
10....
11. Constable from 1912-1918. Co. Trustee years 1918-1920; member of Legislature Jan. 1921.
12....
13. Democrat
14. Methodist
15.....
16....
17. Emily Katharine Thornton, married Nov. 9, 1876, Gladeville, Wilson co., Tenn,; my wife was the grandaughter of John Spinks a minister of M.E. Church also a progressive farmer being the owner of fine farm-her father was a merchant a member of the M.E. Church also a member of the Masonic Order
18.....
19. 1. Francis Annette Hewgley married Cecil Hourne P. O. Milan, Tenn.; Mr. Hourne is clerk for Milan Banking Co.
2. Maud Hewgley - husband Rev.___ ___ Turner (Presbyterian) P. O. St. Louis, Mo.
3. Nancy Elizabeth - husband, Mr.___ Turner, P.O. Memphis, Tenn.

HILL, LEONIDAS CAMPBELL (1882-1939)
Mar. 2, 1922 Dandridge R.2, Tenn.

1. Leonidas Campbell Hill
2. Dandridge, Tenn.
3. Mch. 13, 1882, Hickory Ridge, Jefferson co., Tenn.
4. John W. Hill; Sandy Ridge, Jefferson co., Tenn.; Hickory Ridge, Tenn.; merchant and farmer; Rev. James Maston Hill and Sallie Moore, Sandy Ridge, Jefferson co., Tenn.
5. Francis E. Nichols; Wyatt Faust Nichols and Rhoda Hill; Sevierville, Sevier co., Tenn.
6. Fathers parents first settlers of Jefferson county, Tenn. from Va.; W. F. Nichols foreparents first settlers of Sevier co., Tenn. and his grandfather was a Captain in the Continentals under Geo. Washington; Nicholsville, Bedford co., Va.
7. Common free schools
8. Maury Academy, Dandridge, Tenn.; matriculant of U.S. Grant Univ. Athens, Tenn.; Univ. of Tenn.
9. none
10.Mercantile and agricultural pursuits 1902 till present
11. Justice of the Peace 1906 till present; Chrm. or Judge Jefferson County Court (21 yrs.); U.S. Dept. Collector Internal Revenue 3 yrs.; Member of the House of Representatives, 62nd Gen. Assembly.
12. Assisted in building of macadamized roads of Jefferson Co.- best

system of roads in any county of E. Tenn.; devoted to establishing fine rural school system for Jefferson co., Tenn.
13. Republican - chrm. of Executive Committee of Republican party, Jefferson co., Tenn.; Alternate delegate to Republican National Convention 1920.
14. Methodist.
15. Mason; I.O.O.F., Jr. O.U.A.M.
16. none
17. Josie Kate Fox - married in Knoxville, Tenn., May 18, 1911, dau. of James E. Fox and Hattie Snapp, Dandridge, Tenn.
18. No military record.
19. (1) Herbert Hadley Hill, b. May 18, 1912.
    (2) Francis Hill, b. Sept. 1, 1915.
    (3) Lillian Hill, b. Aug. 7, 1917.

HILL, SAMUEL ELISHA (1872 -)
Knoxville, Tenn., Dec. 8, 1922.

1. Samuel Elisha Hill
2. Knoxville, Tenn.
3. Oct. 6, 1872, Paulette (Milan co.), Union co., Tenn.
4. Isaac Newton Hill; Milan (now) Union, Tenn.; lived at above; Merrill Hill and Miss Day; Claiborne co.
5. Belle Helsley; Henderson Helsley and Elizabeth Fox; Beaver Ridge, Knox co., Tenn.
6. Elizabeth Fox was the grand-daughter of John Fox, Jr., a Rev. soldier who was wounded in the battle at Kings Mountain. Both of my grandfathers were Civil War veterans. Merrell Hill was killed in the Confederate service and Henderson Helsley was in the Union Army.
7. In the public schools of Knox county and in Friendsville Academy of Blount co., Tenn.
8. Attended Carson-Newman College and the Unv. of Tenn.; graduated in law at U. of T. in 1906.
9. See above.
10. Taught school in the public schools of Knox county; also principal of Hancock co. high school.
11. Justice of the Peace, Knox co. 2 yrs., Co. Sup't. Schools, Knox co. 6 yrs.; member of board of Public Works, Knoxville, 2 yrs.; City Comm. City of Knoxville, 8 yrs.; elected to the State Senate, Knox co. 1922.
12. Leader in educational affairs in Tenn.; Ex-president State Teachers Assoc.; organized E. T. Ed. Assoc. in which body he has held an official position since the date of organization in 1904.
13. Democrat
14. Baptist, Deacon in First Baptist Church, Knoxville.
15. Masters Lodge F. & A. M., Paxton Chapter Kerbela(?) Temple, Shrine, Elks.
16. ....
17. Mary Jane Calloway, married Dec. 11, 1899. Wife died Oct. 26, 1914; John Q. Calloway and Eliza Calloway, Ball Camp(?), Knox co., Tenn.; came from North Carolina; Jno. Q. Calloway was a soldier in Union Army.
18. .....
19. .....

HUGHES, WILLIAM NEILL (1850-)
(Veterans form marked "Pioneer") Veterans form #2

1. William Neill Hughes, 1922 Broadway
2. 72
3. Tenn., Maury co., Columbia.
4. No. Tried to enlist in the Federal Army at Cincinnati, Ohio.
5. .....
6. Lawyer
7. Archelaus Madison Hughes; in 1811, Stokes co., North Carolina; Columbia, Tenn.; Attorney General; Circuit Judge, U. S. District Attorney 4 years.
8. Mattie Bedford Neill; John Lambert Neill and Sallie Clay Neill; at Bell Buckle, Bedford co., Tenn.
9. .....

10. no
11. yes, about ten
12. 120
13. $25,000.00
14. two story - half brick the other half frame - eight rooms.
15. Did very little work when a boy - howed then pulled weeds in the onion patch; as a young man carried the mail on horseback between Columbia and Perryville on the Tennessee river; worked in the Express office at Columbia; wrote in the office of the Clerk of the Circuit Courts; never worked on a farm, never plowed.
16. Practiced law; my father owned slaves, they did all the domestic work
17. about ten
18. yes
19. only those who had to
20. this was the rule up to the end of the civil war
21. mingled freely
22. yes
23. yes-were not antagonistic
24. I do not know
25. yes
26. Encouraged
27. All private - there were no public schools at this time.
28. Until I was eighteen years of age - 1868
29. In the town of Columbia, about one mile
30. Several good schools in Columbia
31. Private
32. ten
33. yes
34. First to a woman, then when 14 yrs. of age, to a man
35. .....
36. .....
37. .....
38. .....
39. .....
40. .....
41. .....
42. .....
43. See answer to question 15 and my letter enclosed in this questionnaire stamped: Nashville, Tenn., May 31, 1922 - Col. W. W. Hughes, U. S. Army.
45. and 46. .....

(Separate page - letter to J. T. Moore from Col. W. N. Hughes -"...also my grandfather Neill's commisions in the Tennessee Militia in the last century; one signed by Gov. Willie Blount as Capt., dated 11th of September, 1813; the other one signed by Gov. Joseph McMinn as Lt. Col. of the 3rd Regiment, dated Feb. 25th, 1817; and also, a muster roll of compay of Infantry attached to the 54th Regiment, dated 5th of April, 1923. Samuel Neill was my grandfather's brother...Also, two papers containing some facts concerning my son, Col. W. N. Hughes, Junior, and myself, giving our record as army officers..."

Dated: May 31, 1922, 1922 Broadway, Nashville, Tenn.
(Page 1) COLONEL WILLIAM NEILL HUGHES, U. S. ARMY ....

Born in Columbia, Tennessee, March 10th, 1850; as a young man, carried the mail on horseback between Columbia and Perryville on the Tennessee River. Wrote in the office of the Clerk of Circuit Court at Columbia and worked in the office of the Southern Express Company.

In 1864, while attending Earline College, Richmond, Indiana, he endeavered to join the Union forces, but being small and unknown to the authorities, was rejected.

In March, 1872, went to Washington City, took an examination and was appointed to a clerkship in the Treasury Department, resigned in 1875 to accept the appointment as Postmaster at Columbia. In 1879, resigned as Postmaster to accept a commission as 2nd Lt. in the regular army and was assigned to the 13th Infantry. Was promoted to 1st Lt. in November of 1890, and was promoted to Capt. in April of 1898, while on the way to the Cuban Campaign.

Graduate of the Infantry and Cavalry School, at Fort Leavenworth in Kansas, class of 1897. Commanded Co. H 13th Inf. in battle San Juan Hill,

Cuba in July 1898. Was stricken with yellow fever while in the trenches two days after the battle. Was on mustering duty in the spring of 1899 and mustered out of the service the 8th Regiment of Immunes at Chickamauga Park, Georgia.

From May until November 1899, was in charge of target practice for recruits at the Persidio of San Francisco, California, where he taught ten thousand men how to shoot an army rifle.

(Page 2):

Won first place on the Department of Missouri Rifle Team in 1883 and became a Distinguished Marksman in 1891.

Sailed for Manila, Phillipine Islands, from San Francisco, California with his son, Colonel W. H. Hughes, Jr., in Nov. 1899. When ten days out of Manila was stricken with heart disease, the result of having yellow fever in the Cuban Campaign; after being held in the Manila harbor for 1 month, was ordered back to the United States.

Was retired from active service in October 1901 for disability contracted in the line of duty.

Was Commandant of Cadets at the East Florida Seminary at Gainesville, Florida from Sept. 1902 to Aug. 1905. Was Recruiting Officer at Memphis, Tenn. from Aug. 1905 to Nov. 1907. Was on duty with the Kentucky National Guard from Feb. 1908 to Feb. 1911. Was recruiting officer at Nashville from Mar. 1912 to Sept. 24, 1918, when the Selected Draft went into effect, and all of the recruiting offices in the country were closed. Oct. 7, 1918 to Jan. 7, 1919, was on duty at the Southwestern Presbyterian University, Clarksville, Tenn., as Commandant Student Army Training Crps.

By the act of Congress, 3rd of June 1916, he was advanced to rank of Major, and by the Act of 9th July 1918, was advanced to the rank of Col., having been given credit for doing active duty while on the retired list.

His maternal great, great-grandfather, Abram Martin, was born Feb. 7, 1718, in Virginia, was a soldier under Col. George Washington before the American Revolution and was in the battle known as "Braddock's Defeat".

He, with his family, moved to the Edgefield District, South Carolina and was killed by Indians in Georgia while locating lands before the Revolutionary War. His wife, Elizabeth Marshall, was born Mar. 1, 1776 and they were married Oct. 2, 1744. She was an aunt of Chief Justice John Marshall.

His maternal great-grandfather, Matt Martin, the youngest son of Abram Martin, was born Dec. 26, 1763. There were eight sons and one daughter, all brothers were soldiers on the side of the Colonies in the War for Independence. He took part in the battles of King's Mountain and in the Cowpens. He married Sallie Clary, Mar. 8, 1787. They had thirteen children. He died in Bedford county, Tenn. and his name is on the Court House yard at Nashville as M. Martin.

His maternal grandfather was John Lambert Neill of Bradford co., Tenn. His father was Capt. James Neill of Burke co., N. C. and was in the Revolution Army.

He served under Maj. Gen. Andrew Jackson in the Indian Wars in the southern part of the country, taking part in the battles of Tallegega and the Horse Shoe, in the latter battle he was wounded in the foot. He commanded Gen. Jackson's bodyguard during the New Orleans campaign. After the war he was appointed Capt. of Militia by Gov. Willie Blount, Feb.1813 and in Feb. 1817, was appointed by Gov. Joseph McMinn, Lt. Col. of the 3rd Regiment.

He had three sons in the Confederate Army, one, Archer Neill, was killed at Drury's Bluff, Va.; one, John Lambert Neill, Jr., died in prison at Elmira, N. Y., and the other son, James F. Neill was Lt. Col. of the 23rd Tenn. Inf. and was shot through the body while leading his Regiment in the battle of Shiloh, Apr. 6, 1862.

His paternal great-grandfather was Archelaus Hughes of Virginia. He commanded a regiment of Virginia troops during the Revolutionary War.

His father was Judge Archelaus Madison Hughes, born in Stokes county, North Carolina in 1811. He married Mattie Bedford Neill in 1844. He was elected Attorney General by the Legislature for the Columbia District in 1847, and was afterwards elected by the people for another term. He was a prominent Union man during the Civil War. In 1868, he was elected Judge of the Circuit Court for the same district. He was appointed by President Grant, U. S. District Attorney for Middle Tennessee and held this office from 1873 to 1877. He was elected Railroad Commissioner in 1884 and was elected Chairman by the Commission.

His brother, Archelaus Madison Hughes entered the Confederate Army at 15 years of age, served under Gen. Nathan Bedford Forrest in many of his raids. In October of 1863, was captured by the Federals and imprisoned at Camp Morton, Indianapolis, Indiana. During the Spanish American War, was Lt. Colonel of the 8th U. S. Imunes.

(Separete page - COLONEL WILLIAM NEILL HUGHES, JUNIOR, U. S. Army)

Born in Columbia, Tenn., Mar. 3, 1878. Son of Col. W. N. Hughes and Omie Murphy Hughes. Married Allene Pope Fry of Kansas City, Missouri, Oct. 28, 1907. One son, William Neill Hughes III, born 24 Jan. 1916.
Distinguished graduate of General Service Schools, and Stagg College in 1904. Graduate of Army Signal School, 1907.
Attended grammar school at Leavenworth, Kansas and high schools of Columbus, Ohio and of Buffalo, New York.

Commands:
2nd Lt., 13th Infantry, August 1, 1899
1st Lt., 13th Infantry, March 1, 1901
1st Lt., Signal Corps, September 17, 1907
Capt., 7th Infantry, March 11, 1911
Major of Infantry, August 3, 1917
Lt. Col. of Infantry, August 5, 1917
Colonel of Infantry, October 8, 1918
Resigned, August 11, 1919
Major, Signal Corps, March 18, 1921
Member of General Staff Corps, June 4, 1917 to August 11, 1919
Ass't. Chief of Staff, 42nd (Rainbow) Div., August 13, 1917 to August 2, 1918
Chief of Staff, 42nd (Rainbow) Div., August 3, 1918 to April 25, 1919

The Rainbow Division was no regular troop but was composed of volunteer units from twenty-six states.

Participated in:
Defensive Sector, Baccarat, February to July 1918
Champagne - Marne, July 15-18, 1918
Aisne - Marne, July 18 - August 6, 1918
St. Mihiel, September 12-16, 1918
Meuse - Argonne, September 26 - November 11, 1918

Decorations awarded:
U. S. Distinguished Service Medal
Legion of Honor Officiere (French)
Croix de Guerre (French)
Order of Leopold II, Officiere (Belgium)

JACKSON, GUY WILBUR (1849 -)
(Veterans form used) Veterans form #2

1. Guy Wilbur Jackson, Cumberland City, Tennessee, Route 1
2. 73 years, 13 days
3. Stewart county, Tennessee
4. No
5. ...
6. Farmer
7. Robert Jackson....North Carolina (no other data)
8. Lucinda Cherry; daughter of William Cherry and Maud Cherry, lived near Big Rock, Tennessee.
9. My parents never told me or ever give me any history of my ancestry.
10. ...
11. eleven (11)
12. 800
13. $25,000
14. Log house, one room upstairs, kitchen and dining room.
15. Cut corn stalks with a negro, then plowed with both negroes and also white men, and done all farm work, shoulder to shoulder with them until the whites eat, then the negro.....at night the negro went to his cabin to bed...did not mingle in white society.
16. General farm work. He had no servants only farm help......mother

managed the home, she had one servant black mamie (named Biddie) and plenty of other house help...they kept the cards, spinning wheel, the flax wheel, and loom running all the time making cloth, dying, cutting and making clothes of all kinds for family.
17. one for Mother
18. Certainly everybody worked all kinds jobs and was honored and respected.
19. They did.
20. One only and he had so many slaves he did not know the small one when he met them.
21. If a man was honest, the very highest top notchers mingle freely even the so call white trash - there was no division, every one injoyed the society of all.
22. There was no little I nor big you- all mingle on a footing of equality.
23. There was no ill feeling between any one.
24. No man made any difference between poverty or riches.
25. Money was hard to get in those days, but I did know several of the very poorest to succeed and becom very rich - while maney others seemed to have a better chance completely failed.
26. No one was discouraged by slaveholders-but I knew of many poor men helpted along by his rich neighbor.
27. A very common country school
28. 3 years, 3 months each year
29. Near home, 2 or 3 miles away
30. Every school was a subscription of 3 months duration the studies consist of spelling, reading, writing and arethmatic - then the student would forget all he learned and have to start at the beginning of his book at next year of school.
31. Private.
32. 3 months
33. yes
34. Sometimes the teacher was a man, at other times a woman
35.,36,37,38,39,40,41,42,...no answers
43. I was to young to inlist in either Army, but i rendered the Southern cause as much or more good than many a soldier did. I did not kill a Yankee but had a better way to get shut of him, so he would never shoot one of our boys. Tho I was only 10 years old I was the biggest little boy you ever saw and tough as a pine knot. I went threw all kinds exposure both day and night-better luck than Sam Davis I pull through without a scratch tho a Yankee sent a minnie ball just behind my head.
44.....
45 and 46.......

JACKSON, THOMAS J. (1892-)
(Veterans form) Veterans form #2

1. Captain Thomas J. Jackson, Inf. U.S.A., Columbia, Tenn.
2. 33
3. Tennessee, Maury county
4......
5.......
6. Postmaster at Columbia, Tenn.
7. John W. Jackson; Lewisburg, Marshal co., Tenn.
8. Ida Hayes
9. I am a grandson of Willoughby A. Jackson, who was a son of Col.James J. Jackson; Col. James J. Jackson was a son of William Sherwood Jackson, also an officer, Col. I believe, and a 1st cousin of Pres. Andrew Jackson.
10. through 46 not answered.

(Seperate sheet follows questionnaire)
Information re: Capt. Thomas J. Jackson, Infantry, U.S.Army,,
Attorney at Law, Columbia, Tenn.

Born Jan. 25, 1892, graduate of Maury County High School Cumberland and Georgetown University, Member of the bar. From June 1916 to Jan. 1, 1916 in the foreign service of the State Dept., at London, England, this position was resigned to become private secretary to the President Erie

R. R., which was also resigned to enter First Officers Training Camp on May 12, 1917. Was commissioned May 15, 1917. Assigned to Co. K, 165 U.S. Infantry (Fighting 69th of New York); went overseas inOct 1917, with 165th Inf., 42nd Div,; served with Brittish in Flanders Nov. and Dec.1917 and afterwards in Alsace in the Luneville and Baccarat sectors. Wounded Mar. 20, 1918. On June 5, 1918, transferred to Co. K, 126th Inf., 32d Div. and served in Aisne-Marne, Oise-Aisne and Meuse-Argonne offensives until after the armistice, when he hiked to the Rhine with the 32d. Ad.. Dec. 20, 1918 transferred to the Interallied Railway Commission until Nov. 1919, served later with Interallied Rhineland High Commission, 4th Inf. 50th Inf. and 18th Inf. During 1922 served with the American Relief Adm. in Russia. Graduate of the U.S. Inf. School, and Ass't. Prof. of Military Science and Tactics at the Alabama Polytechnic Institute at Auburn,Ala., for 2 years. Member of the Delta Tau Delta, Phi Delta Phi and Scabbard and Blade fraternities.

JAMISON, HENRY DOWNS (1871-)
Feb. 13, 1922 Nashville, Tenn.

1. Henry Downs Jamison
2. Nashville
3. Jan. 31,1871 near Murfreesboro, Rutherford co., Tenn.
4. Robert David Jamison; Murfreesboro, Rutherford co., Tenn.; near Murfreesboro,Tenn.; he was a member Co. D, 45th Tenn. Reg. C.S.A. President Union University Murfreesboro 1880- ; Henry Downs Jamison and Sarah Thomas; near Murfreesboro, Tenn.
5. Camilla Patterson; Samuel Alex. Patterson and Camilla Butler, (Butler) (t crossed as 4th letter), near Murfreesboro, Tenn.
6. ....
7. Union Unv. at Murfreesboro, the President of which was Robt. D. Jamison.
8. ...
9. ...
10. Retail funiture business in Nashville Tenn. Oct. 12, 1896- later in Wholesale Furniture and Manufacturing Business; later, Apr. 14, 1909, entered the Mattress Mg. business at Nashville.
11. Member City Board of Education 1918 thru 1922; Member 62nd Gen. Assembly 1921-State of Tenn.; Chrm. Municipal Affiars Commission also Education Commission
12.....
13. Democrat
14. Baptist; deacon and treasurer, Immanuel at Nashville; deacon and treasurer, Judson Memorial at Nashville; best work done in helping the building of Judson Memorial Nashville.
15. W.O.W.: Arcium? ; T.P.A.
16.....
17. Marguerite Corinne Spain Jamison, married June 16, 1898 at Salem (near Murfreesboro), Tenn.; Thomas Spain and Mary Dean Fletcher, near Murfreesboro, Tenn.; Thomas Spain, born Apr. 23, 1834 in Belfast, Ireland and came to this country about 1851; made wagons for C.S.A. at Rome Georgia.
18. none
19. 1. Henry Downs Jamison Jr.
    2. Marguerite Spain Jamison
    3. Lucile Spain Jamison
    4. Roberta Bogle Jamison
    5. Eris(?) Spain Jamison
    6. Annie Belle Jamison

(Seperate sheet) JAMISON GENEALOGY:
John Jamison was born in Ireland in 1693.Married Janet Keen. Moved to America in 1713, locating at Little Britain, Lancaster co., Penn.
His son, Samuel Jamison, was born at Little Britain, Pa. in 1723, married 1745, died 1771.
His son John Jamison, born at Little Britain, Pa. in 1748. Married Catherine Cowden. Married Miss Caldwell in 1773. Located in South Carolina 1792.
His son, William Caldwell Jamison, born in Little Britain, Pa. May 11.

1776. Married Jane Downs, June 18, 1794. They had 3 children: Henry Downs, Mary Downs and John. Jane Downs Jamison died in Tenn. William Caldwell Jamison married Eleanor Shelby, May 10, 1801. His son, Henry Downs Jamison was born in Savannah, Georgia, Apr. 12, 1795. Married to Elizabeth Beatty, Jan. 23, 1819. They resided near Murfreesboro, Tenn. and had six children: Mary Jane, William Caldwell, Julia Ann, John Bass, Martha Elizabeth and Eliza Thomas. Elizabeth Beatty Jamison died Feb. 3, 1835. Henry Downs Jamison married Sarah Woodlief Thomas, July 26, 1835 and they had ten children: Susan Cornelia, Robert David, Sallie Gannaway, Lou B., Clarke Moulton, James Henry, Olivia, Samuel Thomas, Dorsey A., Richanna C. Henry Downs Jamison died Mar. 14, 1859. Sarah Thomas Jamison married John L. Cooper, Dec. 5, 1875. John L. Cooper died in 1895. Sarah Thomas Jamison Cooper died Oct. 30, 1898. His son, Robert David Jamison, was born near Murfreesboro, Tenn., Apr. 13, 1838. He married Camilla Patterson, Dec. 26, 1860. They had seven children: Atha Thomas, Eris Campbell, Samuel Patterson, Henry Downs, Ella Patterson, Maddie Woodlief and John Carter. Camilla Patterson Jamison died on July 11, 1908. Robert David Jamison died Aug. 12, 1912. His son, Henry Downs Jamison was born near Murfreesboro, Tenn., Jan. 31, 1871. Married Marguerite Corinne Spain on June 16, 1898. Residing in Nashville, Tenn. They had six children: Henry Downs, Marguerite Spain, Lucile Spain, Roberta Bogle and Annie Belle. Henry Downs, grandfather of Jane Downs, wife of William Caldwell Jamison, was Adjutant of the Second South Carolina Regiment and served through out the Revolutionary War. He was a signer of the "Mecklenburg Declaration", a series of resolutions purporting to have been adopted by the citizens of Mecklenburg county, N.C. on May 2, 1775, declaring their independence of Great Britain, followed by a second series, adopted on May 31, 1775, providing for a local government.
Henry Downs Jamison, 1795-1859, located in Rutherford county, Tennessee, living in Murfreesboro, Tenn. and later nine miles south-east, where he died. Over his grave is a monument with the note that he was the first white man to locate in Rutherford county, this, however, has not been proven as we do not know just when he moved into Rutherford county.
Robert David Jamison, 1838-1912, was a member of Company D, 45th Tenn. Regiment, C. S. A. He served through-out the whole war and was cited for bravery several times. Some years after the War, he became President of Union University, located at Murfreesboro. He was author of a series of articles which were published in several Mississippi and Tennessee papers and called "Reminiscence of a Tennessee Confederate Veteran".
Clarke Moulton Jamison, 1844-1862, was killed in action at the Battle of Perryville, Kentucky, Oct. 8, 1862.

JARRATT, WILLIAM VINCENT (1863-)
Springfield, Tennessee

1. William Vincent Jarratt
2. Springfield, Tennessee
3. Feb. 17, 1863, near Jones Valley, Hickman co., Tennessee
4. William Daniel Jarratt; near Columbia, Maury co., Tenn.; Columbia and Maury county in boyhood and your manhood; resided in and near Nashville just prior to and for a few years after the Civil War; was a confederate soldier; after the war he both studied and practiced medicine and ran a farm on Leifers(?) Creek in Maury co.; son of Daniel Jarratt and Elizabeth Clayton; near Columbia on Bear Creek in Maury co.
5. Mary Carter; Abraham Carter and Mary Bray; Linnville, Giles Co.
6. The Jarratts came from England and first settled in Virginia; my grandfather, Daniel Jarratt and wife were born in North Carolina; the Carters and Brays were of Irish descent. Abraham Carter and wife, Mary Bray were also from N. C. The families of my grandparents migrated from North Carolina to Tennessee early in the 19th century. The Jarratts settling in Maury county and the Carters and Brays in Giles county. Their descendants are rather numerous in these counties at the present time.
7. The foundation of my early education was secured in the city schools of Nashville; later I attended as opportunity afforded, the public schools of Maury co., but I owe much to Prof. T. M.(?) Hogan who conducted a private school at Water Valley, Maury co.
8. Masonic Institute, Santa Fe, Maury co., Bachelor of Science, class of 1887 (a small college which flourished for a few years but like others

of its day, are no more.
9.....
10. Taught school as a young man, before graduating, in Williamson and Maury counties and afterwards in Maury and in Hickman counties.
11. Was County Supt. of public instruction of Hickman co., 1890-1892
12. First public service was in connection with the Campaign for prohibition Amendment in 1887; have been identified with anti-saloon league and all reform movements for the past quarter of century.
13. While not "Cranky" have been intelligently interested in good government;my parents having been Democrats; I naturally lean that way, but am "An Independent Democrat" reserving the right to vote as I pray.
14. Am and have been, a member of the M.E.C.S. since boyhood, been a minister and a member of Tennessee Conferance since 1891; have served several of the best stations among them Lebanon, Monroe Street, west Nashville and Springfield; have served as Presiding Elder of what is now Mt. Pleasant District two years; Lebanon Dist. four years and Fayetteville four years; have also served nine years as Statistical Secretary, etc.
15. Am a Knight of the Pythias, A Knight Templar Mason; a Shriner, and have been prominently connected with the Woman"s Auxilary of the Masonic order, or the Order of the Eastern Star; having been Grand Patron for the state of that order for the years 1918-19
16.....
17. Nannie Bell Porter, near Waverly, Humphreys co., June 9, 1892; James K. Polk Porter and Susan Ross Porter; near Waverly, Tenn.; my wife's father was of the Bedford co. family of Porters and her mother was descended from a prominent family of Hickman and Dickson counties.
18. My military record is as follows: my father was a Confederate soldier for four years and my three sons enlisted in the service of their country in the World War- the oldest volunteering the next day after Wilson declared war. Each of the three went in as a private and each received a commission before it was over. Thats a record of which I am proud, even though I merely served as the connecting link between my father and my sons.
19. 1. Porter Walton, unmarried, Wichita Falls, Texas
2. Paul Reams, married to Katharine Stiles of Lebanon, Tenn. He resides 929 Acklin Ave., Nashville
3. William Vincent, Jr. unmarried, teaches in the Massey Sch.,Pulaski, Tenn.
4. Lucile, married Robert Donald Kelso. They live in Winchester, Tenn.

JETTON, ISAAC NEWTON (1852-)
(Veterans form) Veterans form #2

1. Isaac Newton Jetton, Maury City, Tenn.
2. Passed 70
3. near Murfreesboro, Tenn.
4. neither
5....
6. Farmer
7. John Barnard?; near Murfreesboro, Rutherford co., Tenn;..
8. Isabella; James M. Stewart and (Don't know); near Readyville?
9......
10. none
11. my father owned 9
12. 130 acres
13. sold in 1860 for $10,000
14. part log and part frame, 5 rooms with hall
15. when i was old enough I did most all kinds of work that boy? could do; people as a rule didn't if they could get by without it.
16. as near as I can rember all kinds of work was done at my fathers house; he was a farmer
17. 9
18. It was all concidered resptble by sincible people; there were fools in those days just as there are now.
19. not if they could get by without it.
20. fishing-hunting and whitling gods boxes(?)
21. some did and some did not; it owning to how much since they had
22. dont think they did

23. owing to circumstances
24. not much
25. I think not, as a rule people were honest then
26. dont know
27. The Male Academy at Brownsville, Tenn.
28. dont rember
29. 1 mile
30. The King school near Brownsville in Heywood co., Tenn.
31. private
32. about 6
33. I think they did
34. generaly they were men
35. not at all
36., 37,38,39,40,41,42, not answered
43. I have done a little of several things; I was PM 2 yrs.; I clerked several yrs.; was in business for my self some of the time and farmed some and I have lived in Memphis lived at Louisville, Ky., Quinton, Okla. Bells, Tenn., Tiptonville, Alamo. Brownville, Tenn.; I have been a member of the Church of Christ for 50 yrs. the only one the New Testament says any thing about; I have never been a member of any other.
44.....
45...and 46....

JOHNSON, DANIEL CHERRY (1836-)
(Veterans form) Veterans form #2

1. Daniel Cherry Johnson
2. 86 first day of last February
3. Haywood county Tenn.
4. not either
5....; I was licensed a Minister by Methodist authorities in 1858. And that fall was received into Memphis Conference.
6. He supervised farm, and mercantile business.
7. Isaac Miller Johnson; 10 miles S. Murfreesboro, Rutherford co.,Tenn. 1805; in Rutherford about 20 years on a farm; 1825 with his father moved to west Tennessee Forked deer section
8. Miss Elizabeth Elliott; Major Simon Elliott and ______; my mother was born in Virginia Aug. 14, 1807.
9. Dear Sir: Father being pioneer ___, energetic, etc. became a conspicuous citizen a progressive official in both church and civil affairs. He lived to be 74 years of age died in 1877.; I have a number of articles written by him in Crockett county paper- brief biography, history of early times - formation of Crockett county, etc. I will mail them to you if any service.
10. I went into intinerant Methodist Ministry about 22yrs. of age
11. Father own 3 - one man and two women the man and one woman managed the farm.
12. Perhaps about 100 acres
13. Another hard question - he was also county merchant apparently thrifty - but the war ruined his finances
14. A story and a half frame - two large rooms below and two above and a side bed and dining room, the kitchen was close to diningroom but separate.
15. Outside of attendance school I staid a little in the store, only helped on the farm one season; well remember rough experienc with the plow.
16. In early youth father helped on the farm, but mother was truly a domestic woman - would card, spin and weeve when a little tot she learned me to count on the notches of the spinning wheel while she was spinning.
17....
18. in my youth in Forked deer county say 75 years ago - every person felt duty bound to work, yes manual labor was regarded honorable, etc.
19. yes
20. I do not recall any
21. Not much aristocratic wealth at that date in my knowledge
22 .My recolection is that those was but little discrimination if any
23. friendly association
24. I think not

25. Industrious, ambitious live young men had good opportunity...land was cheap and many made good.
26. the _____ really I am unable to answer - my knowledge is inefficent
27. sugscription
28. most of my attendence was brief
29. sometimes near two miles
30. .....
31. private
32. about three
33. not very regular
34. the last was by a husband and wife mixed - gave academic course term of 9 months
35, 36, 37, 38, 39, 40, 41, and 42...not answered
43. As I have previously stated - when the civil war came I was an itinerant Methodist preacher, but when the first Haywood county regiment was organized, I offered myself and services to the Colonel as Chaplain; at the same time a brother, Mahon, an aged and more matured man tentered his services, finally the Colonel said to me "Bro. Johnson, you are too young inexperienced, etc. and I think it best to secure the services of brother Mahon, he is matured in manhood, etc. - and I think it prudent to appoint him as Chaplian, but all thru the war when opportunity offered, I visited camps, prayed with and preached the Gospel to the Southern boys in Gray; I had two brothers in the Confederate service; I am now at the age of 86, a superannuate of the Memphis Conference.
44. ....
45. Mother died at the age of 55 in 1862 and father married again, a Miss Hale, an ___ lady, of this union one son ____ Robert E. Lee Johnson became a lawyer now resident of Jonesboro, is now active Circuit Judge. He resided awhile in Paragould, Ark. while there his mother, then a widow living with him, suffered a horrid death by fire ignition of her clothing. You may find notice of this article printed enclosed in separate cover. Out of our family of 12 children of first marriage, I and one brother, Dr. James Washington Johnson, now 76 years of age, lives in Paragould, Ark. I was born, reared and loved, in a brood of 12 children, all lived to be grown. Dear Friend - be kind and excuse the use of pencil.
46. J. T. Moore - Dear Sir, having had an interview with D. J. Bowden of Martin...he tells me he has mailed you a full list as best he is able. He is as well prepared as any person of all my acquaintance in every way and he is reliable.

(Separate sheet - handwritten)
3/23/1922
Martin, Tennessee:
J. T. Moore, Director, Nashville, Tenn.
Dear Sir:

In addition to brief given in enclosed cover I take the opportunity to let you know that I am going to mail to your address in a few days a series of articles contributed to local newspapers by my father, giving minute description of the Forked Deer country, West Tenn. in 1825 when he and his father came. He gave interesting reminiciences, history, incidents, customs, settlements, personalities, etc. One fact - he lived 50 years in the limits of 25 miles - farmed, taught school, acted bookkeeper and salesman in general dry good trade...Daniel Cherry....again bought land and farmed...with Mr. Cage of Memphis as partner engaged in mercantile business...at same time, active public churchman, civil official..conspicuous figure in origin of Haywood and Crockett counties... and specially so, as you will find in series of articles, as to Crockett. I also enclose a series of articles paying tribute of esteem and regard had for him by friends and officials, on his demise. You will also find many facts given by me in articles written after his going away. After looking over these notes, you can find them of any use or can make them fill any place in your plan or enterprise you are perfectly welcome to them. If not, be kind enough to return them by mail at your convenience,

And greatly oblige,
Daniel Cherry Johnson

KEATON, HORACE MONROE (1857-)
(Pioneer) Veterans form #1
(See following page #61)

1. Horace Monroe Keaton, Liberty, Tennessee
2. 65 years and 11 months
3. Wilson county, Tennessee
4. was not old enough
5. none
6. Farmer
7. owned none
8. we did not own any
9. about 300 acres
10. about $5000
11. log house with frame added to - six rooms - four downstairs and two upstairs.
12. was not large enough to plow, but used to hoe and thined corn
13. father plowed and did all kinds of work on the farm; mother did the cooking, spinning, carding, dying, weaving, all the cloth for the whole family..made jeans and linsie and sewed and made each garment.
14. none
15. yes, those who did not were counted honorable
16. yes
17. were about three men in the neighborhood who owned slaves..they did not work but their boys worked and the slaves worked
18. there was not but one man who owned a carriage but it did not make any difference in their friendliness; you could not tell any difference with the rest.
19. yes
20. yes all were friendly
21. no
22. yes, land was cheap but you could not get much for your work
23. no
24. one place, framed house 20 X 20, puncheon seats, no back, the other framed house, and one log house, fire places, about 15ft black-board, glass windows, one place there was no school house, just a shed, puncheon seats and stools
25. two or three months out of four or five years
26. 1 mile or two miles
27. Round Top...Cottage Home...Adams school (the shed). Grooms school house
28. Public
29. three or four
30. very well
31. Elizabeth Adams, John Truit, Dr. Turney, Plez Adams and Cinthia Fuston.
32. not at all
33, 34, 35, 36, 37, 38, 39, and 40. no answers
41. Farmer, always lived in Wilson co., moved five times, married at the age of twenty, wife and I lived together for 40 yrs, wife died, I lived widower for 8 mos. and married again.
42. Thomas Keaton; 14th Dist. same place I was; Wilson co., Tenn.; lived and raised his family where he was born, then moved to Cottage Home; he moved to the 20th Dist. of Wilson where he died.
43. (Betsy) Violet Elizabeth Fuston; Jim Fuston and Elizabeth ________; Liberty, DeKalb co.
44. All parents and grand-parents, great grand-parents, was born and raised in the same neighborhood.
45. and 46. no answers

KELLEY, CHRISTOPHER COLUMBUS (1872-1952)
(Senator) Lawrenceburg, Tenn., Feb. 9, 1922

1. Christopher Columbus Kelley
2. Lawrenceburg, Tenn.
3. Jan. 28, 1872, Little Sugar Creek in 4th Civil Dist.; Lawrence co., Tenn.
4. Lewis Kelley, Athens, McMinn co., Tenn.; Carterville, Georgia, Calman, Ala. and Lawrence co., Tenn. where he is still living at the age of 90 years. He was a federal soldier in the 69's; Daniel Kelley and Elizabeth J. Hood Kelley; Winston-Salem, N. C.
5. Elizabeth J. Hood Kelley*; Douise*(probably Daniel and Elizabeth Hood; did he confuse the questions?); Winston Salem, N. C.
6. My grandparents on my father's side came from Ireland; on my mother's

side from Holland. Grandfather Kelley settling in Old Virginia, thence to East Tennessee and grandfather Hood in North Carolina. Both families later moving to Cartersville, Ga. where father and mother met and were married in 1850, moving to Calmon(?) county, Alabama in 1858 and on to Lawrence county, Tennessee in 1870. They raised a family of 13 children: 9 boys and 4 girls, all of whom are living except 4. Mother died 10 yrs. ago at the age of 75 years.
7. In the log school house in the rural districts in Lawrence county. Prof. Andrew J. Hall and Prof. J. J. W. Starr(?) and Prof. William Kelly.
8. none
9. none
10. Real estate Auctioneer. Pr_tical(?)
11. State Senator in 1921; also was appointed to enumerate the Federal Census in 1900 and 1920; also carried mail route #2 at Lawrenceburg from 1903 to 1906.
12. Secured the passage of 21 bills in the legislature and influenced the passage of many more, most important being the repeal of the Dog Law in 53 counties. I was honored with many important appointments on committee work by the Speaker of the Senate; I also got a bill passed by the legislature approving $2000.00 by the State to build a monument on the public square in Lawrenceburg to the memory of Tennessee's hero of the Alamo, Col. Davy Crockett, who began his public life in Lawrenceburg.
13. A Republican, State Senator.
14. Lay member of the Christian Church
15. Woodman of the World
16. A brief sketch of the life of Col. Davy Crockett, Tennessee's Hero of the Alamo and business men's Directory, 24 pages.
17. Sallie Lee Crook, Aug. 10, 1892, at Crowsen Mills, 1 mile west of Lawrenceburg, Tenn.; the late Jacrious Valentine Crook and Mary Pullen Crook, Crowson Mills in Lawrence co., Tenn.; Mr. Crook's grandparents came from Ireland, also his wife's grandparents too. Mr. Crook was a member of the County Court for 35 years, and never had a Judgement reversed by a higher court.
18. I have none
19. Little Marggie, a daughter who died at the age of 7 months in the year 1894, and one son who lived to be about 21 years of age and died with typhoid fever. His name was Lewis Valentine. This leaving us with no children.

KEMPER, JOHN RUSSEL (1881-)
Greenbrier, Tenn., Jan. 30, 1922
(Legislator)

1. Jno. Russel Kemper
2. Greenbrier
3. June 26, 1881, Gallatin, Sumner co., Tennessee
4. Willie Kemper, Gallatin, Sumner co., Tenn.; lived in Sumner co.; Jno. Kemper and Elizabeth _____; Gallatin in Sumner county.
5. Ida Jones; J. R. Jones and Bettie Jones, Robertson county.
6. ....
7. Had an elementary education and practical training.
8., 9. (no answers)
10. Farming since youth; member county court of Robertson county, for 6 years; member high school board for 8 years.
11. Represented Robertson and Montgomery counties in the 65th General Assembly in 1921.
12. Deacon in the Bethlehem Baptist Church since 1905; clerk of said church for 11 years.
13. Democrat. Campaign worker in Red Cross and Liberty Loans Chairman for both.
14. Baptist
15. Junior Order
16. ....
17. Ruth Ethel Maddux Kemper, married at Murfreesboro, Jan'y. 1920; A.V. Maddux and Mary Jane Maddux, Smyrna, Tennessee.
18. ....
19. Kathleen Kemper Wells and her husband, R. H. Wells of Springfield, Tenn.
Van Leer(?) Kemper, at home with parents.

KENNY, WILLIAM DARIUS (1876-)
Memphis, Tenn. Feb. 27, 1922

1. William Darius Kenny
2. Memphis. Tenn.
3. July 29, 1876, Terre Haute, Vigo co., Indiana
4. Thomas F. Kenny;......; lived at Terre Haute, Vigo co., Indiana; father and mother were divorced when (I) 4 years old, do not know where he was born nor anything about parents; was member Odd Fellows at Vicksburg, Miss., had been student at Charleston, S.C. University.
5. Alma Jane Hyde; John B. Hyde and Mahala Jane Hyde; at Staunton, Clay co., Indiana
6. Alma Jane Hyde and Thomas F. Kenny were married at Bowling Green, Clay-co., Indiana,July 22, 1875, Geo. E Hubbard, Clerk. J.B.Hyde was born at Dresden, Ohio, Muskindume? co., Jan. 29, 1832.Died at Terre Haute, Indiana, Aug. 17, 1913. Grand-mother name was Mahala Jane Richcrick, was born Oct. 18th, 1839 Warsaw, Coshocton co., Ohio. Great-grandparents Johnas Richcrick, Dresden, Ohio. Civil war veteran Ohio heavy artillery, Invalid-blind, Rachel Richcrick, Dresden, Ohio.
7. Staunton, Indiana, Clay co., District school; Terre Haute, Indiana, Vigo co. Public school 5th and 7th wards; Effingham, Illinois, Public school, Miss Mary Hasbrook.
8. none
9. none
10. Rail-road, employe, Sept. 1896 Effingham, Illinois; yard & Freight Checker, Switchman March 27, 1900 to Aug. 13th, 1900; Carterville, Illinois. Incapacitated from manual labor, account service in Spanish-American war, all in line of duty.
11. none
12. none
14. Presbyterian
15. none
16. none
17. Emma R. Harvey, May 28, 1900, Altamont, Illinois; Theadore Harvey and Mrs. Theadore Harvey, Effingham, Illinois; Divorced Emma R. Harvey at Effingham, Illinois Msrch 15, 1908. Grand-parent Geo. Harvey, Effingham, Illinois were from Harrisburg, Pennsylvania
18. Spanish-American War; Cuba. Private Co. E 4th Ill. Vol. Inf. 7th Army Corp. Gen. Fitzhugh E. Lee-Colonel Casimir Ondell-Regimental Adjutant Harry B. Parker-Major Chas. E. Ryman, Captain Chas. E. Rudy - enlisted at Mattoon, Illinios June 17, 1898.; muster out of regiment Augusta, Georgia May 2, 1899 on sick furlough from Nov. 10 to Dec. 9, 1898. Per G.O.No 114 A.G.O. 1898. sick in quarters from Sept. 11, to Sept. 14, 1898. Inc. Sept. 19 to Sept. 22. Inc. in 3rd Division 7th A C Hospital from Sept. 23 to Oct. 15, 1898 Inc. absent sick in U.S. General hospital Ft. Monroe, Va. from Oct. 16 to Nov. 10, 1898 Inc. all on line of duty. Mustered out May 2 1899.
19. 1. Mercedes P. Kenny, wife of Herbert Anderson, Charleston, Illinois, son Jack Anderson, Chaleston, Illinois.
    2. Alma Tedema Kenny, Charleston, Illinos

KING,JAMES NEWTON (1850-1932)
Crookville. Tenn. Rt. 5 Feb. 14, 1922

1. James Newton King
2. Cookville, Tenn. Rt. 5
3. Mar. 15, 1850, Paintrock, Roane co., Tenn.
4. Joseph Calloway King; Stogling's Valley, Rhone co., Tenn.;Sweetwater and vicinity after his marriage till 1860 when he moved to Putnam county, Tenn. in the sixties he joined the confederate army he also volunteered in the Mexican war; Robert King and Sarah King, Stogling's Valley, Roane co., Tenn.
5. Fannie Sephire Qualls; John Qualls and Annie Qualls (nee Kelly), Tucheho Creek uper East Tenn.
6. My grandfather Robert King and wife Sarah King came from Ireland to North Carolina when they were children with their parents and Andy Jackson parents they were Scotch-Irish blood. My grandmother Sarah Kings maiden name was McCullough, her father, Joseph McCullough was a teacher he

taught my grandmother and Andrew Jackson their letters. My grandfather Robert King served in Gen. Andrew Jacksons Command in the War of 1812. Was in the battle of horse shoe bend and at New orleans Jan. 8.
7. I was only 11 yr old at the beginning of the civil war. my parents were very poor hence I never attended school but about six months till after the civil war.
8. none I grew to manhood with little or no education but took up books at home then went to a institute school 15 months then taught 32 year my teachers were Prof. Ragsdale, Capps Williams &c
9. I only mastered the common course of Tenn. by getting a bit here and a bit there then put it into practice by teaching in the public schools.
10. I am a natural farmer secondly a teacher I have give most of my time to these two occupations the ballance, misselaneously in office &c.
11. I was a member of the lower house in 1903-1905 and in 1921 I served as tax assessor one term Chairman of the county court 2 yr. Justice of Peace 2 yr.&c
12. I have acted on Special Committees of charitable institutions and relief of poor committees &c.
13. I have served most of my life on the Executive Committee of my party being a life long Democrat of the old school of States rights
14. I am a Methodist and have acted as Stewart lay reader &c most of the time
15. I am simply a Master Mason.
16. I havent wrote any books
17. first wife Mary Tenn. Holloway maried Decr. 22, 1870 at Monterey, Tenn. second wife Annie Mariah Smith Sparta Mar. 25, 1906. (last) dau. of Gillem Smith and Mary Ema Smith, Sparta, Rt. 5, White co., her grandfather and mother on her fathers side was Pleasant Smith and Mary Carline Smith of Sparta, Tenn. and her grandfather and mother on her mothers side Abner Tayler & Mariah Allen Tayler.
18. I have never served in any war at all.
19. 1. Fannie Rebeca King married to Harvey Terry,Cookeville
    2. Joseph Calloway King married to Lou White, Cookeville
    3. William Stephen King married to Minnie Wossom, Cookeville
    4. Lien King married Earnest Clinton, Cookeville
    5. Lillie King married to Charlie Judd, Columbia
    6. Wilburn King married to May Chism, Cookeville
    7. John B. King married to Francis Buck, Cookeville

(followed by several handwritten sheets of data:)

page 1-

....in regard to my great grandfather Joseph McCulloch, his daughter Sally King, my grandmother said that they spelled their name as above but that others spelled it McCullough. She also said that the first school she ever attended was taught by her father Joseph McCulloch and that when her father gave her a lesson he said to little Andy Jackson who also attended to come and say his lesson along with Sally. she said that Andy's father was then dead and that his mother was a widow and very poor and Andy had been deprived of educational advantages on that account so he may have been much over her age at the time as stated before, she was born Mar. 11,1786 named Sally, She further told me that her husband my grandfather Robt. King volunteered under Andrew Jackson in the War of 1812 to 14 and that he Jackson having gone to school with her to her father and then war service together made them great friends. I feel sure that her statement is true not withstandin the defernce in their ages I could be mistaken in some of the miner details as I was only about 8 or nine year old when told these things.

Yours truly
J. N. King

page 2-Dated: Feb.17,1922

To.Mr. Moore

....as stated before, most I know of Gen. Andrew Jackson earley life is traditional given to me by my grandmother Sarah King (called Sally) whose maiden name was McCulloch. She told me that the first school she ever attended was a comon country school taught in north carlina by her father Joseph McCulloch when she was about six year old and that Little Andy Jackson attended the same school as his first school and that he was about her age or perhaps a few months older and that when her fathe called on her around the old time way and gave the letters of the alphabet as a lesson he called out and said here Andy you come and study your letters along with Sally which he did. That must have been about the year 1792-3 for I have a very old family Bible said to been brought from Ireland (for the oldest of all three families came to Carolina from Ireland) by great grandfather Joseph McCulloch and the record in the old Bible shows that grandfather Robert King was born Mar. 15th 1785(?)* that grandmother Sarah (Sally) King was born Mar. 11th 1786(?)* (*These question marks made by Mr. King...cme) There seems to be some different opinions as to whether Jackson was born in north or south carlina he and my grandfathers both was born after their fathers came from Ireland which I think from what grandmother said was before carolina was divided and when Tenn was part of the carolina I can be of any further service........

J. N. King

page 3-
(the incidents of the life of this sketch cont.)

I J N King the subject of this sketch was born mar the 15th 1850 at or near Paintrock Roane county Tenn My great grandparents on my fathers Joseph Calloway Kings side came from Ireland and settled in territory that became North Carolina part of which is now Tenn Andrew Jackson parents came with thim from Ireland hence they all are of the same blood scotch Irish decent my great grandfather the father of my grandfather Robert King was named John King my grandmothers Sarah Kings father and my great grandfather on her side was Joseph McCulloch he taught Andrew Jackson his alphabet he being a school teacher of his day My grandfather Robert King served in the Indian British war of 1812 under Gen. Andrew Jackson. My father Joseph Calloway King volunteered to go to the war of Mexico but peace was concluded while he was enroute there he served also throughout the civil war as a confederate soldier in the 8th Tenn. Regiment under General Bragg as a private of the Infantry he died Jany 2nd 1903 age 79 yr

page 4-
(these pages out of sequence...cme)

My grandfather Robert King was in his early life well to do in lands and negro slaves &c but by going security for all who asked it and the negroes being freed he lost his possessions and in his old age became a very poor man. Hence my father Joseph Calloway King was throuwn upon his own resources as a renter so in Mar. 1860 he with his family of which I was the oldest moved to Putnam county Tenn. and rented lands then in about two years later he joined the Confederate army leaving me at the age of 12 yr in charge of a small crop and the care of my mother and five other brothers and sisters too small to help consequently a good reason can be seen why I could not educate as I had only gone to school up to this time all told but about six months and never went but about six months more till I was 21 yr old and married but always craved an education so after I was married and had accumulated some little means I sold my small possessions took it and my wife and went to Cumberland Institute White county and stayed thru sessions 15 months and completed the primary course to ninth grade. after which I moved back to Putnam county near Cookeville where I have ever since lived when I first rented and took up farming in sumer and teaching in the fall and winter for 32 years In the meantime I bought a good farm or two gave all my children a little home. was in the meantime elected Justice of the peace a number of times and served two terms as chairman of the county court one term as constable one term as tax assessor three terms, in the years 1903-1905 & 1921 in the lower house of the General Assembly of Tenn. My father Joseph Calloway King was a good honest religious man would have been glad to have helped me but could not in the least so I suppose that I am what some folke term as a self made man. but I feel sure that the very hard and trying hardships throughwhich I have undergone did much to prepare me for the duties of life that I have met with from time to time as indicated above for it takes confidence and iron will as demonstrated by Andrew Jackson to meet the trials of life in a manner to overcome the obstacles that many give way to for want of self determination In conclusion I wish to say that I have endeavered in as brief a manner as posible to give to you this short but true history of myself and ancestry as handed down to me I got the most of this information from my grandmother Sarah King whose maiden name was McCulloch an Irish name as she too came from Ireland she was a very learned woman of her day- so use any and all.............

James Newton King

KING, THOMAS BENTON (1875-1968)

Brownsville, Tenn. Feb. 1, 1922
(Representative)

1. Thomas Benton King
2. Brownsville, Tenn.
3. Jan. 16, 1875 Brownsville, Haywood co., Tenn.
4. Thomas Benton King; Maysville, Limestone co., Alabama; Gurleysville, Ala. 1st Lt. D.C. Kellys co. Forest Cavalry, captured and spent two years at Johnson's Island; Thomas M. King and Ann Gurley; Gurleysville, Ala.
5. Belle Thompson; Robert Emmett Thompson; Mary Elizabeth Tolliver; Lebanon, Tenn.
6. Thomas M. King, a Virginian, My grandfathers mother was Ann Cockrell sister of Jno. Cockrell who assisted in establishing American Independence while acting as Major in the Rev. Army under Brig. Gen. McIntosh; Jno Cockrell enlisted under Col. William Christian and was with him in 1776 when he marched into Cherokee country to avenge the ravages of this tribe upon the western settlement; in 1786 he joined the expodition of Capt. John Donelson - they came down the Tennessee and Ohio and the Cumberland to the present site of Nashville- he was given 3 grants of land for his military service by the state of North Carolina- his wife was Ann Robertson who was given a grant of land for her bravery
7. Brownsville and Haywood county schools
8. Bethel College, Russellville, Kentucky 1892
9. Doctor of Dental Surgery; University of Tennessee - Nashville, Tenn. spring of 1897.
10. Dentistry - began practice Mar. 1897
11. Representative Haywood county 1921
12....
13. Democrat
14. Methodist.
15. Mason and K of P
16.....
17.......
18......
19......

KRUESI. PAUL JOHN (1878-)
Chatanooga, Tenn. 6/20/1922

1. Paul John Kruesi
2. Chattanooga
3. Feb.3, 1878, Menlo Park, New Jersey
4. John Kruesi; St, Gall, Switzerland; lived at Schenectady, New York; traveled extensively in Europe in youth; came to U. S. in 1871 became associated with Thomas A. Edison for whom Kruesi made the first Phonograph.....
5. Emily Zwinger; Dr. J. A. Zwinger and Emily....; Pittsburg, Pa. Mother born at Cleveland, Ohio.
6. Family Swiss back to 1412 which is as far as records go. Mother native of Ohio as stated above. Father was General Manager and later Chief Mechanical Engineer of General Electric Co. For full details of career reference is made to Vol. 2 of "The Story of Electricity" by F.? Comm__? Martin - in press June 1922.
7. Private school at Schenectady, New York, preparatory to high school; graduated Union Classical Institute 1896.
8. Union College, Schenectady, N. Y. Entered Ph. D course 1896- left college at end of sophmore year in 1898 for financial reason.Class President.
9....
10. Manufacturer. Started Edison Laboratory Orange, N. Jersey about 1894; various employments during 3 months summer vacations in treasury and other departments of General Electric Co. Schenectady 1898-9; assistant to Chief Statistician Chicago Edison Co. 1899-1902; Ass't to sales Mgr. of affiliated Insul? Electric interests in Newport City 1902 to date, American Lava Cor'n, Chatta. (of which President)
11....
12. Vice Pres. Chatta. Chamber of Commerce 1912; President 1913-4 of Chatta. Chamber of Commerce; Vice Pres. for some years Chatta.Mfrs. Ass'n.

President 1914 Commercial Club Director (1920) Rotary Club; Member Exec. Comm. all War Loans;Vice Chairman 4th Liberty Loan; Chairman United War Work Campaign; Director Chatt. Chap. American Red Cross (cont'd on p. 4 under question #18); Director Hamilton Trust & Savings Bank; Dir. O. B. Anderson Paper Mills Co.; Dir. Chatt. Elec. Metals & Co. and Pres.; Dir. American Lava Corp. and Pres.; Dir. Southern Ferro(?) Alloys Co. & Pres.; Dir. Tenn. River Milling Co. and Vice-Pres.; Dir. Tenn. River Muscle Shoals Improvement Assoc. Vice-Pres. Dir. 1912-3 Chamber of Commerce,USA; Appointed June 1, 1922 by Hon. Herbert Hoover as "Acting Ass't. Sec. US Dept. of Commerce"; Trustee-University of Tenn. 1921 to (present) date.
13. Republican; member Hamilton Co. Exec. Comm. and Vice-Chairman 3rd Congressional Dist.; Republican Comm.; Active manager campaign 1920-3rd Cong. Dist. when Hon. Jos. Brown, M.C. unhorsed Hon. John A. Moon, M.C. after 24 years service. Appt'd Mar. 1922, State Campaign Mgr. for Hon. Alf A. Taylor, candidate for re-election for Governor.
14. Board of officers; Third Presbyterian Church.
15. No secret orders except at college where member of Sigma Phi.
16. ...
17. Myra Kennedy Smartt, July 26, 1906, Walden's Ridge near Chattanooga; late Capt. James Polk Smartt and Rowena Kennedy, Chattanooga; Capt. James Smartt was a Confederate survivor of battle of Chickamauga and to date of death in 1914 was Government Historian of "Chattanooga & Chickamauga National Military Park Comm."; originally from McMinnville and Smartt's Sta., Tenn. indirectly related to many of old families of Middle Tenn. (ask for interesting details re: historical names on both sides of family if interested.)
18. None
19. (1) Peggie Kruesi
    (2) Margaret Kruesi
    (3) Rowena Kruesi
    (4) John Kruesi
    (5) Mary Eleanor Kruesi

LARKINS, JAMES ALEXANDER (1859-1940)
White Bluff, Tenn., Jan. 31, 1922
(Legislature)

1. James Alexander Larkins
2. White Bluff, Tenn.
3. 4 Nov. 1859, place I now live, Dickson co., Tenn.
4. James Calvin Larkins; Charlotte, Dickson co., Tenn.; the place I now live on all his life; James Larkins and Mary McAdoo; the place I now live on.
5. Susan Gatewood; Richard Gatewood and Sarah ____; near Lexington, Ky.
6. My grandfather, James Larkins and his wife, Mary McAdoo Larkins emigrated here about 1795 from North Carolina. My great grandfather, Hugh Larkins came with them, he having got a grant from the state of N. C. to one thousand acres of land the grant states that it is his for signal bravery as Sargent in the Continental army; he was born in Ireland and came to America when quite a boy. I still own part of the original 1000 acres; I don't know anything about my mother's parents.
7. The most of my education I received in Charlotte, Tenn. from Prof. E. E. Larkins - I never had the advantage of mutch education.
8. ...
9. ...
10. My occupation is farming. I have followed it all my life here on the farm I was born on.
11. Justice of Peace 12 yrs. beginning in 1900, chairman of county board of Education, chairman of the local draft board of Dickson co. during the world's war; member of the 1921 Legislature.
12. Took great interest in abolishing the saloon.
13. Private in the Democratic Party.
14. Christian
15. Royal Arch Mason
16. ...
17. Mary Tennessee Larkins, Feb. 10, 1886, Dickson co., Tenn.; Samuel Putman Larkins and Louisa Palestine Larkins, Dickson co., Tenn.; her father is a 3rd cousin of mine, a descendant of our great grandfather, Hugh Larkins. I don't know anything of her mother's ancestry.
18. None

19. 1. Alice Gilliam,her husband Guy Gilliam, Charlott, Dickson co.Tenn.
2. Clara Hooper,her husband Homer J. Hooper,212-15 Ave N Nashville Tenn.
3. Leslie Dobson Larkins, wife Maude Graham Larkins, White Bluff,Tenn.
4. Mary Nicks,husband Charles Emmet Nicks,Murfreesboro, Tenn.
5. Eddie Lee Buttrey, husband William Boyd Buttrey,White Bluff, Tenn
6. Lucille Nicks,husband Dallas Nicks, Dickson, Tenn.
7. Alline Larkins
8. Susan Larkins
9. Samuel Calvin Larkins

LARSEN, CARL ALFRED (1870-1934)
Memphis, Tenn. Jan. 31, 1922
(Legislature)

1. Carl Alfred Larsen
2. Memphis, Tenn.
3. Mar, 27, 1870, Kristiania, Norway
4. Hans Larsen; Norway; Lived Norway (no more information)
5. Karen Olsen (Norway) (nothing more)
6.....
7. Rec'd 6 yrs. of public school education in Kristiania, Norway
8. none
9. .....
10. Painter and Decorator
11. Member of Tenn. Legislature in 1913-1915-1919 and 1921 and was elected member of the Shelby county election Board 1921
13. Democrat
14. Lutheran Church
15. Mason, 32d and Shriner
16......
17. Rosa Lee Sowers, married at Memphis, Tenn. Sept. 28, 1899; Joseph Sowers and Sarah ____; Memphis, Tenn.
18.....
19......
(followed by letter dated Dec. 6, 1922 to J. T. Moore from Carl Larsen: ....My full name is Carl Alfred Larsen I was born in Kritiania Norway March 27th 1870. My fathers name is Hans Larsen and my mothers name is Karen Larsen. They were also born in Norway. I came to America in 1890 and to Memphis in 1892, which has been my home ever since. I am a Painter, I am a Democrat, I am a 32nd degree Mason, and a Shriner. Served in the Tenn. lower House four terms representing Shelby county, in 1913-15-19 and 1921. was elected to State Senate during november of this year. I married Rosa Kinsey Sowers in Sept. 1899. My wife was born in Memphis,

Yours truly
Carl Larsen

(Note: on letter head of the above note is: John Brown, Chairman, Commissioner of Purchasing and Finance; E.W.Hale, Secretary. Comm.of the Dept. Health and Bridges; Luther F. Jones, Comm. of the Workhouse and Roads; Commission Government, Office Shelby County Commissioners.)

LAWRENCE, RACHEL JACKSON (1832-1922)
(Veterans questionnaire) Veterans form #2/part of Females questionnaire

1. Rachel Jackson Lawrence, Hermitage-" Bird Song", Tenn.
2. I will be ninety years old Nov. 1st, 1922.
3. Hermitage Home, Davidson co., Tenn.
4. I was thirteen years old when my grandfather Gen. Andrew Jackson died; I remember him well.I loved him dearly I am his only grand daughter and named by him for his wife.
5.....
6 Being only son (adopted) of Gen. Andrew Jackson, attended to all business on Hermitage plantation and private and personal matters
7. Andrew Jackson Jr.; Hermitage district on plantation of his father. Severn Donelson; lived at Hermitage, having been adopted when three days old; he attended to all personal matters of Gen. Andrew Jackson correspondence and business on Hermitage plantation.

8. Sarah Yorke; Peter Yorke and _______; Philadelphia, Pa.
9. (See my accompanying papers)
10. Plantation of 560 acres, with home similar to Hermitage which was burned soon after completion in 1858; real estate in Nashville, Tenn. on Broad St., valued then at 25,000 dollars.
11. My husband, Dr. John Marshall Lawrence, and I, owned six families - my mother and father owned hundreds.
12. Hermitage plantation.
13. ...
14. Hermitage home, a brick building, 14 rooms and large halls and porticoes.
15. Raised in luxury, did not know what work was until I became married and the mother of nine children and endured the hardships of the Civil War.
16. As the (adopted) son of Pres. Andrew Jackson, my father attended to all of his business and correspondence, supervised the work, and managed all the affairs of the Hermitage plantation. Was with him in Washington while the president attended to personal correspondence and business. He made trips to Hermitage supervising affairs there. He was a natural biologist and a great lover of nature.
17. Hundreds of slaves.
18. All manual labor was done by slaves. A paid overseer supervised their labor, but my mother and father kept in touch with their personal needs and gave them every care.
19. No, they supervised.
20. Those who had slaves supervised the work. Those less fortunate did it themselves.
21. As has ever been the case, class distinctions were drawn, but no Christian gentleman or lady looked down upon a fellow creature - Were always gracious and helpful.
22. (See answer above)
23. ...
24. ...
25. Yes
26. Encouraged
27. Governess at home first; neighborhood school (pay) held in historic Hermitage Church, music and dancing tutor at Hermitage; attended private exclusive school held at Mrs. Wm. Nichols home in Lebanon Road; I went every Monday morning and returned Friday evening; boarded at the home of Mrs. Nichols as a special privilege; after that I attended a Catholic (Sisters of Charity) school for one year; after that entered Mrs. Mercers school for young ladies at Belmont, Va.; took final course and graduated
28. (Above answer covers this space)
29. 1/4 of mile
30. Pay school at Hermitage Church
31. Private
32. eight or nine
33. Yes
34. Man
35. through 42. (No answers)
43. I have lived at our home "Bird Song", about two miles from my Hermitage home since the close of the war with the exception of a four year residence in Nashville, Tenn., from 1885 to 1889; the occasion of our moving was because of continual ill health of my family; each member had a severe spell of typhoid fever; my husband died in the fall of 1882; my mother, Mrs. Sarah Yorke Jackson (Mrs. Andrew Jackson, Jr.) died in 1886. My oldest child, a daughter, Sarah Jackson Lawrence married Dr. Charles Winn in 1880 and died in 1882, leaving a son one month old, Chas. Lawrence Winn, who was raised as one of my sons; my next oldest child,Annie Laurie Lawrence was married in 1888 to Mr. Joshua W. Smith; in 1889, we built this present home at Bird Song and moved back to our plantation;my oldest son, Dr. Andrew Jackson Lawrence was married about 1884 to Emma George of Fort Worth, Texas; my third son Dr. Samuel Jackson Lawrence was married about 1889 to Miss Maud Clifton of Fort Worth, Texas; these two sons are leading dentists of Ft. Worth and have resided there with their families since before their marriages; in 1890 my youngest daughter, Marion Yorke Lawrence was married to Mr. John Cleves Symmes of Nashville, Tenn.
44. ....

45. (Q. #43 cont'd): In 1882 my third daughter, Carrie Minerva Lawrence was married to Mr. William Daniel Bradford of Texas; in about 1898/1899 my fourth son, William Walton Lawrence married Miss May Flisher of Nashville, Tenn.; my two other sons, John Marshall and Thomas Donelson Lawrence, have not married but have resided here with me in our home at Bird Song; this give a record of my five sons and four daughters. About 1911/1912, I was made Honorary Regent for life of the Ladies Hermitage Asso'cn; in 1904 I was chosen to be hostess of the Tenn. Bldg. at the Louisiana Purchase Exposition held at St. Louis, Mo.; the building was a perfect replica of the Hermitage house; many beautiful and complimentary articles were written in the daily papers; I resided at the Hermitage building during the 6 months of the exposition returning in Dec. 1904; upon my return a large reception was tendered me at the Hermitage House ...also been given an honorary position with the Society of the Daughters of 1812...(Note: Following are numerous pages, both typed and hand written concerning events, socials, political, etc., as recalled by Mrs. Lawrence, of her years at Hermitage and the White House. Not included here, this is interesting reading) Some of the names mentioned in this correspondence are: Andrew and Sarah Yorke Jackson (her parents), Dr. Foster, Dr. Gynne; Chief John Ross; old Alfred -Pres. Jackson's body servant; Mrs. Adams (sister of Mrs. Jackson, Jr.); Dr. Esselman; Mr. Healey (an artist); Gen. Sam Houston - includes her personal recollection of this famous man; Major Donelson; the artists, Longacre and Peyton; Col. Earle; Jane Caffrey, who married Col. Earle and was a niece of Mrs. Lawrence's grandmother; (Note: Col. Earle's people were all residents of Connecticut and he was then a young man at the time of Pres. Jackson's death and had studied in England, France and Italy. On coming to the U. S., he arrived in South Carolina just before the Battle of New Orleans. His wife died in six months after their marriage and he lived with the Jacksons at the Hermitage. ...he also painted a great many portraits while living with them in Washington and returned with the family to Hermitage in 1837. Col. Earle is credited with laying off the grounds at the Hermitage. He died shortly after of a congestive chill.) Mrs. Lawrence discusses the death of her grandfather, Pres. Jackson (General Jackson); Miss Eliza Peale of Phildelphia, an artist; Marcell B. White, who was in the Battle of New Orleans and a close friend of Gen. Jackson; discusses her mother, Sarah Yorke Jackson..."My mother went abroad to school, and was there for seven years. Her father and mother both died, and three little girls were left orphans. Her younger sister, Jane, married Samuel Wetherill. Her older sister, Mrs. Adams, had property in New Jersey and married John Adams whom she met in New Jersey. It was said that Mr. Adams was related to President Wilson. The Adams couple were married in Philadelphia and had three boys: John (who went into the Navy); Earle (who was killed at the Seige of Vicksburg); and the third (not named) was in Gen. Morgan's command and was killed in Kentucky. Mrs. Adams died at the Hermitage and is buried there." Also mentions Mrs. Mallon's School for Young Ladies in Philadelphia.

(Here follows part of a questionnaire for women; no copy is available as to the other questions on form)

34. As a young girl I delighted in making dainty doll clothes; as a young woman, exquisite fancy work, applique or transfer work being much done in those days; my dresses were made by the best dressmakers; my underclothes was most beautifully made by "Gracie" whom my mother owned and who was wife of "Uncle Alfred". She also made my grandfather's (Jackson) linen shirts with ruffled front and cloth collar.

35. Not considered dishonorable (for women to work) but manuel by slaves; the daughters of a wealthy southerner not supposed to work.

36. (None of my friends taught school or did clerical work.)

37. My home "The Hermitage" was ever noted for unbounded hospitality. Guests were always welcomed and entertained royally. As a child I delighted to ride with Grandpa on "Sam Patch" who was his war horse in front of him on a pillow was my accustomed place until I became large enough to ride my own horse "Black Satin".

38. I was always taught that Home was Woman's sphere. She was "Queen of the realm called Home" - Social pleasures were enjoyed, receptions, the old dances, games, horse back riding, etc.

39. Most horrible! Crops destroyed, livestock and poultry all taken, our house ransacked, lives threatened, plantation devastated, husband captured, I alone with six young children! (Conditions during Civil War)

40. When the Civil War was declared there were five sons of age at the

Hermitage home; my two brothers, Andrew Jackson III and Samuel Jackson and Mrs. Marion Adams's three sons (she was the widowed sister of my Mother) - John, William and Andrew Adams. These five boys immediately volunteered their services and entered the Confederate army. Andrew Jackson III, my brother, was soon promoted to Col. of artillery and Samuel Jackson to Captain of a company. Two of the Adams boys, John and Andrew, were killed in active service. William died of yellow fever . My brother, Capt. Samuel Jackson was mortally wounded at Chickamauga; my mother and father were notified and left the Hermitage in a buggy to drive thru the country to Marietta, Ga. to his bedside. A trunk containing clothing and personal effects was strapped on back of the buggy. This was stolen by bushwhackers one night as they stopped at an inn; they later discovered its absence. My brother had been carried to the home of Gov. Atchison who was then Gov. of Ga. His daughter and my brother were engaged to be married. But death claimed him before my mother and father reached him. His body was brought back to the Hermitage and now rests in the family burying ground under the shadow of the tomb of his grandfather, Andrew Jackson. My brother, Col. Andrew Jackson was the only one of the five boys to return to the saddened house. He had won honors, was a brave and fearless soldier,a beloved officer to the men under him...he returned home broken in health from extreme exposure and hardship. During his absence, our father Andrew Jackson, Jr. died from an accidental gun shot thru the hand, causing lockjaw. He was a man about sixty years of age. At the time of the war my husband, Dr. John Marshall Lawrence and I and our family of six little ones were living on our plantation near the Hermitage. My husband was the only doctor for a radius of about fifteen miles in this part of the country. He was torn between his desire to serve his country in the war and his clear duty to serve the sick and suffering ones who looked to him alone. He and his bosom friend, Frank McNairy of Nashville went so far as to organize a company and made all preparations to leave early the next morning. I will never forget the night I spent in agonized prayer to our Father in Heaven to show him HIS will concerning as to what was his duty. The answer came...to remain at his post....he was once captured upon suspician...was taken to headquarters and a mockery of a trial was enacted...he was to be shot next day.. ...a friend and a Mr. Hudson found out the circumstances, proved his innocence and secured his release.....(This is followed by a small notebook filled with more reminiscence of Rachel Jackson Lawrence, daughter of Sarah and Andrew Jackson, Jr.. This material is much the same as the above and for those interested in this particular family, the editors suggest reading the entire series of notes and letters...cme)

This is an interesting series of notes at the end of the note-book on Andrew Jackson, Jr.:

Andrew Jackson, Jr. was one of twin boys born to Severn and Elizabeth (Rucks/Rucker?) Donelson, Dec. 22, 1809, a mile or two from the Hermitage ...Severn Donelson was the 7th brother and favorite brother of Mrs.Rachel Jackson wife of Gen. Andrew Jackson. She was born Rachel Donelson..very early in the morning of Dec. 22, 1809, she and Gen. Jackson were told by a servant that "Miss Betsy and Massa Severn" had twin boys that night.. Jackson remarked "we must have one of those boys"...they went across to the home (Donelson), chose one of the infants, named him Andrew Jackson, Jr., tied a string around his wrist, returned the 3rd day and carried him home to The Hermitage. The Legislature being in session, Gen. Jackson visited Nashville, had young Andrew legally made his lawful son and heir, his name changed from Donelson to Jackson ..henceforth and forever was known, called, spoken to or of as this name..attended an excellent old field school until old enough to go to Nashville to Dr. Priestly, who prepared him for college.....he entered the University of Nashville.... Dr. Phillip Lindsley, President....received his diploma at the First Presbyterian Church in October 1828....among those attending were: Gen. Andrew Jackson, Judge Catron, Major Daniel Graham......(Note: There is also a vivid description of her father)

LITTLEFIELD, JAMES LUTHER (1856 -)
Adamsville, Tenn., Feb. 17, 1922

(See the following page #72)

1. James Luther Littlefield
2. Adamsville, Tennessee
3. Feb. 2, 1856, Adamsville, McNairy county, Tennessee
4. Luther Rice Littlefield; Spartenburg, Spartenburg co., S.C.;Adamsville, Tenn.; was farmer - never held office; born at Spartenburg, S.C. Dec. 25, 1826-moved with his father to Tenn. in 1831, then to Ala. in 1837 and to Tipah Co., Miss. in 1845 where he married-moved to McNairy Co. in 1850; William Littlefield and Sarah Turner Littlefield; Spartenburg, S. C. until 1831-then moved to Carroll co., Tenn.; he was a school teacher by profession-was born in 1756.
5. Nancy A. Wolverton; James and Sarah A. (Williams) Wolverton; Columbia, Tenn. until 1831 - then moved to West Tennessee
6. My great grandfather William Littlefield was born in England-Stratford on Avon near London-came to America, settling in the state of Maryland prior to 1700, married Miss Rebecca Lee, who were the parents of William II, born in Maryland, educated and married Sarah Turner and who followed teaching as a life-time profession - who was a soldier and private under Gen. Nathaniel Green in the Revolutionary War-just what particular organization, I do not know. William Littlefield II was a first cousin to Mrs. Catherine Green, wife of Gen. Nathaniel Green. William Littlefield III was the father of Luther Rice Littlefield and was reputed to be one of the ablest scholars of his day.
7. Early education in country schools of which only lasted two to four months of the year, where I was raised just after the Civil War, hence very limited and forcing me to study at home and around the fireside at odd times until I was 18 years old, when I began teaching country school ...Prof. M. R. Abernathy being my principle teacher.
8. I had no college course, hence no degrees, a matter of much regret and which lacking has always been a great drawback in filling positions imposed upon me, with the duties to fulfill.
9. I had no professional education-my father asking me to take a medical course of which I turned down, believing as I did, that it did not suit the trend of my desires. I then selected law and my father opposing me, and dissuading me with all his power, resulting in my declining.
10. ...
11. In 1882 I was elected County Trustee of McNairy county then again in 1884 and 1886; I then invested in the mercantile line of life work, which I followed until 1921; I was elected the the Gen. Assembly of 1909, one of the primary election Comm. but the law was determined unconstitutional by the Supreme Court. I was again elected a member of the State Tax Equalzation in 1921, which position I still fill.
12. When the state wide prohibition movement was before the people of Tenn., I took a greater interest in and was active in aiding in making Tenn. legally dry; I have always felt a greater degree of pride in my actions along this particular moral issue than almost any other, believing as I do that use and sale of intoxicating beverages has been a great draw back and curse to the masses, hence I have always been proud of my stand on this line.
13. I am and have always affiliated with the Republican party but have held no important position in the state organization of same, however, held some minor places as Congressional Committeeman. While I have been fully identified with the party, yet never seeking places of position.
14. I have always (belong) to Baptist church; Deacon of local church.
15. Mason in 1887, been treasurer of local lodge for about 25 years.
16. Never wrote any books...been too busy.
17. Elizabeth J. Bolton, raised near me and was a school mate in childhood days; John Lindsey Bolton and Miss Kittie Surratt, Purdy, Tenn.; he John Lindsey Bolton was son of Joseph Bolton who was one of McNairy co.'s first settlers, coming from Alabama to Tenn. and formerly from North Carolina to Alabama.
18. No military record; born in 1856-was too young for the Civil War and too old for the World War, however had two sons who served in World War. My father was a staunch Union man when the Civil War came up but having a large dependent family, rendered no soldier services for either side.
19. (1) John Luther Littlefield, b. Nov. 10, 1878, married Ollie Orr (he is a Merchant)

(2) Ornie Eveline, b. Jan. 2, 1880, married J. W. Hickman (Teacher)

(3) William H. L., b. Oct. 12, 1881, Postmaster, Anson, Texas

(4) Mary E.(?) L., b. Jan. 2, 1883, married Mark Perkins (he is a Lumberman)

(5) Edgar B. L., born Sept. 11, 1884, married Ethel LaGrone (he is a Salesman at Spur, Texas)
(6) Neill B. L., born Mar. 4, 1886, married Zella Phillips (Farmer)
(7) Ella P. L., born Nov. 1, 1887, married W. M. Messer (he is Lumber Dealer)
(8) Artye C., born July 7, 1890, married J. J. Tidwell (Farmer)
(9) Jas. M. L., born Jan. 14, 1893, married Lois Ivoery (he is Salesman in Corinth, Miss.)
(10) Henry E.(?) L., born May 16, 1894, married Maxie Pettigrew (he is a Merchant of Adamsville, Tenn.)
(11) Charlie L. L., born Nov. 18, 1899, single (Watchmaker of St. Louis in Missouri)
11 children, of which 7 are sons and 4 are daughters.

MC DANIEL, NICHOLAS MARION (1872-1937)
Madisonville, Tenn., 3-30-1923

1. Nicholas Marion McDaniel
2. Madisonville
3. May 13, 1872, Tellico Plains, Maury co., Tenn.
4. Peter McDaniel, Tellico Plains, Maury co., Tenn.; Tellico Plains of near Jala__; Pally(?) McDaniel and Caroline Stillwell; near Tellico
5. Caroline Stillwell; John Stillwell and Rebecca Strickland.
6. My fathers people came from S. C. Had two uncles, Peter and James in the Mexican War who were officers and Peter was a Confederate Captain. My mothers people came from Buncomb co., N. C.
7. Country school at Brown(?) Hill, Jalapa, Tenn., teacher-James Cline.
8. Hiwassie College, Maury co., Tenn.; S. G. Gilbreath, Pres. 1893/4/5
9. U. S. Grant Univ. near (now) University of Chattanooga; graduated in Law dept. June 1899.
10. Admitted to the Bar at Madisonville, Dec. 1899 in Chancery Court and Jan. (June?) 1900 in the Circuit Court - sworn in.
11. Represented Maury co. in (Monroe co.?) in the Lower House 1917 & 1923 as a Democrat. Elected both times by a 21 majority.
12. Was sworn in as Federal Prohibition ___ for East Tenn. in Nashville on Feb. 5, 1920 and resigned same to get back to the practice of law in November 1920.
13. Democrat, now secretary of Committee.
14. Baptist
15. 3rd Degree, 32nd Degree and Shriner Mason.
16. ...
17. Lillie L. Hicks; Hugh and Bettie Hicks (Bettie Webb), Madisonville and later in McMinn county
18. ...
19. Cecil McDaniel - 16
Dora McDaniel - 14
Bryant McDaniel - 11
Ray McDaniel - 7
Wanda Bill McDaniel - 8 mo.

MC DONALD, JOHN QUINCY (1885 -)
Byrdstown, Tenn., Mar. 4, 1922

1. John Quincy McDonald
2. Byrdstown, Tennessee
3. Aug. 8, 1885, Alpine, Overton co., Tenn.
4. John Roberts McDonald, West Fork, Overton co., Tenn.; Ci McDonald & Jane (Roberts) McDonald, Nettle(?) Carrier (now Alpine), Tennessee
5. Loretta Smith; John Smith and Hannah (McDonald) Smith, West Fork, Overton co., Tenn.
6. ...
7. High school-Alpine, Monroe, Livingston and Hillwin(?), Tenn.; my teachers: Gov. H. H. Roberts, A. R. Hogin, A. J. Taylor and Monroe Seals.
8. ...
9. Law at Cumberland Univ. at Lebanon, Tenn.; LL.B., Jun. 1914; Post graduate Vocational student in Law(Low?) Univ. Tenn. Dec. 1920.
10. Att'y; began practice at Byrdstown, Tennessee in October of 1914,Con-

tact Representative U. S. Veterans Bureau since Feb. 1, 1922
11. Republican Elector on Hughes-Fairbanks ticket for 4th Cong. Dist. 1916, member of 1911 and 1921 Gen. Assembly from 12th Flo-___? Dist.
12......
13. Republican
14. Christian Church
15. Mason, I.O.O.F., K of P, Modern Woodmen of America and member of American Legion
16.......
17. Maggie Mattie Winton; married at Alpine, Tenn. May 25,1902; John Lesley Winton and Mattie (Farley) Winton, Alpine, Tenn.
18. (1) Private (2) Commander? Cols. C. B. Rogers?, J. B. Van Mitz, and Luke Lea
19. Addie Rems? McDonald, Mattie Loretta McDonald and Caesor Kent McDonald at home in Brydstown, Tenn.

MC KENZIE, BENJAMIN GORDON (1866-1938)
Dayton, Tenn. Feb.4, 1921
(terrible writing)

1.Benj. Gordon McKenzie
2. (living)
3.26, Feb. 1866 near Big Spring, Meigs co., Tenn.
4.Jerremiah McKenzie, Meigs co., Tenn.; lived near Big Spring, Tenn. was in War with Mexico in Capt. Geo. W. McKenzies? Co. was also Lt. in War between States in the 60's. was in Col. Geo. W. McKinzies Reg. Capt. William Lillards? Co. was in Battles Chickamauga and other battles around Chattanooga when war closed was in prison at Johnson Island; Benjamin Franklin McKenzie and Nancy Grubb in Meigs co., Tenn.
5. Margaret Masoner; Issac Masoner and Mahalia......., near Kincannons Ferry, Meigs co., Tenn.
6. Ancestry were of Scotch extraction on fathers side and graet grandfather came from Scotland settled in Meigs co. The McKenzies in Scotland our relatives were many of the clan Kenzie especially John McKenzie who was an uncle of my grandfather Benj. F. McKenzie. My father Jeremiah McKenzie held every office in Meigs county from Justice of Peace to Judge of County Court he is now 91 yrs of age and only surviving Mexican Soldier living in E. Tenn. He is still been interested in politics being a staunch democrat.
7. Rec'd early education in common schools Meigs co., Tenn.
8. only rec'd high school education in high school of Meigs co. graduated in 1887.
9. Read Law under Judge V. C. Allen of Decatur, Tenn.
10. Licensed to practice law in 1887 Feb. 6, removed to Dayton, Tenn. May 1888 and practiced profession law there since.
11. Legislature 1899 Special Court Judge 1901 County Atty. Rhea Co., 1901-2. App'td by Gov. R Atty General 1915 Elected 1916 and 1918 without opposition has 5 yrs to serve
12. Often mention for Cong....from 4th Dist. have stumped the state several times for Dem. Ticket
13. Democrat from this (His?) youth up as an (are?) all the McKenzies in E Tenn.
14. Baptist - Deacon
15. belong to Masons and K of P
16. Author of Lecture entitled "From the Cabin to Castle" pronounced by Govr. R. L. Taylor to be one of the best.
17. married twice 1st wife Luna? Leota Todd daughter of Geo. R. and Sarah Todd who died in 1890. 2nd wife, dau. of Geo.W. Foust and Emma Foust, Rhea Springs. 1st wife's people came from Va. 2nd wife, natives of Rhea co., Tenn.
18......
19. By 1st wife:Marjorie McKinzie;by 2nd wife:Jas. Gordon McKenzie, Gladys McKinzie, Wendell McKenzie and Emma Jean McKenzie. Jas. Gordon McKenzie married to Maud Hallaran? has one little grand daughter, Margery Dean; Wendell McKenzie Nov. 7, 1920 married Bessie Mae Godsey and have one little girl born Sept. 14, 1921 named for her grandfather the subject of this sketch name Bennie Godsey McKenzie. All my children reside Dayton, Tenn.

MC KNIGHT, ALBERT DOLLARSON (fl 1891-1918)
Murfreesboro, Tenn., Feb. 9, 1922

1. Albert Dollarson McKnight
2. Murfreesboro, Tennessee
3. (no date of birth), Rutherford co., Tennessee
4. John A. McKnight; on farm - Rutherford co., Tenn.; lived at the farm east of Murfreesboro, Tenn.; served as a private in 45th Regiment, Confederate army 1861-1865; was Magistrate from 17th Civil Dist. of Rutherford co. for 22 years; Madison McKnight and _____ Thomas, on a farm in Wilson co., Tenn.
5. Ludie Barker; Don Barker and _____ Hooper; Milton(?), Tennessee
6. ...
7. Milton (Milten), Tenn. Halls Hill and Lascarras, Tenn., Walla Walla, Washington.
8. No
9. None
10. Farmer, merchant, traveling salesman.
11. Co. Crt. Clk., Sept. 1914-Aug. 1, 1918. Resigned after being nominated for second term. City Councilman.
12. Foreman of Grand Jury.
13. Democrat; member of State Board of Equalization; member of State Executive Committee from 8th District.
14. Church of Christ.
15. Mason, Scottish and York Rite; Shriner; Odd Fellow; Knight of Pythias and Elk.
16. ...
17. Emma Catherine, June 28, 1891, Walla Walla, Washington; William King and Jane Catherine Wiley, Walla Walla, Washington.
18. ...
19. Luda Catherine, wife of Marvin Wright Lea(?), Murfreesboro, Tenn.
Ben Scott McKnight, married Mary Forrest Batey, Murfreesboro, Tenn.
Eva McKnight, died at age of 28 months.
Robert Dixon McKnight, Murfreesboro, Tenn.

MC LEAN, RIDLEY (1872-1933)
Washington, D. C., 30 May 1923

1. Ridley McLean
2. U.S.S. Arkansas, % Navy Dept., Washington, D. C.
3. 10 Nov. 1872, Pulaski co., Tenn.
4. Thornton McLean, born Oct. 1838, Elkton, Todd co., Ky.; Elkton, Ky. until about 1869, when he married and moved to Pulaski, Tenn.; becoming cashier of Giles Co. National Bank; in 1872 he became a widower, moved to San Francisco, Calif. until 1880, when he returned to Murfreesboro, Tenn. where he died Oct. 1887; Hon. Finis Ewing McLean and Lucy Amanda Gray; Elkton, Ky.; the former after becoming a widower, moved to Greencastle, Indiana where he died about 1875.
5. Sallie Caruthers Ridley; Hon. Bromfield L. Ridley and Rebecca Crosthwaite; Murfreesboro, Tenn., Old Jefferson, Tenn. and McMinnville, Tenn.
6. Descended from Charles McLean, who with his brother, John, emigrated from Scotland in 18th century; John settled in N. Y. Charles in N. C. - married daughter of Ephraim Moore; grear-great-grandson of Charles McLean of Mecklenburg co., N. C. a wealthy planter, prominent for aid furnished American forces during the Revolutionary War, who married Susan Allison Howard, daughter of Dr. Howard of Philadelphia. Gr-grandson of Rev. Chas. Ephraim McLean who with his father, Charles, migrated to Ky. about 1790. He was the first ordained minister of the C. P. Church; he married Elizabeth Byers(Ayers?), dau. of Edward Byers(Ayers?) of Va. and S. C. in 1788 - 5 sons and 4 daughters. Grandson of Hon. Finis Ewing McLean of Elkton, Ky., youngest son of above union; member of House of Representatives 31st Congress and Lucy A. Gray of Elkton, Ky. Only child of Thornton McLean (1838-87) and Sallie Caruthers Ridley (1849-72, daughter of Chanceller Bromfield Lewis Ridley, Murfreesboro, Tenn.
7. Attended school in Murfreesboro: (1) Electic & Normal School, Rev. J. M. Waters, DD, at the Old Union University Bldg. on Mary St. about 1885, (2) Public school, Murfreesboro, 1886-87, Prof. E. C. Cox, Supt., (3) the Sweetwater College, Sweetwater, Tenn., Rev. J. W. Bachman, DD, Pres. - 1887-1888.

8. Entered University of Tenn., Knoxville, in autumn of 1888 in sophomore class, Dr. C. M. Dabney, Pres.; won Allen Prize medal in mathematics in 1889; received appointment to U. S. Naval Academy, Annapolis in the spring of 1890 and entered Annapolis, May 20, 1890; appointed by Hon. Jas. D. Richardson, M.C., from 5th Dist. Tenn.
9. Graduated from Naval Academy, June 1894, since which date have .... continuously in various ranks and grades in U. S. Navy; Judge Advocate General of the Navy in 1913-1917; Capt. U. S. Navy since 1918.
10. See Q. 18, last page
11. None
12. None
13. Registered voter in Murfreesboro, Tenn. during absence ____ to military service of Federal government.
14. Born a Cumberland Presbyterian; raised a Presbyterian; married and now affiliated with Unitarian.
15. Member of Kappa Sigma fraternity, Lambda Chapter (Univ. of Tenn.)
16. Bluejackets Manuel - A Catechism and Aid in Professional Education and Training of Enlisted Men of the U. S. Navy. 800 pp. now published as an official publication by the Navy Dept.
17. Olive Gale, of Washington, D. C., married 8 Nov. 1916; Thomas Monroe Gale and Ida May Fisher, Washington, D. C.; descended on fathers side from William Fuller who emigrated to America in the Mayflower, on mothers side from union of French and German ancestry being the grand-daughter of the late Thomas Jefferson Fisher of Washington, D. C.
18. ...
19. Olive Beatrice McLean, born 22 Feb. 1905
Gale McLean, born 20 Jan. 1908

The above children of Olive Gale McLean by a former marriage, having been adopted by the subject of this sketch after his marriage to their mother in 1916.

(Followed by a set of 5 typewritten pages, in part, discussing the remarkable improvement in the Navy and its advances - headed: Captain Ridley McLean, U.S.N., Washington, D.C. - first part is much the same as the ancestry: i.e. - parents, grandparents; second part: Capt. McLean born in Pulaski, Tenn. and lost his mother at birth, was taken back to the old home in Elkton, Ky. and reared by his uncle and aunt, Major and Mrs. Jerome S. Ridley, during his early years, and later made his home in Murfreesboro; then gives a detailed list of Capt. McLean's service in the Navy. There follows a summary account of the development of American gunnery for a collection of historical data by Capt. McLean in 1920.)

MC MURRY, JAMES DALE (1873-1945)
Hartsville, Tenn., Feb. 1922

1. James Dale McMurry
2. Hartsville, Tennessee
3. Apr. 13, 1873, Hartsville, Trousdale co., Tennessee
4. John Saunders McMurry; Dixon Springs, Smith county, Tenn., lived at Dixon Springs for many years, but was living at Hartsville, Tenn. when he died Apr. 1909; served in the Civil War under Morgan and was in the service the full four years from 1861 to 1864; Charles McMurry and Frankie McMurry; near Hartsville, Tennessee.
5. Caroline McClain; Dr. Jesse McClain and Elizabeth McClain; Nashville, Tennessee.
6. ...
7. At Hartsville, Tenn., Dixon Springs, Tenn.; teachers: Mrs. Kate Wilson, Prof. S. A. Minors, Prof. Boon, Prof. Gross, Prof. Clark, Prof. Mcconnell, Miss Mary Winston.
8. ...
9. (Read law under my father, John Saunders McMurry).
10. Lawyer; admitted to the bar, August 1898.
11. Legislature of 1919, Extra Session of 1920 and 1921 Regular Session
12. ...
13. Democrat
14. Baptist; Deacon
15. ...
16. ...

17. Laura Puryear McMurry, married January 1, 1899 at Hartsville, Tenn.; Lafayette Puryear and Bettie Bass Puryear; Hartsville, Tennessee.
18. ...
19. John Puryear McMurry m. Leona Anthony Puryear, Hartsville
Jesse Saunders McMurry, Hartsville
Elizabeth McMurry, Hartsville

MC REYNOLDS, JAMES CLARK (1862-1946)

(No form used; extra pages only)

First sheet is entitled: "War Time Prohibition Act of the U. S. held valid by the Supreme Court of the U. S. - Dec. 15, 1919. Members of Court: Chief Justice-Edward W. White; Associate Justices - Joseph McKenner, Oliver Wendell Holmes, William R. Day, W. Van de Vanter, Mahlon Pitney, James Clark McReynolds, John H. Clark and Louis Brandeis.
Second sheet: James Clark McReynolds, Assoc. Justice of Supreme Court of the U. S., was born in Elkton, Ky. in 1862. His mother was Ellen Reeves who was a great grand-daughter of John Edwards, elected with John Brown as Senators to U. S. Senate by the 1st Legislature of Kentucky in May of 1792. His father was Dr. John O. McReynolds, a celebrated physician - a man of commanding influence in the southern part of the state. In a district torn by a divided allegiance to the North and South, he was a pronounced seccessionist - always a man without fear in the expression of his political and religious convictions. Mr. McReynolds graduated at the Vanderbuilt University at Nashville, Tenn. at the head of the class. In the law department of the University of Virginia, he ranked high; he received his degree in little over a year by taking during one summer,a special course under the private instruction of Prof. John B. Minor, one of the greatest teachers of law. In 1885-6, Mr. McReynolds spent some time in Washington as a private secretary to Senator Howell Jackson of Tennessee, then went into practice in Nashville, Tenn. until 1903. At this date, Att'y. Gen. Knox, a Republican appointee of Pres. Roosevelt, selected this Democrat as an Assistant Attorney General. Within a few months he was recognized as an able assistant. He performed these duties of office for 3 years. In 1907, he went to New York City ...was asked to act as advocate for the government in the suit against the tobacco trust ....involved the real test of the Sherman Anti-Trust Law....(Note: there continues many accomplishments during his career.)..
This article was prepared by Mrs. John O. Street, Sr., War Historian of Todd County for files in that county. The latest pictures of him can be obtained from Harris and Ewing, Photographers, Washington, D. C.

MC REYNOLDS, SAMUEL DAVIS (1872-1939)
January 30, 1922

1. Samuel Davis McReynolds
2. Chattanooga, Tennessee
3. April 16(?), 1872, Pikeville, Bledsoe county, Tennessee.
4. Isaac Stephens McReynolds; Pikeville, Bledsoe co., Tenn.; on a farm near Pikeville, was a prosperous farmer, born Sept.(?) 17, 1845 and died July 8, 1915; Samuel McReynolds and Annie McReynolds, near Pikeville.
5. Virginia Addie Davis; Robert R. Davis and Harriet Boggess Davis; in Meigs co., Tenn. six miles north of Decatur, Tenn.
6. My great grandfather, Samuel McReynolds, was one of the early settlers of Sequachee Valley, settled about 8 miles south of Pikeville; of Scotch-Irish descent.
7. Peoples College at Pikeville.
8. Cumberland University at Lebanon, Tenn.; did not graduate.
9. Went to no law school, studied law in the office and home of Senator James B. Frazier of Chattanooga who is a first cousin, his mother and my father being brother and sister.
10. Lawyer, admitted to bar Apr. 16, 1893 at Pikeville, Tenn.; moved to Chattanooga, Jan. 1895-formed partnership with Jno. H. Cantrell; quit practicing Apr. 16, 1903 and went to Criminal Bench Judge of Criminal Court, 6th Cir.(?) which place I still hold.

11. Appt'd. Judge of Criminal Court 6th Cir. by Gov. Frazier, Apr. 16, 1893, been elected three times since and am still in this position.
12. ...
13. Democrat
14. Souther M. E. (Methodist Episcopal)
15. Mason - including Chapter, Commandery Temples and Shriner; Odd Fellows, K. of P., Elks, D. O. O. K.
16. ...
17. Mary Caldwell Davenport, Mar. 10, 1910 at Chattanooga, Tenn.;Rodolph Blevins Davenport and Maggie Caldwell Davenport; Chattanooga, Tenn.; he was born and reared at Valley Head, Ala., came to Chattanooga as young man,-he and his brother, George, engaged in wholesale dry goods as Davenport Bros., very successful. Mrs. Davenport's mother was a Gordon before marriage, came from Georgia, related to Gen. Hardin and Gordon Lee.
18. ...
19. Only one child, a little girl nine(?) years old: Margaret Henriette McReynolds, born here in Chattanooga, Oct. 21, 1912.

MAJOR, HOWARD (1893-)
Big Rock, Stewart co., Tenn., Dec. 8, 1922.

1. Howard Major
2. Big Rock, Tenn.
3. May 7, 1893, near Roaring Springs, Ky.; Trigg county.
4. Lester Major; Belvey, Christian co., Ky. - in Christian co., Ky. untill he was 30 yrs. old then married and came to Stewart co., Tenn. for yr., to Trigg co., Ky. for 7 yrs., back to Stewart co. in 1898(?); Howard Major and Rachel Major; 1 mile near Beverly(?), Ky.
5. Hope Killebrew; S. R. Killebrew and Mary Killebrew; 1 m. of Weaver's Store, Tenn., Stewart county.
6. My great grandfather Chas. Major came from Virginia about 1824, my grandfather Howard Major was then 17 yrs. of age. They settled near Beverly, Kentucky and became farmers.
7. Miss Flora Shelby was my first teacher, I being 8 years old; school was at O. K.(?) Stewart county.
8. Graduate of M. B. A. at Nashville in 1914; some college work at S. P. U., Clarksville.
9. None
10. Farmer, with exception of what time I was in school, have spent all my time working on farm.
11. None
12. Acted as Chairman of organization committee in my county to organize Dark Tobacco Growers Cooperative Assoc.
13. Democrat
14. None
15. Mason
16. None
17. Sallie Belle Greenhill, Nov. 8, 1920 at Clarksville, Tenn.; Chas. F. Greenhill and Nannoe(Nannie?) ______ near Big Rock, Tenn.; of Irish descent.
18. None; physically unfit.
19. No kids

MALONE, SOPHIA KEY (1827-)
(Veterans form) Veterans form #2

1. Sophia Key Malone
2. 98 on March 12; born March 12, 1827
3. Sumner county, Tennessee
4. and 5. (no answers)
6. Farmer and Speculator
7. Peter W. Key; near Bethpage, Sumner co., Tenn.; near Bethpage; father was a Colonel in the Indian War.
8. Mary Rippey (nothing else)
9. My mother died when I was very young and I made my home with grandfather William Key-grandmother Elizabeth Gaines Key. He was in Rev. War.

10.......
11. My parents owned slaves but I dont remember how many
12. They owned land a good size place.
13....
14. log house with three rooms on lower floor and two on upper floor
15.....
16. My father bought and sold tobacco and my mother would spin and weave but a slave always did the cooking.
17. My parents kept three servants and cook, house girl and boy.
18. It was considered honorable but the best people did not do such work.
19. no, only the poorer class.
20. most of the white men were idle
21. all slave owners considered themselves far above those who did not own slaves.
22. slave owners and non slave owners attended the same churches and schools but did not mingle much
23. no the feeling between slave owners and none slave owners was not very friendly
24. no the fact that one man owned slaves did not help him to win
25. no
26. he was not encouraged much by the slave holders
27. country school
28. about 10 years
19. the nearest school was in sight of my house.
30. this was the only school in operation in my neighborhood
31. the school was a public school
32. the school was run about the same as now days
33. yes the pupils attended pretty regularly
34. first a man. then a woman
35 - 44......
45. use this page and as many more as you wish to write the story of your life - JTM:

I married John J. Malone when I was twenty years old and in 1840 I moved to Covington, Tipton c., and have lived here since.

(Followed by a letter to Mr. Moore from W. A. Owen, (Judge of Court of Appeals) Jackson, Tenn. dated Sept. 20, 1926; says he is enclosing a picture of Mrs. Sophia Key Malone who was 99 on Mch. 12 .. she is now 99½ he had seen her that day and she was bright and cheerful as if she was seventy..the child is her great-great-grandchild....there being now 5 generations in her family. Her grand-daughter filled out the questionnaire at Aunt Sophia's dictation. I always send her flowers on her birthday. Some ladies presented her with 99 dimes her last birthday. She has a wonderful lot of pleasure giving these dimes to children of town, admonishing the child when the dime was presented to keep it until he or she reached 99 years and to remember an old lady 99 years was the giver. Numerous children have carried Aunt Sophia fruits and flowers all this summer and have been rewarded with one of the shower dimes.
.....hope Aunt Sophia lives far beyond the century mark,

W. A. Owen

(note.. no picture was included in this file for microfilming..cme)

Letterhead includes these names as Judges of Court of Appeals: Arthur Crownover, John H. Dewitt, F. H. Heiskell, J. D. Senter, Hal E. Portrum, C. O. ? Snodgrass and Neal L. Thompson, plus Owen.

MARABLE, SAMUEL ADDISON (1889-)
Ashland City, Tenn. Feb. 1, 1922

1. Samuel Addison Marable
2. Ashland City, Tenn.
3. Feb. 17, 1889; Palmyra, Montgomery co., Tenn.
4. Samuel Addison Marable, M. D.;Palmyra, Montgomery co. Tenn.; Palmyra, Tenn. where he was recognized as one of the prominent physicians of the county.; John Hartwell Marable; Palmyra, Tenn.
5. Elizabeth Jackson; James Madison Jackson and Mary Corbin Jackson; Palmyra, Tenn.
6. The original family from which the subject of this memoranda descended,

was French, the original name being spelled "Mirabeau". At a period just prior to the Revolutionary War, three Mirabeau brothers fled from France to England due to political disturbances and religious persecution. They later came to America, settling in Virginia. One of these brothers was named Champion Mirabeau. A descendant of one of these brothers, Henry Hartwell Marable emigrated from Virginia to Tennessee and settled in Rutherford county. He was a Methodist minister. He had seven children - six sons and one daughter. One of the sons was named John Hartwell Marable who was a member of Congress from Tennessee during the 19th and the 21st sessions. He married Miss Ann Jones Watson, whose father owned a large plantation adjoining the "Hermitage". Subsequently he removed to Montgomery county, settling about five miles west of Palmyra on the south side of Cumberland river, where he accumulated a large body of real estate. He had nine daughters and one son. The latters name was John Hartwell Marable, who enjoyed wide reputation as a physician of ability and prominence prior to the Civil War. The last named John Hartwell Marable had eight children, one of whom was Samuel Addison Marable, now prominent physician in Montgomery county, Tennessee and father of the subject of this memoranda. Another son was Thomas Howard Marable, who was a prominent physician of Clarksville and served several terms as Mayor of that city. Three of the brothers were physicians. During the period between 1830 and 1840, one member of the Marable family in Virginia served as Governor of that state.

7. Attended Taraus, Palmyra and Union public schools of Montgomery co., Tenn. and graduated at Union High School in April 1906, being first graduate of that school which is now one of the largest public schoolsof Montgomery co. In June 1906, attended State Teachers Institute at Cumberland City, Tenn. and passed examination, receiving State Teachers Primary Certificate. Taught school at Toler public school in Montgomery co. during fall of 1906. Early teachers were Misses Emma Rogers and Cornelia Glase, and Profs. Clayton Bumpous and A. C. Outlaw. Entered Cumberland City Academy and graduated in May 1909. Studied during fall of 1909 at Battle Ground Academy, Franklin, Tenn., Prof. D. E. McClearen was principal of Cumberland City Academy and Profs. R. G. Peeples and R. H. Peeples were at head of Battle Ground Academy.

8. (above answer in this space)

9. Graduated from Law Dept., Cumberland Unv. at Lebanon June 1911-LL.B.

10. Passed State Bar examination held at Nashville in Jan. 1911 after only five months study of law. Cont'd. studies at Cumberland Unv. ,graduated in May 1911 and admitted to the bar at Clarksville on June 1911. On Aug. 14, 1911, formed partnership with Lyttleton J. Pardue at Ashland City, Tenn. and have practiced there since continously under firm name of Pardue and Marable.

11. Mayor of Ashland City, Tenn. during 1920-1921; represented Floterial District of Tenn. comprising counties of Cheatham, Robertson and Williamson in 1921 session of the General Assembly of Tenn. as a member of the House of Representatives. Nominated and elected without opposition. Was mentioned by newspapers as probable candidate for Speaker of House, but did not enter contest. Member of most important committees of the House.

12. ...

13. Democrat. Have served as Chairman of Democrat Executive Committee of Cheatham co., Tenn. continously since 1914.

14. Methodist Episcopal Church, South

15. Member Independent Order of Odd Fellows; Masons, being an 18th degree Mason. At present Worshipful Master of Ashland Lodge No. 604, F. & A. M.; served three previous terms as such.

16. ...

17. Pearle Allen Chambliss, married Dec. 2, 1914 at Methodist Church in Ashland City, Tenn.; James Carrol Chambliss and Nannie Emma Allen; Ashland City, Tennessee.

18. Enlisted Jul. 4, 1918 at Ashland City, Tenn. as volunteer; inQuartermaster Corps of U. S. National Army. Sent to Fort Logan H. Roots, Arkansas. Arrived at latter place which is about four miles from Little Rock near Camp Pike, Arkansas, on July 6, 1918. Assigned to duty with the detachmant at Fort Logan H. Roots, and entered the finance department of Quartermaster's Office. Served under: G. J. Jeuneman, Col. M. C.; C. M. Walson, Lt. Col. M. C.; Frank C. Walesh, Major Q. M. C.; O. K. Marshall, Capt. Q.M.C. and C. A. McAteer, 2nd Lt. Q. M. C. Served as a Private until Aug. 1918 when given the rank of Corporal.
Was offered sergeancy in February of 1919,...(cont'd next page)

after signing armistice, but did not accept as advised discharge would be given immediately. Granted honorable discharge from military service at Ft. Logan H. Roots, Ark. on Mar. 15, 1919. Prior to being accepted for service in July 1918 had in Jan. 1918 offered as a volunteer but rejected upon physical examination; at second attempt in July 1918, again placed on limited service list, but after repeated requests finally was accepted for service in Q.M.C. as above stated.
19. No children.

MARSHALL, JOHN LEONIDAS (1867-1942)
Sevierville, Tenn., Mar. 8, 1922.

1. John Leonidas Marshall
2. Sevierville, Tenn.
3. Mar. 3, 1867, Middle Creek, Sevier county, Tennessee
4. Robert Marshall; Middle Creek, Sevier co., Tenn.; Middle Creek, Tenn. Robert Marshall and Jemima Marshall; Middle Creek, Tenn.
5. Asa Trotter; Amos Ranier Trotter and Polly Trotter; Beaver Ridge, Knox county, Tenn.
6. Paternal great-grandfather was John Marshall from Ireland. His son Robert Marshall married Jemima Butler, daughter of Henry Butler from Fairfax co., Va. Maternal grandmother was Polly Gamble, who married Amos Rainer Trotter, who was the son of John Trotter and his wife, Appie (?) White from England.
7. Middle Creek, Pigeon Forge and Sevierville, Tenn.; teachers: Prof. Sam McCallie, Pleas A. Wear, D. H. Ernert(Emert?) and Joseph Duggan.
8., 9. and 10. (no answers)
11. Member of the Legislature in 1921.
12. ...
13. Republican
14. ...
15. Mason and Odd Fellow, Past Grand (Master?)
16. ...
17. Mabel Reese Hicks, married Oct. 26, 1921 at Sevierville, Tenn.; Abraham Jackson Hicks and Mary Pasteur Hodsden; Sevierville; grand-daughter of Dr. Robert Hatton Hodsden (Member of Tenn. Legislature 1861) and wife Mary Reece Brabson. English descent. Abraham Jackson Hicks was a Confederate soldier and a member of the 19th Tenn., Co. G. He was the son of Isiac Hicks and his wife, Rebecca Hull. The Hicks are of Scotch-Irish descent and the Hulls are Dutch.
18. ...
19. Conley McSpadden Marshall, Sevierville.
Asa Trotter Marshall, wife of Hugh Henderson, Sevierville.
(P. O. Sevierville, Tenn.)

MATTHEWS, ALBERT ROSS (1874-1958)
Columbia, Tenn., Dec. 8, 1922

1. Albert Ross Matthews
2. Columbia, R. R. #7
3. Nov. 2, 1874, McCains, Maury co., Tenn.
4. John Galloway Matthews; McCains, Maury co., Tenn.; McCains, Tenn.; Joseph Anderson Matthews and Louisa Jane Matthews, McCains, Tenn.
5. Mary Ellen Morgan; Joseph Morgan and Elisebeth Morgan; McCains, of Maury co., Tenn.
6. My great-grandfather, Joseph Matthews was born in Mecklenburg co., N. C. in the year 1779 and came to Tenn. with his father, James Matthews whose wife was a Doak. James Matthews was born in or near Dublin, Ireland in the (year) 1739, and was a member of the Scottish covennanters. Joseph Morgan, my grandfather on my mother's side came to Tenn. from Va.
7. Public schools of Maury co. and private schools, same county.
8. One year at Erskine College, Due West, S. C.
9. ...
10. Farmer from boyhood to present time.
11. Elected Justice of Peace from 6th Civ. Dist. of Maury co. in 1917 - 1922 elected as Rep. from Maury co. to Lower House of General Assembly.

12. ...
13. Democrat of the rank and file.
14. Member of the Associate Reformed Presbyterian Church; am a ruling elder and clerk of the Session of Hopewell, Tenn.; assoc. Ref. Pres.
15. Am not a member of any fraternal order.
16. ...
17. Rachel Elma McDaniel; Joseph Carpenter McDaniel and Margaret Orr McDaniel; Belfast, Marshall co., Tenn. Joseph Carpenter McDaniel was a son of Allen McDaniel who came to Tenn. from N. C. Margaret Orr McDaniel was a daughter of John Orr who came to Marshall co., Tenn. from N. C.
18. No military record.
19. Joseph Ralph Matthews, who is in his senior year at Bryson College, Fayetteville, Tenn.

MAXEY, TONY BLACK (1897-)
Celina, Tenn., 12-18-1922

1. Tony Black Maxey
2. Celina, Tenn.
3. June 30, 1897, Celina, Clay county, Tenn.
4. Oglesby Black Maxey; near Center Point, Monroe co., Ky.; Center Pt., Ky. until 17 yrs. old when he moved to Clay co., Tenn. Has taught school in Clay co., Tenn. Held the offices of J. P., County Judge and County Court Clerk. Is a practicing attorney; Pennington Gee Maxey and Emily Oglesby Maxey; near Center Point in Monroe county.
5. Louisiana Hampton; Jno. Reed Hampton and Sarah Hawkins Hampton; Butlers Landing, Clay co., Tenn.
6. ...
7. Local schools of Celina, Tenn.
8. ...
9. Cumberland Univ., June 1919, LL.B
10. Practice of Law commenced in August 1919, in Clay co., Tenn. Moderate success.
11. Deputy County Court Clerk for 4 yrs.; Ass't. Postmaster, 7 yrs.; acting Postmaster at Celina, Tenn., 1 yr.
12. Sec'y. of local Chamber of Commerce for a number of years.
13. Democrat; Sec'y. of Clay co., Tenn. Democratic Executive Comm. for 4 yrs.; made active campaign fight for entire Democratic ticket in the years 1918, 1920, 1922.
14. Christian - preference; no connection with any church.
15. Member of Masonic Lodge Canton Lodge No. 635 F & AM
16. ...
17. Mary Kate Stone, married in Celina, Tennessee on Sept. 25, 1920; William Lovell Stone and Eva Williams Stone, Celina, Tenn.
18. ...
19. Note - Genealogy attached. Filed seperately under genealogy - Maxey Family
(Editors Note: This family history was not included on microfilm)

MITCHELL, EDWARD BACON (1850-)
(Veterans Questionnaire) Veterans form #1
Washington (no date)

1. Edward Bacon Mitchell and wife, Amanda Gray Mitchell
2. 72
3. Washington co., Tenn.
4. ...
5. farming
6. farmer
7. ...
8. no
9. 200(?)
10. $4000
11. framed 4 room
12. both planting and hoeing
13. my Father done vey kind of worke on the farm. my Mother cooked spin wove and evry kind of worke

14. none
15. yes
16. yes
17. very few - most evry man worked
18. not in this part of the state but further south they did
19. yes
20. yes
21. for evry 5 slaves he got a extry vote
22. yes
23. not very much encouragement
24. subscription schools - very poor
25. about too (2) years
26. about one mile
27. primary
28. private
29. about foor (4) months
30. no
31. man
32. i warent in the army
33. ...
(Editors note: This next sheet was form for women to answer)
34. the women wove and made there own cloth from flax cotton and wool.
35. no
36. taught school
37. ...
38. very little
39. very hard times in this state - evy thing destroyed by the armyes
40. ...
(Editors note: Next sheet is veterans questionnaire)
34. - 40. (no answer)
41. Christian Church. I was magistrate for 18 yrs. Post master 2; Road (commissioner) 18 yrs.
42. Robert Mitchell; some where in Virginia; ..
43. Catherine Beals; David Bales (note spelling) and Rachel West(Wert?)
44. ...

MITCHELL, FRED GOULD (1874-1921)
Sparta, Tenn., Feb. 5, 1923

1. Hon. Fred Gould Mitchell
2. (Died Nov. 22, 1921, Sparta, Tenn.)
3. Aug. 7, 1874, River Hill, White Co., Tenn.
4. Thomas Lafayette Mitchell; River Hill, White co., Tenn.; lived Sparta, Tenn.-was a lawyer and real estate man. Also lived at Guntersville, Ala. later at West Point, Miss.-was President of Mitchell Optical Co.; Joe Gould Mitchell and Susie Parker Mitchell, Sparta and River Hill; was a cashier of the Bank of Sparta when Civil War came up and carried money to Nashville and saved it.
5. Sallie Frances Crook; John Crook and Sallie Brown; Old(?) Zion, in White co., Tenn.
6. Parents and grandparents always Democrats. The Mitchells were peace loving, quiet people.
7. Doyle College, Doyle, Tenn. Prof. J. N. Huff, Prof. Wm. Smith, Prof. Bryant (always witty and favorite of teachers), also at Sparta, Tenn.
8. (Above answer cont'd here)..Prof. McIlhearen, Prof. Bryant and others.
9. ...
10. Merchant and Drummer at Sparta, Tenn. Hotel man at Crookeville and Sparta.
11. Was member of Legislature 3 terms 1915-1917-1921; was seeing after paroled convicts for Middle and East Tenn. at time of death.
12. Always on moral side - was anxious to help humanity always.
13. Democrat
14. Presbyterian N. S.(?); was elder for 30 years
15. Was Mason, Odd Fellow and Junior Woodman of the World.
16. ...
17. Nannie Sims, married February 24, in 1900 at (home) of Henry Sims, (her father)..........Sparta, Tennessee. Grandfather on fathers side was Jeff and Kate Sims. Grandfather on mothers side was Capt. Jeff Leftwich who was captain in General George Dibrell's company; was a brother-

(cont'd from p. 83; Q. #17)..in-law of General Geo. Dibrell. Grandmother was Lousetti (Clark) Lisk, whose father was Dan Clark (very wealthy and eccentric pioneer).
18. ...
19. One son died in infancy
(Editor's note: This form was filled in by Mrs. J. L. Sims, sister of the deceased).

MOFFITT, PATRICK NAVE (1882-)
McMinnville, Mar. 17, 1923
(Senator)

1. Patrick Narve (Nave) Moffitt
2. McMinnville, R. #2
3. Mar. 26, 1882, Irving College, Warren co., Tenn.
4. Venus Moffitt; Irving College, Warren co., Tenn.; Irving College, all his life; none; Gilbert Moffitt and Celia Moffitt; Irving College
5. Magie Bauldin; Narve Bauldin and Nancy Bauldin; Irving College
6. ...
7. County school and Irving College; Dr. I. (J.?) M. Smoot(?), Prof. E. B. Ettes(?), Miss Georgia Ettes, Miss Linda Hill, Etta Booms.
8. None
9. None
10. Entered mercantile business 1904 at Irving College also lumber and mfg. 1906. Have continued in the mercantile business since 1904 - also stock raising and farming.
11. Elected member of County Court 1918
12. ...
13. Democrat
14. Christian Church
15. Mason
16. None
17. Margie Meadows; date of marriage Nov. 1908; Jerome J. Meadows and Emma Meadows, Irving College, Tennessee.
18. None
19. None

MOORE, ARTHUR DAVID NATHANIEL (1852-)
(Veterans form) Veterans form #2

1. Arthur David Nathaniel Moore
2. 70 years old last September
3. Henry co., Tenn.
4. No, save about 3 weeks and that I acted as courier for Col. Faulkners Confederate Cal.(?)
5. I know not; its captain was Posser(?); Faulkners & Forrests
6. Cumberland Presbyterian minister, farmer and merchant
7. William Boswell Moore; near Tennessee river in Benton county, I think Tenn.; Caladonia, Henry Co., Tenn. and at Christianville, Carroll county, Tenn.; died 1861.
8. Eliza Jenkins Smith; _____ Smith and _____ Smith; near Raleigh, N.C. where she was born in 1811.
9. I have always understood that both my grand sires (were) Irish. My grandfather Moore was raised at or near Kilkeny. My grandmother _____ at Belfast.
10. ...
11. Yes, a few. I do not know now.
12. In my boyhood my father owned a 20 acre farm.
13. About $3000 or $4000
14. A frame, two stories, 7 or 8 rooms and halls.
15. I plowed, hoed and cut wood, hauled wood and goods and milked and did chores about the house.
16. My father kept a store, but often worked on the farm. We had a cook most of the time, but my mother sewed, churned, wove a little and spun a deal.
17. All were workers, and the whites toiled side by side with blacks.

18. All honest work was honorable; idleness was deemed a sin.
19. The large majority did.
20. In all my youth I never heard of but one, and he was a drunkard and looked upon as an imbecile.
21. In company with the neighbors one could not tell a slave owner from a hired man.
22. They did
23. They were mutual agreeable and friendly
24. I never observed or believed that it did
25. Decidedly so, and just as good as todays
26. Always encouraged and aided
27. Common schools and two terms at academies at McKenzie, Tennessee
28. Abt. 30 months
29. From 1/2 mile to as far as two miles except when I lived at McKenzie
30. ...
31. Private but all children of the community attended
32. From 3 to 10 months
33. Yes
34. More often both
35. As intimated herein before, I joined Capt. Penn and Co. of Colonel Faulkner's regiment at Huntington, Tenn. in the fall of 1862 but was in service only about 1 month, when I was "captured" by my folks and carried back home at Christianville. I was only a little past 10 years of age.
36. It started to Newbelle(?) Cross Roads, when I was overtaken by the home folks.
37. Only a few weeks
38. The unforgettable flogging my mother gave me for running away to the army.
39. ...
40. ...
41. It was neither long nor tedious, nor romantic, save my oldest brother was escorting me, and he stopped for a night at his then sweetheart's house and that night gave me 100$ in cond(erate) to go to bed.......
42. The same that I had done
43. At 17 I began teaching in the public schools and for several years was thus engaged and quietly reading law. In 1874 I went to Trenton in Smith co., Miss. and sold (goods) for W. J. Bell that year and the next. Studying law of nights. In Jan. 1876, I moved to Raleigh, the county seat of Smith County, Miss. and began the practice of Law with A. J. McLouwin(?), who was afterward governor and U. S. Senator of Mississippi. I have met many prominent men of several states. Professors, circuit and chancery judges, supreme court judges, editors, senators, lecturers and preachers. I have published two small books of rhyme - "Fallen Leaves" and "Pine Knots" and am now arranging for another, which I shall entitle "Tennessee Bubbles". My present address is Huntington, Tenn.
Mar. 30, A.D. 1923 David Moore
44. ...
45. ...
46. David Moore,Huntington, Tenn.

MOORE, JOHN ALERSON (1872-1943)
Saltillo

1. Johnny Alerson Moore
2. Saltillo, Tenn.
3. Aug. 24, 1872, Saltillo, P. O., Hardin co., Tenn.
4. Edward Nelson Moore; in country, P. O. Lexington, Henderson co.,Tenn. -Henderson co...Moved to Hardin co. in 1870(?); William(?) __blurred___ Moore and Rachel Moore; in Henderson co., Tenn.
5. Perlina Beasley; John Lenton Beasley and Martha Beasley; Henderson co.
6. My grandparents all come to Tennessee from North Carolina
7. In district schools and at Saltillo, with Prof. Robt. Logan as teacher and at Sardis (Henderson co.) with Yates and McKenney as teachers.
8. Had high school work at both Saltillo and Sardis but at death of my father in 1898 it became necessary for me to quit and keep house with my mother.
9. Took one course of teacher training at Sardis with Prof. Yates

Taught school and worked on farm from 1892 to 1897. Worked on farm and in timber from 1897 to 1911, worked on farm, taught school and held office since.
11. Justice of the Peace from 1906 to 1912. Member of high school board from 1917 to 1921. Member of Legislature from 1919 to present.
12. Introduced the resolution in co.court and worked Hardin's first farm demostration agent-voted and worked in co. court for cooperation with state and national authorities in the eradication of the cattle fever tick from Hardin co. - In the legislature voted against ratification of the 18th amendment.
13. Have been a member of the Republican ex. comm. of Hardin co. for ... more than 20 yrs. Served six yrs. as chairman of the committee.
14. (...scratched out....) "I dont believe that there is but one church and that is the church of Christ and I believe every Christian belongs to it. I dont mean the so called "Christian church".
15. and 16. ...
17. Single
18. and 19. ...

MURREY, JOHN BUCHANAN (1822-)
(Veterans form) Veterans form #2
"Pioneer"

1. John Buchanan Murrey, Franklin, Tenn.
2. born July 6, 1822
3. In Williamson co., Tenn. about 2½ miles south west of Triune on the farm laterly owned by Jack Patton.
4. No
5. No
6. Farmer
7. Ennis Murrey; Maury county, Tennessee; Maury county, Williamson co. and Davidson county, died March 11, 1874; he was an early settler and helped cut cane for the road from Franklin to Columbia.
8. Joanna Buchanan; John Buchanan and Margaret Edmondson; near Triune, Tennessee
9. ...
10. I owned 300 acres near Beechville, Williamson county, Tennessee on Hillsboro Pike.
11. I had 14 negroes at that time.
12. 350 acres
13. My property at outbreak of the war was approximately worth $1500000. (Note: this was typed and appears to have been corrected to - $1500.00)
14. Brick house 5 rooms in main building with ell.
15. Farmer, with the exception of 14 years while I was a constable serving as Deputy Sheriff in Davidson county (to) Sheriff James Hinton.
16. My father operated his own farm, and my mother ran the house, weaving, and spinning.
17. 3 men and 3 women, slaves
18. Yes
19. Yes
20. You did not find many loafers in those days
21. They mingled with people of their own class. Of course, there was classes among the people. The rich people of course associated with each other; the richest owned large numbers of slaves.
22. Yes
23. Not a bit antagonistic to each other.
24. No difference
25. Yes; I do not think there was as much class difference in those days as there is today.
26. Encouraged
27. Common schools of the country
28. I was delicate and couldn't go to school much. However, I received a good common school education.
29. 2½ miles
30. Claybrooke school near Triune; Hardeman Academy
31. Private schools; there were no public schools in the country districts then.

32.About 10 months
33. yes
34. man
35. I was in delicate health and was not physically able to go into the Army. My sympathies were with the South, and I assisted in running contraband goods, cattle, negroes, etc. for the use of the military authorities. I was commissioned by Gov. Harris to raise negroes to build the fortifications at Nashville and was engaged in building them when Donaldson fell.
36 - 42......
43. My first vote was for Henry Clay and against Jas. K. Polk. In 1844 I heard Clay speak at Nashville. I was Lieutenant of a militia company which was called the Clay Guards, Geo. Armstrong was Captain. I was 2nd Lt., we attended the speaking in a body, and after the election, and Clay's defeat, we disbanded. I saw Gen. Andrew Jackson in 1834 in Nashville as he was driving around the Square at a Democratic meeting, in his carriage and with his bee gum hat. I have seen all the Governor of Tennessee beginning with Gov. Newt. Cannon, and have been acquainted with a number of them. I remember when there were only three stores in Nashville all on or near the present Square, they were run by Jno. B. Snowden, Josiah Vaulx and Josiah Nichols. At that time I was a boy, living on a farm which was about one mile from the city as it then was, the farm being about 700 acres, and is now Edgefield. I have seen the following Presidents, Andrew Jackson, William Henry Harrison, Jas. K. Polk, Grover Cleveland, Benjamin Harrison,Rutherford B. Hayes, Wm. H. Taft, Wm. B. McKinley, Andrew Johnson and Wm. Jennings Bryan.
44......

(Following is with the Murr<u>a</u>y material)

MR. JOHN B. MURRAY

It is a cardinal doctrine of Kiwanis, to recognize and emphasize true manhood, and a high type of citizenship wherever found.

To no one would these principals be more correctly, and appropriately applied, than to our esteemed friend, Mr. John B. Murray, who reaches the remarkable age of one hundred years, on this July 6, 1922.

(Then continues a letter of recognition and his qualities, etc.) Signed by: Thos. B. Johnson, J.F.Eggleston, Lynn R. Walker, Bernard? Campbell and W.A. Roberts.

(This also follows): The additional addenda to his questionnaire was secured from Mr. John Buchanan Murrey, at his home in Franklin, Tenn. by a representative of the Tenn. Historical Commission and made part of the original, by the consent of Mr. Murrey:

"At the time I lived in Edgefield, no one lived in that section from the old wooden bridge at the north-east corner of the Square, to a mile and a half from town. Beyond lived George Smith, who kept a tavern on what is now the Gallatin Pike. Dr. Shelby owned a large farm adjoining ours, on which were a few negro cabins. Ours was the only residence in what is now known as East Nashville. My father, Thomas Hardeman and a "blue Yankee" named Benjamin Tappan owned our farm jointly.

Four miles out on the road was a little church and schoolhouse. The Methodists were the only people who had services in it in my day. Near this school, on the hill, lived the Hintons. Other families in the same neighboorhood were the Williamses, Stulls, Robert and Sam Weakley and Nicholas Hobson, for whom Hobson Chapel was named, Finally my father sold 100 acres off the North-east corner of this farm to Col. Andrew Johnson, for $100 an acre.

The plows we used to cultivate this farm were made of wood, only bolts and rod being of iron. I well remember the wooden paddle we carried along to shovel the dirt from the plow. The hoes were made at the blacksmith shop and were very heavey. But the ground was in such a virgin state of richness that it was easy to make a living. With the implements we had then a man would starve to death trying to make a living farming today.

We lived in a frame house with stone chimneys at each end, two stories with three rooms below and two above. the kitchen was off from the house in the yard. Downstairs there was a large passage or hall, in which was the stairway.

All cooking was done over an open fire-place, in pots, ovens and skillets. I never saw a stove until after I was grown. The sweetest bread I ever ate was the old fashioned ash-cake. This was made by brushing the ashes from the stones of the fire place or hearth, putting the batter there and covering it with the hot ashes. Another bread very much like it was made by spreading the dough on a clean board in front of the fire. Cabbages, beans and other like vegetables were cooked in the large pots over the open fire. Our principal meats were pork, beef, chicken and turkey. We had little wild meat. Most of our bread was from meal, very little flour used on account of its scarcity.

I did the marketing for the family. There was no grocery store then in Nashville at the time. There was a very small market-house on the site of the present one near the Court House. There were not stalls as it is at present. The principal object of market-measure was a large set of balances, called in that time "Stilliards", used in weighing flour. Near these scales were bags of flour, set along in rows for sale. Each customer selected the flour he wished to buy and the trade was made direct with the owner. It took me some time to learn how to select white flour. Much of it showed up dark when baked. Finally I learned to take a piece of white paper and rub the sample on it. If it left no dark mark I knew that it would bake into white bread. As everyone had their own smoke house, there was little sale for meats at the market, though some people would come to Nashville, put up at the little log shanty on top of Cedar Hill, now Capital Hill, and in the morning bring their ham, butter and eggs down to sell to those visiting the market. Many people bought meat and smoked it in their own smokehouse.

Our sugar was obtained from sugar-maple trees. There were few imports of cloth or food. What little came in was brough mostly on horse-back. Exports were carried down the river on flat boats, with New Orleans the principal destination.

Funerals in those days were simple and the method of burial crude. In every neighborhood was a cabinet maker, who made furniture and coffins. These latter were made usually of black walnut. I have often seen four men make a swing of ropes, pass these under the coffin and tie the other end to stakes and thus carry the coffin miles to the grave, often set it down that they might rest. Attending funerals and church often men would mount their horse, take the wife up behind them and the baby in the lap and thus ride to service. After primitive method of burial named above, the next I remember was hauling the coffin in a rude cart drawn by steer. Then came the old-fashioned "express" or four-wheeled light wagon. Finally the hearse.

Harvesting grain was at first done by means of a small scythe, such as now used to cut grass. The reaper would grab a handfull, cut with the scythe and finally secure a bundle. As the large scythe and cradle, and fianlly the reaper, came into use, the acreage of wheat naturally increased. Threshing was also progressive. The first method I can remember was to build a pen, in the bottom of which was place a sheet. This pen was built of rails and others placed on the sheet. The regular motion of those handling the sheets as they waved them up and down, finally seperated the chaff. The next method was to scrape out a large, clean place in the ground, and tramp it out with horses. This wheat had to be washed and dried in the sun before it could be used. Next, the wheat was taken to the mills to be ground on the same burrs used for corn. A reel with an incline was used for bolting, with the customer turning the reel. Men wore jeans -clothing as a rule. Store-cloth was the exception. Cloth for dresses. underclothing and other purposes was also spun and woven in the home.

As to the war, in this community, it must be said to the credit of the negro that most of them proved loyal to the wives and mothers of their masters, who were in the army. These slaves, or ex-slaves, worked on the farms, did the cooking and looked after the interests of the women left behind.

(Note: - Asked as to what he attributed his extra long life, Mr. Murrey replied: "Prudence and care; regular habits and a strict diet. All my life I have been delicate, for many years of my life was despaired of. Physician after physician advised with me and each outlined a diet, but I have always made it a rule to eat nothing that I found did not agree with me and everything that did agree. My physicians forbade me to drink coffee, but I have never found that it hurt me, so I have continued the use of it to this day. I never ate to excess and never used stimulants except as a medicine. I have spent a great deal of time on horse-back, in the open and it has helped me. When seventeen years of age five physicians diagnosed my trouble as tuberculosis and despaired of my ever getting well.")

MUSGROVE, PARALEE MATILDA (ROBERTSON) (1829-)
(Veterans form was used) Veterans form #1

1. Para Lee Matilda Robertson Musgrove, 308-49th St., St. Elmo, Chattanooga, Tennessee
2. 92 (years old), 3rd of last Dec. 1921.
3. Middle Tennessee, Montgomery county.
4. ...
5. General house work and fancy work, i.e. - made fancy work and sold it.
6. Farming
7. I did not own any property at this time.
8. No
9. My parents were dead at the beginning of the war.
10. ...
11. Hued log, two story, 4 room house - the kitchen and dining room were off from the house.
12. The men did hoe and plough before the war.
13. My father was a farmer, but gave mot of his time to blooded stock. He sold dressed hogs and shipped tobacco to New Orleans. Had lots of sheep and curried the wool off to have it carded and brought it back home, then my mother spun and wove. G___ knitted sox, made comforts and coverlids. Did the milking and all house work. They also raised geese and sold the feathers for beds.
14. They had white help for the farm. The busy time of the season they kept more help, but always had two or more.
15. It was. Everybody did this and were respected.
16. They did.
17. None that I knew anything about.
18. They just as friendly and couldn't tell any difference.
19. They did. Everybody went together and were social and mingled same as one.
20. They were friendly indeed and were helpful and kind.
21. Yes. The non-slaveholder worked just as hard for the slaveholder as he would for a non-slaveholder and harder.
22. Yes. All were willing to help.
23. Encouraged very much. They were always glad to see prosperity.
24. Country, county schools.
25. 1 year.
26. 1 mile from my house.
27. County school.
28. Public
29. 7 months.
30. They did.
31. Man
32 & 33. ...
34. (Female questionnaire) - I helped do all the house work, wove and spun, and made my own clothes. In those days each girl tried to see which could make the prettier dress to wear to Church. Every girl did the same as I did, all kinds of house work.
35. It was a credit.
36. My friends did.
37. Quilting, log rolling, corn shucking, house raising. All young people came together and had games such as guessing contest, but no "dancing".
38. All went to church and did their duty. Took no part in politics. The women did all they could for the schools to rebuild them. Had religious teachers.
39. I didn't see any of the battles or war until the Raid to the Sea and burned the iron works. Major Hunt had charge of the Mining Bureau business of the south.
40. Down south the bushwhackers killed 3 to 5 men at night for quite awhile. The railroad was torn up and we had to leave Ala., so we went in wagons for 15 days on the road back home to Middle Tenn. The slaves were all as a rule friendly and some of them stayed with their masters. My older brother enlisted, one of the first ones. The company was made up of home boys and he went through the war in many hard battles, went days

without anything to eat and often tramped with bleeding feet. He had a gun shot out of his hand at one time, but didn't receive a scratch. He wasn't ever home till after the surrender. Times were hard, but soon built up. I am the oldest of four children. My mother died when I was ten and left a little baby. Father lived four years after her death. I rented the house and farm and educated the children. I married in 1855 and moved to Ky. We sold the farm and divided it after I was married. We never had any children. My husband has been dead 29 years and I haven't a kinsman. I am keeping house and doing all my cooking and most of my house work. Keep very well and always happy with the Lord.
(39th question) - Recollections of the war and conditions following it. My husband was employed there at this time, is why he was not in the army. Conditions: Times was right hard and everything was high for awhile and we left Alabama and came to Chattanooga in '65 just after the war.

NELSON, HUNTER BITHAL (1869-)

1. Hunter Bithal Nelson
2. Jefferson Barracks, Missouri
3. Mar. 14, 1869, Mount Pleasant, Maury county, Tennessee
4. Willoughby Howard Nelson; Mount Pleasant, Maury co., Tenn.; Mount Pleasant until his death in 1894; served under Gen. Forest in Civil War.
5. Laura Miriam Nelson; Douglas Crook(Crock?) and Kate Gillespie Crook; Mount Pleasant, Tenn. and Paris, Texas.
6. Data called for under this (question) can be secured from my mother: Mrs. Laura Nelson, Mount Pleasant, Tenn.
7. Mount Pleasant Public Schools and Mount Pleasant Academy; Giles College, Pulaski, Tenn.
8. Univ. of Tenn. 1886-1888; U. S. Military Academy, West Point, New York 1889-1893.
9. West Point, N. Y.; graduated.
10. U. S. Infantry since June 12, 1893.
11. & 12. No
13. ...
14. Episcopal church
15. Master Mason
16. ...
17. Annie Hazel Block, Dec. 31, 1895, Butte, Montana; Charles M. Block and Annis Daniels, Boise, Idaho.
18. (See attached slip)
19. Hazel Katherine Nelson, born at Ft. Douglas, Utah, Feb. 16, 1898
Willoughby Block Nelson, born at Ormoc, Island of Leyte, P. I., Apr. 25, 1906.

Signed: Hunter B. Nelson, Col., 6th Infantry

(Note: This questionnaire is followed by a list of military assignments).

NEWMAN, JAMES BRYAN (1870-)
Court House, Nashville, Tenn., Feb. 8, 1922

1. James Bryan Newman
2. Nashville, Tennessee
3. Dec. 19, 1870, Grove Hill, Clarke county, Alabama
4. James Addison Newman; Orange, Orange county, Va.; Grove Hill, Ala. He was Lt. of the Montpelier Guards (Orange Co., Va.) in 1859. That was the military escort of John Brown to the scaffold. A Confederate soldier; Reuben Newman and Mark Clark; Orange, Virginia.
5. Anne Elizabeth Boroughs; Thomas Boroughs and Rebecca Kimbell Morriss; Vashti, Alabama
6. My paternal great-great grandfather, Alexander Newman, and my maternal great-great grandfather, William Armistead, were officers in the Revolutionary War. The Newman-Clark-Boroughs and Morriss families came from England and settled in Virginia between the dates of 1620 and 1640.After the Revolutionary War, the Boroughs and Morriss families, from whom I descend, removed to North Carolina. I am a descendant on the paternal

side of the Daniel, Barbour, Towles and Terril families of Orange county, Virginia and on the maternal, of the Armistead and Bryan families, also of Virginia, and the Waddell family of North Carolina.
7. Grove Hill Academy and Newton Academy.
8. ...
9. University of Alabama, 1889, LL.B.
10. Lawyer. Began practice at Grove Hill, Alabama, January 1890. Remained there until September 1891, when I removed to Talladega, Ala. where I engaged in the practice until February 1899 and then came to Nashville.
11. Was prosecuting Attorney of Clarke co., Ala. 1890-1. Held same office in Talladega co., Ala. 1892-3. Chancellor, Part II, 7th Chancery Division of Tennessee 1915 to ---(present)
12. ...
13. Chairman Democratic Executive Committee, Davidson county, Tennessee 1906-8. Member from the 6th Dist. and Sec'y. of the Democratic Executive Committee of Tenn. 1912. Delegate from the 6th Dist. of Tenn. to the Democratic National Convention at Baltimore 1912.
14. Member of the Immanuel Baptist Church, Nashville, Tenn.; Chairman of the Board of Deacons, 1921-22.
15. 32nd degree Mason, Odd Fellow; Knights of Pythias and Red Men.
16. ...
17. Lilah McDaniel, Nov. 19, 1901, Demoplis, Ala.; John McDaniel and Mary Knox; Sumpterville, Ala.; My wife's mother was a daughter of Dr. Jas. C. Knox and Jane Bowie, daughter of Chancellor Alexander Bowie of Alabama.
18. & 19. ...

NEWTON, SAMUEL S. (1886-1959)
Appleton, Feb. 4, 1922

1. Samuel S. Newton
2. Appleton
3. Oct. 24, 1886, Appleton, Lawrence county, Tenn.
4. James A. Newton; Appleton, Lawrence co., Tenn.; Appleton, Tennessee; he is a farmer and a merchant; Joshua Newton and Eliza E. Newton; Appleton (Tennessee).
5. Nancy Tennessee Ezell; Harbert C. Ezell and Cynthia Ezell, Appleton.
6. Harbert C. Ezell came from South Carolina to Tennessee in his early manhood.
7. In rural schools - teachers were: J. P. Canvay and E. O. Coffman.
8. None
9. None
10. Rural school teaching. I began in 1907 and have been teaching ever since. I am a farmer and a merchant.
11. 1921
12. ...
13. Republican Committees - I served on Commerce, Education, Federal Relations and Horticulture.
14. None
15. Odd Fellows, Past Grand Mason.
16. None
17. Rhoda J. Hood; Thomas Henderson Hood and Eda Malinda Hood; Appleton, (Tennessee); Her grandfather, David Hood, his wife, Jane Hood, lived at Appleton. Her mother's parents are Leggett Jenkins and his wife, Tabitha Jenkins, they lived at Anderson Creek, Alabama.
18. I never served in any wars. I was the Register in 1917 and 1918 to register the men for service in the World War.
19. (1) Ruby P. Newton, age 10 years
(2) Joshua K. Newton, age 8 years
(3) Bernice C. Newton, age 5 years
(4) Opal Leon Newton, age 2 years

NORMANT, WILLIAM MENEFEE (1829-)
Pioneer (Veterans questionnaire) Veterans form #1
(See data from Hardeman Co., Tenn. at end of this questionnaire)

1. Rev. William Menefee Norment, Whiteville, Hardeman co., Tennessee
2. 92 years last Sept. 21, 1829.
3. Tennessee, Hardeman county.
4. I was an ordained Minister, a brother preacher proposed if I would preach to two of his churches, he would join the Confederate Army.
5. (Above is written over this space. More on last page of his notes.)
6. Farming and built a cotton factory.
7. I owned land and slaves, probably about $50,000.
8. We owned slaves, but I don't know how many.
9. About 640 acres
10. Parents were dead, when the war opened; Father died in 1839.
11. Log house, four rooms.
12. Did not work much.
13. My father managed the farm and factory. My Mother kept house.
14. Yes; don't know.
15. Yes
16. Yes
17. There were none.
18. All on an equality.
19. Yes
20. Friendly feeling.
21. No
22. Yes
23. Encouraged
24. Common school of the country.
25. Until 16 or 17 years of age; from 5 years when I started.
26. Not a mile.
27. Lafayette Academy, 4 miles off; male and female
28. Private
29. 10 months
30. Generally regularly.
31. Both
32. & 33. ...
34. (This space used for Q. # 4 and 5): Which he did and was Chaplain of the __ Regiment ___ ___, a most successful revivalist. Was ____ over by everybody. G. W. Winchester(?) __ after a great revival was taken sick and died a month or so before the close of the War.
34. - 41. ...
42. Nathaniel Ellis Norment, near Richmond, Virginia; he moved to Hardeman county, in 1826.
43. Sallie Menefee Norment; born and raised in Alabama.
44. ...

Letter to Mr. J. T. Moore, Feb. 5, 1924 from G. H. Rhodes, Senator from Whiteville (Benton, Decatur, Hardeman, Hardin and McNairy counties) ...."Dear Sir - A few days ago I noticed an article carried in the Associated Press relative to an old gentleman (I have forgotten his name) - being the only living person that looked upon the face of Andrew Jackson that is now living. In the interest of accuracy and I know that you will be interested to know, desire to inform you that in this town lives Rev. W. M. Norment, now in his 95th year, who visited Gen. Jackson at the Hermitage in 1845 in company with a number of Rev. Norment's school mates from Cumberland University. At the time, Bro. Norment was 16 years old. About six weeks later, Rev. Norment attended Andrew Jackson's funeral at the Hermitage. No doubt Brother Norment is the only living person that attended the funeral of Gen. Jackson.

Rev. Norment while somewhat feeble in body has a very active mind and reads the daily papers with interest. He has preached here at the Cumberland Presbyterian Church since he was 21 years of age and only gaveup the pastorage about three years ago. He frequently fills the pulpit. About two months ago he preached in Memphis at one of the Presbyterian Churches there, the occasion being "Old Folks Day".

Rev. Norment talked with Jackson, Polk and Johnson, Tennessee's three Presidents.

Brother Norment introduced William J. Bryan here about 5 years ago and the "Commander" declared him to be the most remarkable man that he ever met at that time, having preached 70 years in one pulpit and in one town.

Whiteville is very proud of its distinguished citizen and his birthday is always the occasion of his friends gathering to wish him many happy returns of the day.

(Another letter, dated Feb. 15, 1924, from Mr. Rhodes of Whiteville,...)

Whiteville, Tenn. Feb. 15, 1924

....am returning herewith clipping concerning Rev. Norment....received letters from various sections of the country, people that read this article . The old man was delighted.....called on him this morning and turned over the questionnaire to him and ...his daughter is to fill out and he would sign it.....(Follows letter from Mr. Moore to Senator... Feb. 13, 1924).....

Acknowledgement of article to Associated Press..on Norment; letterhead includes these names: Committee: Mrs. Chas. W. Allen, Greenville; A. V. Goodpasture, Clarkeville; Gen. L. D. Tyson, Knoxville; R. H. Yancy, Nashville; Robt. S. Fletcher, Jackson; S. G. Heiskell, Knoxville; Chas. R. Evans, Chattanooga; Mrs. Clara Cox Epperson, Cooksville; Col. Luke Lea, Nashville; Rev. S. A. Stritch, Nashville; Geo. H. Armistead, Franklin; Sam. L. King, Bristol; Prof. G. W. Duer, Nashville; Miss Lizzie Bloomstein, Nashville; Col. W. J. Bacon, Memphis; J. I. Finney, Columbia; Col. Harry S. Berry, Hendersonville; Col. Carey E. Spence, Knoxville; E. M. Boyd, Cooksville; John H. DeWitt, Nashville; Miss Daisy Barrett, Chattanooga; W. E. McElwee, Rockwood; Hallam W. Goodloe, Nashville; Judge John S. Cooper, Trenton - all members of the committee of Tennessee War History with Mr. John Trotwood Moore as Chairman.

(Another letter from Moore to Rhodes:....mentions daughter of Rev'd. Norment...Frances Norment (Note: not clear if this is daughter or granddaughter).

See <u>History of Tennessee-Hardeman County</u> (Goodspeed) reprinted 1979 by Southern Historical Press:

Martha B. Miller, born 6 Nov. 1831 in Virginia; married William Menefee Norment; had 12 children - 7 sons and 5 daughters...all living 1887.

NUCHOLS, THOMAS LAMAR (1875-)
Maryville, Tenn. R.F.D. 1, Dec. 13, 1922

1. Thos. Lamar Nuchols
2. ...
3. July 20, 1875, 6 miles east of Maryville, Blount county, Tennessee
4. James Waters Nuchols; 6 miles east of Maryville, Blount co., Tenn.; lived near Maryville all of his natural life. Was a boy of 11 years age at the close of the Civil War. His education was meager, being taught by his wife after marriage; Thomas Nuchols and Mary (Waters) Nuchols; six miles east of Maryville.
5. Mary Jane Broady; Thos. Brown Broady and Martha (Clemens) Broady; 4 miles east of Maryville, Tenn.
6. Great grandfather Nuchols came to Tenn. from near Petersburg, Va. Thomas Nuchols was born near Petersburg and lived to manhood and married there. Volunteered for service in the Mexican War and while making preparations to go, word came that Santa Anna had surrendered and that the war was over. Believed to be of Scottish descent. Thomas Broady's father was an Englishman and his mother a Scottish maiden. He was exempted from service in the Civil War on account of a physical disability.
7. Public schools at the 14th Civil Dist. of Blount co., Tenn.
8. Left college in middle of Junior year (Maryville)
9. ...
10. Taught school, farmed, run a dairy for four years and have been dealing in real estate and trading for eight years.
11. Justice of the Peace from 1900 to 1909; good roads commissioner from Apr. 1920 to present time and 4th ____P.M. at Seaton from 1897 to 1901.
12. ...
13. Republican
14. Deacon of the 1st Baptist Church, Maryville, Tenn.
15. & 16. ...
17. Rachel Susan Davis, married Apr. 6, 1902 near Hibbard (Hubbard) Sta.; Samuel Davis and Margaret Ann (Snider) Davis; Hubbard Station; The Davis' are of English descent and the Sniders were of Dutch and Irish extraction.
18. ...
19. Samuel Davis Nuchols, born Feb. 25, 1903, and is now ranked as 3rd Class Fireman and is on the U. S. S. Nokomis.

James Homer Nuchols, born Oct. 2, 1904, M___ R Park, Cal.

Mary Ann Nuchols, born (no month) 23, 1906, Maryville, R.F.D. 1

(Cont'd from p. 93-children of Nuchols):
Sarah Susan Nuchols, born Feb. 4, 1909, Maryville, R.F.D. 1

ODLE, JOSEPH FRY (1880-1965)
Camden, Tenn., 11-7-1923

1. Joseph Fry Odle
2. Camden, Tenn.
3. May 29, 1880, Coxburg, Benton county, Tennessee
4. Hiram Dorsey Odle, near Sugar Tree(?), Decatur county, Tenn.; Coxburg and Camden in Benton co., Tenn. early life a school teacher and for 30 yrs. or more a merchant; Richard Odle and Lucretia (Tippell?) Odle, near Sugar Tree, Tenn.
5. Victoria A. Odle; Joseph Fry and Nancy (Wesson?) Fry; Sugar Tree, Ten.
6. ...
7. County schools, McTyeire Institute, McKenzie, Tenn.
8. McTyiere Inst., McKenzie
9. Lebanon Law School, graduated with LL.B degree in Jan. 1908.
10. Lawyer since 1909, member of Camden Bar.
11. Mayor of Camden 1917, Member of Legislature 1911-1919 and 1921; State M.W.A. for 3 yrs.
12. ...
13. Democrat former chairman ex. comm. of Benton co.
14. M. E. Church, Steward and recording Sec'y. of Home ch. for many years
15. Royal Arch Mason, W.O.W. and M.W.A., Macabees
16. ...
17. Robert E. Paschall (this not clear), Hazel, Ky. married Nov. 24, 1913 -J. Frank Paschall and Ella (Clark) Paschall, near Hazel, Ky.
18. ...
19. Virginia Madaline Odle
Mildred Claire Odle
Joseph Fry Odle
Frank Paschall Odle

OFFICER, A. H. (1831-) (Veterans questionnaire) Form #2

1. A. H. Officer, Algood, R. #1, Putnam county
2. 91
3. Overton county, Tennessee
4. & 5. (no answers)
6. Slave
7. Bill Hawes (father)
8. Charlotte Hulford (mother)
9. - 13. (no answers)
14. Log cabin - 2 rooms
15. Worked on farm
16. - 26. (no answers)
27. Never went to school a day in my life.
28. - 42. (no answers)
43. I stayed on the Officer farm until March 1871, then moved ten miles west to where I live now. I have been a blacksmith up to about 15 years ago. I made a crop every year. Rented until I bought land. I now own 132 acres. I sold my son 72 acres off this place. I now own a house of six rooms. I have 4 living children.
44. ...
45. W. A. Officer stayed away from home a great deal last two years of war on account of guerrillas. Union soldiers under Cpat. Stokes forced him to take the oath of allegiance at Sparta. He came home now and then. During one of these visits some of his men - 7 of them - were there after he took the oath. Six of them were Texas Rangers: Bill Lipscomb of Ala. -Billy Slaughter, Bob Davis, John Shipp, ___ Garritt and ___ York. Johny King, a small boy was the 7th and only one that escaped - I think his home was at Manchester. He went in the house, hid in a corner and I told them - the Yankees- that he was an orphan boy going about from house to house. Mr. Officer's son John was there are the time, but they never saw him. I fixed a place for him to hide. John Shipp , as they shot at him,

run through the house and caught Mrs. Shipp by the hand and she was shot through the back. She got well. Shipp was killed. Al the others except young King were shot down. Capt. Zeke Bass of Stokes men told Officer that it was a shame you(r) wife got shot, but it was a blessing to you for we were going to kill you and burn the house, but I am going to ... leave you to take care of your wife. You shant be hurt.
46. As they shot Bob Davis, I was six feet of them - He was wounded and couldn't walk. They carried him out of the house and stood him up by the gate post and shot him. As they prepared to shoot, he said "You ought not to do this. I have never done anything but my sworn duty." He never flinched. After this was all over, John Officer was allowed to come out of hiding and took to the woods. He went up a neighbor's house and got an old hat ...not being satisfied, he run about a mile to get on a high hill. As he crossed the road he was halted but did not stop. The reason they did not shoot was because they expected to run on a bunch of men near there and did not want to make a racket.

A. H. OFFICER

OFFICER, WILLIAM ROBINSON (1872-)
Livingston, Feb. 2, 1922

1. William Robinson Officer
2. Livingston, Tenn.
3. June 18, 1872; Mouth of Wolf (now Lillydale), Clay co., Tenn.
4. John Holford Officer; Mouth of Wolf (Lillydale), Carthage, Smith co. and Nashville, Tenn.; was a farmer and live-stock man; at age of eighteen enlisted in Confederate army year 1862, served in Capt. Joe Bilbrey's Co. 8th Tenn. Cavalry until surrender. Was detailed for special scouting service under Gen. Joe Wheeler. Held no commission. Died at his home in Nashville, Tenn. on Gallatin road, March 1912; William A. Officer and Cynthia Holford; Sinking Cane in Overton county where he owned a large and valuable farm. It is under the Mountain near where the town of Monterey now is.
5. Ida Chowning; Dr. Zach. R. Chowning and Rebecca McMillin; Fox Springs on Obed's river in Clay county, Tenn.
6. Dr. Zacharia R. Chowning was a member of the Constitutional Convention of 1870, elected as delegate from Overton county, his residence was in that part of Overton, that was afterwards a part of Clay county, Tennessee. He was a practicing physician and lived upon a high hill on Obed river and traveled horseback over a wide territory, his practice extending for forty or fifty miles from his home, and was in the active practice of his profession until his death in 1881 or 1882 at the age of 70 years. His father was Chatten Chowning, a farmer who lived on Obed's river, farmed and run boats out with produce, tobacco, -etc. to New Orleans. He died with cholera contracted on a boating trip down the Mississippi to New Orleans. William A. Officer was a prominent farmer and also stock-man in Overton county. His ancestors, his father being one of four brothers who came from North Carolina and settled on Cumberland Plateau, as the writer understands. He owned a number of slaves who were emancipated and had little left at the close of the Civil War in the way of world's goods, but accumulated a competency and a comfortable estate for his section again before his death.
7. Common schools of the community, and by home reading, under direction of Mother and attended high school at Oak Hill in Overton co. under Prof. Henard, Alpine Academy under B. O. Bowden and A. H. Roberts.
8. ...
9. By reading at home, and later for awhile under the instruction of Judge E. L. Gardenhire at Hartsville, Tenn.
10. Began practicing law at Livingston in 1893; in Jan. later practiced in partnership with Albert H. Roberts, under the firm name of Officer & Roberts.
11. Clerk and Master of Chancery Court, Overton co. 1895 to 1901 by Appointment of Chancellor Thos. J. Fisher. In Aug. 1902, elected Att'y.Gen. for the 5th Judicial Dist. of Tenn.; re-elected in 1910 and served until Sept. 1, 1918. Aug. 1918, elected Chancellor of 4th Chancery Div. Aided in organizing Farmers Bank, also Citizen's Bank & Trust Co., was Pres. of Farmer's Bank until organization of Citizen's Bank & Trust Co. 1910 and has been its Pres. and Gen. Mgr. since. Besides banking, mining, has

engaged in Mercantile, timber mfg., farming and other pursuits. Was active in effort to get railroad facilities into Overton co. and likewise better roads and schools.
13. Democrat - served as democratic Committeeman on co. Comm. most of the time since his majority, for many years as Chairman of the committee.
14. ...
15. F. & A. M.; served as Master of his Lodge; also as High Priest of Chapter; Royal Arch Mason.
16. ...
17. Nanie Belle Windle, was married at Livingston, Tenn. June 1903 by Rev. J. Ridley Goodpasture; Alfred Lafayette Windle and Mary Armstrong Windle; Livingston, Tenn. Wife's grandfather, Robert S. Windle, was son of ______(Sevier) Windle, who was a daughter of John Sevier, First Governor of Tennessee. Wife's mother, Mary Armstrong, daughter of P. M. Armstrong of Livingston, Tenn. Grandmother, Mary Cullom Armstrong, daughter of Judge Alvin Cullom of Overton co., who was Circuit Court Judge and member of Congress from Tenn. prior to the Civil War. Alfred Lafayette Windle, was elected 2nd Lt. of the first company of Volunteers organized in Overton co., for the service of the Confederate States, and served until captured and imprisoned on Johnson's Island in 1863. He was held as a prisoner of war until the close of the conflict. Was many year in mercantile business in Livingston.
18. ...
19. Gertrude McMillin Officer
Ida May Officer (died in early childhood)
Albert Fitzpatrick Officer
Ruth Officer
Jessie Burks Officer
William Robert Officer
Cynthia Officer (died in early childhood)
Margaret Frances Officer
Residence of children: Livingston, Tennessee

O'GUIN, WILLIAM WALKER (1886-)
Nashville, Tenn., April 13, 1922

1. William Walker O'Guin
2. Nashville
3. Feb. 1, 1886, Hohenwald, Lewis county, Tenn.
4. Sydney L. O'Guin, Coble, Hickman co., Tenn.; Coble, Hohenwald and Centreville, Tenn.; is a member of the County Court of Hickman County; Thomas O'Guin and Mary Bates O'Guin; Coble, Tenn.
5. Sarah Jane Coble; James Coble and Rosa Allison Coble; Hohenwald, Tennessee.
6. Both of my grandfathers, Thomas O'Guin and James Coble, were soldiers in the Confederate army. Thos. O'Guin contracted tuberculosis in the army and died before the close of the war. James Coble was a member of Forrests Cavalry and was killed at Pinson Station in Madison county during a charge on a block house at that point. Both my grandfathers were volunteers.
7. Public schools of Hickman county. Fairview Academy at Centreville and Murray Institute, Murry, Ky., W. P. Morrison, Principle.
8. Not a college man.
9. None
10. Teacher in schools of Hickman and Lewis county for 10 years. Newspaper publisher at Hohenwald, Centreville and Camden, Tenn. Reporter on Nashville Tennessean in 1919, now chief clerk in State Mining Dept.
11. Sergeant-at-Arms in House in 1917. General Assembly. Chief Clerk of State Mining Dept. from 1919- (present).
12. Led fight in my section for enactment of Prohibition Laws.
13. Democrat; Sec'y. to Democratic Committee of Lewis Co. 1912; Sec'y. of 20th Senatorial Dist. Comm. 1912.
14. Layman in Christian Church.
15. W.O.W., M.W.A. & K. of P.
16. none
17. Ruby Faye Poore, Apr. 21, 1907, Centreville, Tenn.; her parents are John Wesley Poore and Harriet Lancaster Poore; Centreville; her grandfather, Gilbert Lancaster Poore was a minister of the Baptist

Church and her grandfather, Pleasant Poore, was a veteran of the Confederate Army.

O'MEARA, CHARLES HAYES (1894-)
Westmoreland, Tenn., 2-10-1922

1. Charles Hayes O'Meara
2. Westmoreland, Tenn.
3. Apr. 28, 1894, Westmoreland, Sumner co., Tenn.
4. Hardy Wilburn O'Meara; Westmoreland, Tenn.; Westmoreland, Tenn.; James O'Meara and Sarah Caldwell O'Meara; Westmoreland, Tenn.
5. Cora Wakefield; James Wakefield and Jane Wakefield; Gibbs Cross Roads in Macon co., Tenn.
6. ...
7. In public schools of Sumner co., mostly at Westmoreland, Tenn. My teachers: John Doss, U. D. Moss, Thomas Perry. High school work done in Hawkins Training School in Gallatin, Tenn. under Charles E. Hawkins, the Principal. Graduated in 1915.
8. & 9. ...
10. Postmaster at Westmoreland, Tenn. since Jan. 1, 1917.
11. & 12. ...
13. Democrat
14. ...
15. Member of Trammel Lodge No. 436, F. & A. M.
16. & 17. ...
18. Enlisted at Nashville, Tenn., June 17, 1917 in the 2nd Tenn. Infantry, Col. Chas B. Rogan. Later transferred to 119th Inf., Col. J. Van. B. Metts, with which I served overseas. Regiment sailed from N. Y. on May 13, 1918. On returning landed at Charleston, S. C., Apr. 2, 1919. Was in Ypres, Somme and Hindenburg line offensive. Discharged at Columbia, S. C., Apr. 7, 1919.
19. ...

PATTON, ERASTUS EUGENE (1874-)
Knoxville, Tenn., Jan. 30, 1922

1. Erastus Eugene Patton
2. Knoxville, Tenn.
3. Aug. 7, 1874, Dry Creek, Carter co., Tenn.
4. Drury Morrow Patton; Dry Creek, Carter co., Tenn.; lived at Dry Crk. also Johnson City, Corryton, Knox county, Tenn.; wrote no books; had no war record; served for a short time as Justice of Peace in Carter co., but resigned; Samuel E. Patton and Temperance Morgan; Dry Creek, Carter co., Tenn.
5. Joanna Lucinda Hyder; Michael E. Hyder and Sabina Williams; Powder Branch, Carter co., Tenn.
6. My ancestors on my father's side came to this country from the north of Ireland in the early part of the 18th century and settled near Carlisle, Pennsylvania; removed to Carter co., Tenn. in the early settlement of the Watauga Association; my great great grandmother is said to have made the powder with which was fought the battle of King's Mountain. My great great grandfather on my mother's side came from Holland and settled on Powder Branch, Carter co., Tenn. between 1769 and 1773,fought on the American side in the Revolutionary War in three battles in S.C.; signed the Watauga Assoc. Compact, which fact is mentioned in Ramsays Annals.
7. Patton's Chapel. Piney Grove, Carter co., Johnson City, Walnut Grove Academy in Knox county; Holbrook College, Fountain City, Knox co., Tenn. Teachers: J. M. Martin, member Tenn. Leg. 1917-1919, Wash. co., Tenn.; W. A. Evans, Confederate soldier at Johnson City, Tenn.; John C. Webster, W. C. Gibbs and H. B. Clapp at Walnut Grove Academy, Knox co., Tenn. High school there.
8. Holbrook College, Fountain City, Tenn. Graduated with degree of B.S. (Bachelor of Science) 1900 at 26 yrs. of age; waited on tables and also swept floors to help pay my way through. Class orator.
9. None
10. Teacher-stenographer. Began teaching in country schools of Knox co. 1895 at $25.00 a month; taught one year in Holdbrook College; two years

(Q. #10 cont'd): in Douglas, Georgia, where Billy Bond once taught;five years in Central High School, Fountain City, Tenn.; five years in city high school, Knoxville, Tenn. and was principal of each school. Now, in 1922, Superintendent of the Draughon Business College, Knoxville, Tenn.
11. Elected in 1918 to the 61st Session of the Tenn. State Senate and re-elected in 1920.
12. Made speech in Senate and converted one member, Walter M. Cameron, to the support of woman suffrage and his vote put this bill over in 1919; author of Mother's Pension Bill in 1921 and also the law to confiscate pistols and other felonious weapons when found on arrested persons. Supported and voted for every piece of progressive school legislation before the sessions of which I was a member.
13. Republican; member of Rep. Co. Exec. Comm. in Knox county for many years. Private Sec'y. to Hon. Nathan W. Hale, Rep. in Congress from 2nd Congressional Dist. of Tenn. for 3 yrs. from 1906 to 1909.
14. Presbyterian - an old line, blue stocking.
15. None
16. Government of Tenn., written and published in 1919.
17. Lula Belle Smith, Aug. 7, 1906, Halls X-Roads, Knox co., Tenn.; Dr. J. Worth Smith and Harriet Elizabeth Harris; Graveston, Tenn. Her great grandfather, Josiah Smith was one of the commissioners who laid off old Union co., Tenn.
18. ...
19. Charles Hyder Patton, born Jan. 15, 1908, Fountain City, Tenn.
Elizabeth Jane Patton, born Aug. 29, 1909, Fountain City, Tenn.
Eugene Smith Patton, born Dec. 19, 1919, Fountain City, Tenn.

PEEK, GROVER CLEVELAND (1879-1945)
March 29, 1923

1. Grover C.(leveland) Peek
2. Livingston
3. _______, Overton co., Tenn.
4. John Wesley Peek; Bolivar, Hardeman co., Tenn.; Bolivar until four years of age, then moved with his mother to Overton co., Tenn. where he lived until his death, Sept. 6, 1918 at age of 83 years; Elisha Peek and Nancy Moore Peek; Bolivar and after her husbands death, she emigrated to Overton county.
5. Mary Gibbons; Edmond Gibbons and Evelin Dillon Gibbons; Overton co., Tennessee.
6. My grandfather, Elisha Peek, and grandmother, Nancy Moore Peek, emigrated from Virginia to West Tennessee and grandfather Gibbons and his wife emigrated to Overton co. from Virginia, all of them and their ancestors are of Scotts Irish and and English descent.
7. Attended common schools. Good Hope Institute, Fisk College, Peabody College, Cumberland University Law Dept.
8. ...
9. Graduated from Law Dept. of Cumberland Univ. at Lebanon (Tenn.)
10. My profession is Law.
11. Never held any nor asked for any until Member of 1923 Session of the General Assembly of Tennessee.
12. ...
13. Democratic Party and believe in the original Jefferson fundamental kind.
14. Southern Methodist
15. & 16. ...
17. Ofa(?) Buna Cooper, married Jan. 25, 1922 at Richman, Overton co., Tenn. by Rev. G. W. Baxter; William Charlie Cooper and Lillie May Cooper, Oak Hill, Tenn.
18. ...
19. Have one child, Mary Lillian, who was born Jan. 18, 1923.

(There follows the above, a typed manuscript, listing Mr. Peek and brief history: Sources: Livingston Enterprise, June 12, Sept. 18, 1918; Mar. 2, 1945; Moore - Biographical Questionnaires, 1923 in the Tennessee State Library and Archives, Tennessee. Vital Statistics, Death Certificate - 29051.
(Peek, Grover Cleveland - 1879-1945).

(Continuation of manuscript on Peek):
House - 63rd General Assembly, 1923-1925; Representative Overton Co.; Democratic. Born in Overton county, Jan. 10, 1879; son of John Wesley and Mary Gibbons Peek. Attended "Common Schools"; Good Hope Institute, Fiske College, Overton co.; George Peabody College for Teachers, Nashville, Davidson co.; Graduated in law from Cumberland University, Lebanon, Wilson co.; married at Richman, Overton co., January 25, 1922 to Ofa Buna Cooper, daughter of William Charlie and Lillie May Cooper; children: Mary Lillian and Grover Cleveland, Jr. Taught school for a time, began practice of law at Crossville, Cumberland co., after seven years moved, in 1918, to Livingston, Overton county, to continue the law practice; secretary and treasurer Overton county; Farm Loan Assoc. ten years. Secretary board of Education; superintendent of public instruction; mayor of Crossville, Member of the Methodist Episcopal Church, South. Died at Cookeville, Putnam county, Feb. 26, 1945; buried in the Zion Cemetery at or near Richman.

Note: This following information was found at the bottom of the brief manuscript on G. C. Peek. The page number is shown as #37, what publication is not indicated.

PHILLIPS, ALVIN BUNYAN (1873-1956)

House, 59th General Assembly 1915-17; Representing co.'s of Overton,Clay, Fentress and Pickett; Republican; born in Overton co., Apr. 3, 1873;son of Moses and Antine (Batey) Phillips; married (date and place not shown) to Lula Bilbrey; children: five sons and four daughters (names not included); farmed at Monroe.

PERRY, WILLIAM ALBERT (1854-1930)
Feb. 16, 1922

1. William Albert Perry
2. Jackson, Tenn. R. F. D. #1
3. July 14, 1854, in 9th Civil Dist., Madison co., Tennessee
4. Herbert Perry; Oct. 28, 1823, Rutherford co., Tenn.; his father removed to Madison co., Tenn. in 1824. He was a member of the Baptist Ch. and a Mason. He was relieved of military service on account of physical disability; son Albert Perry and Susan Perry; in Madison co., Tenn.
5. Mary Howlett; Grandison Howlett and Louise Howlett, Nashville, Tenn.
6. Grandfather Albert Perry served in the War of 1812 as a captain. He died in Madison co., Tenn. in 1832. Grandfather Grandison Howlett served in the War of 1812 as a private. He died in Davidson co., Tenn. 1828.
7. In the county schools of Madison county, Tenn. My first teacher was Rev. Y. A. McLemore, a Presbyterian preacher and next and last was Alonzo Day.
8. None
9. Graduated from Evanville, Ind. Business College, Apr. 1872.
10. Kept books for Moore & Exum, Jackson, Tenn. from Sept. 1872 to Oct. 1873. My fathers health failing, I returned to the farm to see after his farming interest.
11. Member of Gen. Assembly 1895 and '97 and again in 1921-22; Ass't. Commissioner of Labor 1898-9 and '10. Justice of Peace 40 years.
12. Advocated local option in the House in 1895, have been a temperance advocate since.
13. Democrat; local committeeman for 40 years.
14. Missionary Baptist Deacon
15. W.O.W.
16. None
17. In Apr. 1897 was married to Carrie Montague Jennings of Mt. Pleasant (Tenn.) in Nashville; Capt. W. S. Jennings and Cordelia Kindel, Mount Pleasant, Tenn.; Her father, Capt. Walter Scott Jennings was Captain of the 3rd Tenn. Regiment in Civil War and served the 4 years of litter(al) struggle. Hon. Jno. A. Pitts, a distinguished lawyer of the Nashville bar is her kinsman, both being scions of the good, old pioneer Montague family. (This filled in by someone else, probably Mrs. Perry, as the writing is different from rest of form.)
18. I was 11 yrs. old at the end of the war between the states and 62 when we entered the war with Germany, consequently, too young for the

(Perry, cont'd):
first and too old for the last.
19. Clyde Perry and wife, Nina Hamlett Perry, Tampa, Florida
Fred Gambetta Perry, and wife, Attona (Altona?) Webb Perry, Tampa
William Thomas Perry and wife, Zila(?) Rubush Perry, Tampa
Gladys Alleen (Perry) Pope and husband, John Pope, Jackson, Tenn.
Jennings Perry, Editorial writer for Tennessean, Nashville, Tenn.
Howlett Hugh Perry, Jackson, Tenn.
Nell Perry, Jackson, Tenn.
Christeen Perry, Jackson, Tenn.

PILE, OTUS PROCTOR (1874-)
Cowan, Tenn., May 6, 1922

1. Otus Proctor Pile
2. ...
3. March 21, 1874, Pall Mall, Fentress co., Tennessee
4. Stephen H. Pile, Fentress co., Tenn.; Fentress co., Tenn., was farmer and dealer in real estate - served as Justice of the Peace for 18 yrs. Par.: William Pile and Pollie Pile, Fentress co., Tenn.
5. Ermiece(?) (Ermine?) Miller; Amstead Miller ___________; Fentress co.
6. ...
7. In the common schools of Fentress county
8. Was in Hiwassee College 4 yrs. graduating May 1893, B.S. degree
9. ...
10. Civil and Mining Engineering, 1902 to 1912; E. M. for Fentress Coal & Coke Co. 1908 to 1922; Chief Eng. of Davidson Hicks & _____ Co.;in R. R. constructional work besides having charge of engineering of the Highland Coal & Coke & Lmbr. Co. The Overton Coal & Coke, The Davidson Coal Co.
11. Justice of the Peace, Fentress county 1908-1914; Justice of Peace, Franklin co., at present and Appointive Chief Mine Inspector of Tenn. Dec. 10, 1920.
12. ...
13. Democrat, served as Co. Chairman, Fentress Co. 1898 to 1902, and am at present Election Commissioner for Franklin county.
14. Christian
15. Odd Fellows, Knights of Pythias, Past Chancellor Commander K. of P.
16. ...
17. Willa Littrell, July 14, 1907, Nashville, Tenn.; Cololus(?) Littrell Nov. 21, 1897, Albany, Ky.; T.(?) Mack Littrell and Mollie Littrell of Savage, Ky. Mollie Littrell was a daughter of Daniel Powers of Wayne co., Ky., who was a very prominent merchant and one of the leaders of Republican politics in Wayne county.
18. ...
19. Mack Litrell Pile, Chattanooga, Tenn.
Clarence Delman Pile, Harlan, Ky.; wife - Lucile.
Stephen Elmer Pile, Cowan, Tenn.

POLK, GEORGE WASHINGTON (1847-)
(Veterans Form #1)

1. George Washington Polk, 423 Ogden St., San Antonio, Texas
2. July 7, 1847 (date of birth)
3. Maury county, Tenn.
4. Did not enlist in the Confederate or Federal army
5. School-boy
6. Planter
7. Owned no property of any description
8. Yes, about 50 or 60
9. My father owned one thousand and twelve acres
10. Landed property was valued at $75.00 per acre, including improvements (this valuation as near correct as possible to estimate)
11. Brick house, containing thirteen rooms and large hall.
12. I did not perform manuel labor of any kind.
13. My father managed his plantation. Mother died when I was infant.

Spinning and weaving was carried on on the plantation;Work about the residence such as cooking, house cleaning and sewing was performed by servants.
14. Yes, about 5 or 6 who performed work about the house and premises.
15. In our community all of the free holders owned slaves in more or less numbers. I have known many small slaveholders to work in the fields and otherwise, with their slaves. Such men were regarded as respectable and honorable citizens by their neighbors and others.
16. (Answered in #15.)
17. I do not recall any white men in our community who lead lives of idleness or luxury.
18. As I said in answer to Q. 15, all land owners in our community owned slaves in a more or less degree. In our county seat there were near as I can remember several non-slave holders with abolition tendencies. Such men were naturally disliked and abhored by law-abiding citizens.
19. There was free and friendly intercourse between slaveholders and respectable law-abiding non-slaveholders who attended to their own business and did not interfere with the property rights of the slaveholder. Of course social lines were drawn then as now.
20. I think this question is answered in the foregoing #19.
21. I don't think so.
22. Yes, I think there was.
23. I cannot recall any cases of this kind.
24. I attended the usual country schools in vogue at that time.
25. About 6 or 7 years
26. About 2 miles
27. Stevenson Academy in the "Frierson Settlement", about 2 miles from my home.
28. Private
29. 10 months
30. Yes
31. Man
32. I did not enlist in either army.
33. ...
34. - 41. (no answers)
42. Lucius Junius Polk, Raleigh, N. C.; Wake co., N. C.; Hamilton Place seven miles west of Columbia, Tenn.; member of the Upper (House) of the State Legislature in 1832 or thereabouts.
43. Mary Ann Eastin; William Eastin and Rachel Jackson Donelson; Nashville, Tennessee
44. (See separate sheets attached)
(Q. 44) ...Remarks on ancestry: My paternal great grandfather, Thomas Polk, was a great grandson of Robert Pollock and his wife, Magdelen Tasker, the common ancestors and founders of the Polk family in America. Robert Pollock was the son of John Pollock, gentleman of some estate in Lanarkshire, Scotland, not far frm what was the small but important cathedral city of Glasgow. During the reign of James, Sixth of Scotland, and First of England, John Pollock, who was an uncompromising Presbyterian, left his native land to join the new colony of Protestants which had been established in the North of Ireland.

Sometime between 1672 and 1686, Robert Pollock emigrated with his wife and children from County Donegal in the Province of Ulster, North of Ireland, and came to America, landing at Dame's Quarters, Somerset co., Maryland, soon after this emigration the surname Pollock was abbreviated to Polk, as appears in the will of Robert Pollock, dated May 6, 1699 and signed, Aug. 8, 1703. Also in the will of his wife, Magdalen Tasker Polk, dated April 7, 1726.

Thomas Polk's father was William Polk, the progenitor of the southern branch of the Polk family. About the year 1695, William Polk emigrated from Maryland to Pennsylvania, settling near Carlisle in Cumberland co. where he married Margaret Taylor, and where all of his children were born and reared. Thomas Polk was born about the year 1730, left parents home about 1753 to seek his fortune in a country which would furnish him a greater scope to his active mind and energy. He traveled south through the country on the east of the Blue Ridge, crossing the Dan and the Yadkin (rivers) until he reached Sugar creek, a branch of the Catawba river, in the vicinity of a few settlements, the area now forming a great portion of Mecklenburg county, near the present city of Charlotte, North Carolina. He married Susanna Spratt, daughter of the pioneer Scotsman, Thomas Spratt, at whose dwelling the Colonial Judiciary first held trial courts in Western North Carolina. Thomas Spratt emigrated from County Down, Ireland in 1730, and was among the first of the earliest permanent settlers in Western Carolina.

Thomas Polk fitted himself for the occupation of surveyor, and by his industry and enterprise, soon acquired property and with it an extensive popularity, which he always enjoyed. In 1767, he was appointed one of the Commissioners and Town Treasurer of the newly chartered town of Charlotte, which was chartered by Chapter 11 of the Private Laws enacted by the Colonial assembly. In 1769, he was chosen a member of the Provincial Assembly. One of his acts was to secure the charter of Queens College, located in Charlotte. He was made trustee of this institution when it was chartered as Queens College, and when it was re-chartered in 1777, as Liberty Hall Academy. In 1771, as captain of a company under command of Col. Moses Alexander, he marched troops from Charlotte to Salisbury to act against the Regulators. During this year he was also engaged as surveyor in establishing the line between North and South Carolina by appointment of the Governor. Just before the Revolution, the Committee of Safety was organized in Mecklenburg county and Thomas Polk was named presiding officer. The celebrated Mecklenburg Declaration of Independence was proclaimed May 19, 1775, and was read from the Court House steps on May 20th by him, who was recognized as a leader in the movement. On September 9th, the Provincial Assembly appointed Polk a Colonel of the second battalion of militia in the Salisbury district, and marched to South Carolina at the head of 900 men to assist in suppressing the Tories. In April of 1776, the Provincial Congress at Halifax appointed him colonel of the 4th Regiment of Continentals and marched under Gen. Nash to join the army of Washington in the north, where he served two years participating in the battle of Brandywine and the hardships of Valley Forge. He was in command of the escort which conveyed the heavy baggage to a place of safety at Bethlehem. Among the impedimenta was the famous Liberty Bell, which was removed from Independence Hall at Philadelphia. He sent in his resignation in June 1778. The Board of War appointed him Superintendant of the District of Salisbury in 1780. After the fall of Gen. Davidson at Cowan's Ford, Feb. 1781, the field officers petitioned Gen. Greene to appoint Polk to take command of the forces in the District, and he was accordingly commissioned brigadier general which appointment the Assembly refused to confirm, but commissioned him Colonel Commandant, which he declined and retired from further military service. He returned to his residence in Charlotte, where he died in 1793, and was interred in the cemetery of the 1st Presbyterian Church at Charlotte.

Thomas Polk was an elder brother of Ezekiel Polk, the grandfather of Pres. James K. Polk. Letters Patent was issued by the State of North Carolina to Thomas Polk for 2191 acres of land in our County of Tennessee on Defeated Camp Creek the North Waters of Duck River signed by Richard Dobbs Spaight, Esq. our Governor, Capt.-General in Chief of Newbern the 26th day of Dec. in the 18th year of our Independence and in the year of our Lord 1793. The original is on file among the archives of Tennessee Historical Society at Nashville.

My maternal great great grandfather, Colonel John Donelson was the only son of John Donelson I and his wife Catherine Davies. He was born ab. 1718 in Delaware or New Jersey, on the Delaware Bay or river at the place where his father settled. Whether he received his education in Delaware or Pennsylvania is not known, but it has always been said his mother had him thoroughly taught the art of navigation and surveying. He married Rachel Stockley in Accomac co., Va. There is a tradition that he lived on the western shore of Delaware Bay, where his oldest children were born, a majority of them however were born in Pittsylvania county, Virginia. His father emigrated from England in 1670.

The earliest date we have on him in Pittsylvania county is November 25, 1744 on which date there was patented to him 200 acres of land on both sides of Sandy Creek, etc. Other entries made by him were between 1744 and 1765 and aggregate about 3000 acres.

In addition to these entries, the deed records show that he purchased between 500 and 600 acres from various individuals. The records also show he was acting Surveyor while Pittsylvania was still a part of Halifax county, but being cut off from the parent county and established as an independent county until 1767. He was appointed Justice of the Peace in June 26, 1767, March 1770, March 1774 and Feb. 23, 1777; Colonel of

Militia of the County, June 26, 1767.

Was elected vestryman of Camden Parish, Pittsylvania, 1767,1768,1769. At the beginning of the Revolution, the militia in each county of Virginia, was reorganized in Pittsylvania and Colonel Donelson was app'td head of the County Militia (27 companies)

He represented Pittsylvania in the House of Burgesses 1769 to 1774 (both inclusive); app'td Commissioner to treat with the Indians; in 1770, app'td Commissioner to treat with the Five Nations of Indians, at Long Island on the Holston River, for the purpose of extinguishing the Indian title to a portion of the Kentucky country. At a meeting of the principle Chiefs and Warriors of the Cherokee Nation, with John Stuart, Esqr., Supt.of Indian Affairs, etc. at Lochbar, S.C., Oct. 18, 1770-present Col. John Donelson (by app't of Right Hon. Lord Botetourt in behalf of the Province of Virginia), Alexander Cameron, Esqr., Dty.Supt.of Indian Affairs, etc.(and others). In 1772, he was app'td surveyor to run the state line west, to designate certain limits for Indians and secure a route for emigrants to Kentucky; at an early day he established iron works on the Banister River in Pittsylvania co., which he operated for some time ; he disposed of this property in Jan. 1779, settled his business and determined to emigrate West. Left Pittsylvania co., with his family-proceeded to Fort Patrick Henry near Long Island on the Holston river in what is now Sullivan co., Tenn. There he assembled a company of 30-40 families, including his own and that of Capt. James Robertson; embarked in a flotilla of some 30 rudely constructed boats on the 23rd Dec. 1779, proceeded down the Holston and Tennessee, up the Ohio and Cumberland rivers to the French Lick (present site of Nashville), arriving Apr. 24, 1780; Donelson kept a journal of this voyage, the original preserved among the Archives of the State Historical Society of Nashville. He settled at Clover Bottom on Stone River which flows into the Cumberland above Nashville.After a short time removed to Kentucky and took an active part in settlement... of that state;returned to Tennessee with his family short time prior to his death, which occured not a great way from Nashville, on his return from a trip to Virginia; he was murdered from ambush (supposed to have been Indians), in Oct. 1785.

Among the members of Donelson's family with him on his voyage was his daughter Rachel, who was to the wife of Gen. Andrew Jackson.

My paternal grandfather, William Polk, 2nd son of Thomas Polk and wife Susanna Spratt. was born in Mecklenburg, N. C., July 9, 1758; educated at Queen's College, Charlotte, which he left in Apr. 1775 to accept a commission as 2nd Lt. in Capt. Ezekiel Polk's company of the 3rd S.C. Mounted Infantry, under Col. William Thompson (know as"Old Colonel Danger") He was wounded in the left shoulder at the battle of Great Cane Brake, Dec. 22, 1775 and incapacitated him from duty 8 or 9 months. On Nov. 1776, he was elected by the convention at Halifax, N. C. Major of the 9th Reg't; resigned his commission of Lieutenant in the S. C. line, joined his regiment at Halifax in March 1777,.....preparatory to the march to join the army of Gen. Washington in New York. The Colonel and Lt. Colonel....dispatched on recruiting service, William Polk being next in command as Major, took charge and marched 4 companies with the 3rd Div. of the line into the Jerseys...they joined the main army under Washington; participated in the battles of the Brandywine and Germantown; in the latter battle he was shot in the mouth; served in the 9th Reg't, for 2 yrs. and 8 mo's;in 1779 and 1780 volunteered in the militia, served as aid to Gen. Caswell at Gate's defeat at Camden; in the fall and winter of 1780, was app'td. Lt.-Col. of the 3rd and 4th S. C. Regiments; his total active service in the Rev.War was 5 yrs and 2 mo's; participated in battles of Brandywine, Germantown, Camden, Guilford C.H.,Quimby and Eautaw Springs; at the last battle named his oldest brother was killed. He was also at the sieges of Orangeburg, Forts Mott and Waboo. After the war he settled in Charlotte, then moving to Raleigh about 1800; appt'd surveyor-general of that part of N.C. which is now the State of Tennessee and lived for a short time in Nashville in 1786 he represented Davidson co. in the Gen. Assembly of N. C. represented Mecklenburg co., in the N. C. House of Commons in 1787, 1790, and 1791; appt'd supervisor or collector of internal revenue for the district of N.C. on March 4, 1791 and held that office for 17 yrs.; trustee of the Board of Trustees of the Unv. of N. C. ,pres. of the board from 1802 to 1805; trustee of the Davidson Academy at Nashville; (above - change to: from 1792 until his death he was a member of the Brd of Trustees of the Unv.) Grand Master of the Grand Lodge of N. C. and Tenn. from 1799 - 1802 (when the two states formed one Masonic jurisdiction; from 1811-1819 was pres. of the State Bank of Raleigh; was offered commission as Brig. Gen. in the War of 1812 by Pres. Madison; declined as he was a Federalist and had opposed the declaration of war; later on when degrading conditions were demanded by England as a price of peace, he wrote a letter to his brother-in-law,Gov. William Hawkins, tendering his services to the state of N. C. in any station that the Gov. might designate; he was twice married: (1) on Oct. 15, 1789, to Grizelda Gilchrist, dau. of Thomas Gilchrist a Scotch merchant and his wife Marth Jones, dau. of Willie (Wylie) Jones of Northampton co., N. C. and his wife Mary Mumford. Grizelda was born in Suffolk, Va. Oct. 24, 1768, died at Willswood near Charlotte, N.C. Oct. 22, 1799; (1) Sarah Hawkins, married on Jan.1801, dau. of Philomen Hawkins, Jr. and was born at Pleasant Hill, the residence of her father in Warren co., N.C.on Mar. 6, 1734; died at Raleigh Dec. 10, 1843, and is bur. beside her husband in the cemetary there.

William Polk died on 14 Jan. 1834 in the 76th year of his age, at his residence in Raleigh; bur. in the cemetary there; at the time of his death was the sole surviving field officer of the N.C.line.; was an original member of the "Order of the Cincinatti".

(Follows is a letter from Mr.Polk to Mr. J.T.Moore:):
Dec. 30, 1921....."I am sorry I cannot give you a Confederate Record, one of my regrets of my life is that I did not run away and join the Confederate Army"........"I am certainly glad to know that some steps are being taken to write a true history of the old South, the Lord knows that it has been long enough neglected, for which our people alone are responsible. Those who are now living and who can tell the story of the old South and its life as they saw it should hasten to do so before it is too late. It is well to leave a record of a life that has passed beyond recall. The like of which will never be seen again.".....

My paternal great great grandfather, Philomen Hawkins, Sr. was the son of Philomen Hawkins, 1st. and Ann Eleanor (Howard) Hawkins, his wife of Devonshire, England. He was born Sept.28, 1717, on Chickahominy river, near Todd's bridge in Charles City co., Va.He married Della Martin in 1743; the dau. of Zachariah Martin,Esq. who lived in an upper county of Va...They were married in Va. in a church in Brunswick, Parson Beatty presiding. He resided in Province, N.C. at the mouth of Six Pound Creek on Roanoke river ab. 10yrs.; removed to Pleasan Hill in Warren co., where he raised and reared a family; in 1757 he was elected High Sheriff of Granville co., (which consisted of what Granville is now, added to Franklin and all of Warren lying south of the Roanoke river.Held this office for several years; in 1771-72-76 took an active part in the trying events of that period; was a member from Bute co. to the Provincial Congress Apr.-Nov. 1776; 1776-1781 Col. of N.C. Militia; Counselor of State from Warren co., May 6, 1783,Nov. 19, 1790-Jan. 2, 1792; Representative from Franklin co., 1779-82 to 86; served under Col.Gov. Tryon in the Alamance campaign against the Regulators, as Capt. of the Bute Light Horse; was detailed as chief Aid-de-Camp to the Gov.; bore the Gov's commands through the action exposing him to fire of the enemy his clothing & hat being pierced by bullets; was ___ continental Congress at Halifaxin.1776; was made Lt.Col. of cavalry at the age of 60; later resigned & raised a battalion of his own; died at his residence at Pleasant Hill, Warren co., N.C. Sept. 10, 1801;

My parental great grandfather,Philomen Hawkins Jr., was the 2nd son of Philomen Hawkins and his wife Delia (Martin) Hawkins; he was born in Bute co., N .C. Dec. 3, 1752; married Lucy Davis, Aug. 31, 1775; served in the campign against Regulators; was a member of his father's company of Bute Light Horse; was courier on the Gov's staff and later a Col. in the war of the Revolution; was a long time in public life Councilor of State from Granville co., June 26, 1781; Representative from same county 1779-80, 1782-1786, from Warren co., 1787-1789,1803-05-06; State Senator from Warren co., 1807-08-10-11; Member of Constitutional Convention 1789; died in 1833 (family then consisting of 130 members).

REMINE, INGERSOLL OSEA (1891-)
(several forms filled

1. Ingersoll Osea Remine
2. Loudon, Tennessee
3. Aug. 6, 1891, Chuckey, Greene county, Tennessee
4. Calvin Keezel(?) Remine.......; served as Postmaster 18 consecutive years during part of which he was a member of the County Court of Greene county and also served three terms (6 yrs) as chairman Greene Co. Republican Exec. Comm.; born near Limestone, Greene co., Tenn.; until 18 yrs. of age..(cont'd below on form)
5. Laura Painter (Remine); Osea Painter and Mary Painter; on Horse Crk. in Greene co., Tenn.
6. My great great grandfather ____ Remine (name originally spelled with capital M-ReMine) emigrated from France to America ab. 1795, settled in southeastern part of Virginia, moving shortly afterwards to what is now Scott co., Va.; my great grandfather, William Remine, farmer and tombstone maker moved from Scott co., Va. to Green co., Tenn. in 1845 during the boyhood of my grandfather Daniel Webster Remine; my grandmother Phoebe (Keezel) Remine of Irish descent was the daughter of ____Keezel, pioneer Methodist minister. She was born near Keezeltown(?), Rockingham co. Va. and moved to Tenn. with her father some years before the outbreak of the Civil War.
(Q. #4 cont'd) teacher in public schools of Greene co. and Washington co. until marriage in 1890; merchant at Chuckey, Tenn. until appointed postmaster at that place during McKinley's first term (see attached note); a son of Daniel Webster Remine and Phoeby (Keezel) Remine; near Limestone, Tennessee.)
(Q. #6 cont'd) my grandfather D. W. Remine and Phoebe Keezel were married 1859 and lived in same house on farm lying in western(?) portion of Greene and western portion of Washington co.'s from that date until the death of grandfather in 1913, a period of 54 yrs.; in 1870 grandfather Remine organized the Methodist sunday school, Limestone, Tenn. and served continually as Superintendent until his death in 1913, a period of 43 yrs.; parents of grandfather Osea Painter and his wife Mary Painter-(whose name was Painter before her marriage); moved from Va. ab. 1830 & settled on Horse Creek, Greene co., Tenn.; grandfather, Osea Painter was a farmer and merchant on Horse Creek and before his marriage was a rail way contractor and as such participated in building of the East Tenn. & Va. Railway (now Southern) through Greene and Washington co.'s. Painters are of English descent.
7. Private school, Chucky, Greene county, Tenn., taught by Effie Huffaker; public school (same place); Wesleyan Academy (same place)-Principal, S. H. Thompson.
8. .....
9. .....
10. Telegraph operator; entered service Southern Railway System Apr. 10, 1906; served this co. continually since as Telegraph Operator, station agent, etc. at Colteway(?), Johnson City, Concord, Athens, Afton, Musselville __, New Market, Newport and Loudon, Tenn., Hot Springs and Marshall in N. C. and various other points - Knoxville Division, S. R. S.
11. & 12. ...
13. Republican Party; chairman, Loudon co.; Repub. Exec. Comm. since Apr. 1920-Repub. campaign manager in Loudon co., Presidential campaign 1920 in which campaign the usual county Republican majority of 400 was increased to 1295.
14. M. E. South
15. Free and Accepted Masons, Master of Tenn. Lodge 204(?), Loudon, Tenn. -Royal Arch Mason-Master First Vail(?); Junior United American Mechanics
16. ...
17. Bertie Pearl Fisher, married Lenoir City, Loudon co., Tenn. Aug. 14, 1912; Marion Parker Fisher and Dorcas (Fouts) Fisher, Lenoir City, Loudon co., Tenn.; my wife, of English-French stock, grand dau. of Jacob Henry Fisher and his wife, Elizabeth Ann Lowery of McMinn co., Tenn. on the Fisher side of the family; her great great grandfather, Jacob Foute (or Fouts) of French ancestry, was born in Frederick county, Maryland on Nov. 29, 1769 and came to Tenn. in 1792 and located at Dandridge, Jefferson county. Her great grandfather, William L. Foute was born at Dandridge, Tenn., Nov. 30, 1798 and died in Roane (now Loudon) co., October 5, 1856. Her grandfather, Geo. Washington Foute, born Sept. 25, 1829 - died July 27, 1891; was a private in the 26th Tenn. Infantry, Confederate Army.
18....
19. Samuel Thompson Remine, b. Nov. 17, 1913 (died in infancy)

Marian Fisher Remine, b. Nov. 17, 1914, lives Loudon, Tenn.
Daniel Calvin Remine, b. June 10, 1916, lives Loudon, Tenn.
Laura Nelle Remine, b. Jan. 6, 1919, lives Loudon, Tenn.

Form dated: Dec. 14, 1922. This material is difficult to read - several copies of the same page, typed and microfilmed with distortions.

RICE, JAMES WILLIAM (1851-1949)
Dover, Tenn.
Jan. 30, 1922

1. Jas. William Rice
2. Dover, Tennessee
3. April 28, 1851, Dover, Stewart county, Tennessee
4. Jas. E. Rice, Robertson county, Tennessee; Springfield afterwards at Dover and after the Civil War, now at Clarksville. He was a Major in the Confederate Army. After the battle of Fr_____(this may be battle of Franklin) (Ft. Donelson?) he served as Gen. Wm. B. Bates....on staff till the close (of the war). After the war he practiced law at Clarksville; served as Attorney General of the 10th Judicial Circuit until September 1869. He was elected Circuit Judge in August 1869 and was re-elected in 1870 or 1871. (Parents): Edwin Rice and _____Diamond (may be Dionnus?) Rice; Robertson county, Tennessee.
5. Julia A. Rice; Parents: Stephen N. Dowson and Anna White (or While ...."t" not crossed) Dowson, Logan county, Kentucky.
6. My father's father came from Killarney, Ireland; fought on the American side in the Revolutionary War. My father's mother was named Diamond. She was of Welsh ancestry. My Rice grandparents came from North Carolina ...on my fathers side we are said to be descended from Baron Rice of Ireland and his mother is said to be a descendant from Gower Glendower. On my mothers side.....her father, Stephen N. Dowson came from England with two brothers, Geo. and Joseph. They settled in Montgomery county, Maryland. They are descended from Count D'Osson (or D'Orson) of France, who went to England with the Conquerers in 1160.The name was afterwards changed to Dowson. My _________grandfather came from Maryland to Kentucky in 1820 to Logan county. In 1844, he bought a large farm near ______, Tennessee, which is still in the family. My grandmother's family (was) named White, a prominent family in Montgomery county, Maryland. She was of Scotch and English ancestry. I neglected to say my father served in the Seminole War in Florida in 1836. He enlisted in the _______war but the command was stopped in New Orleans.
7. I went to the Mission schools in Dover until 1860. I then went to ______to A. L.(?) Johnson, near Clarksville and then continued with him until 1865. We then moved to Clarksville and I went to ______ after I attended a school taught by Prof. Marshall in 1869. I went to Kentucky University at Covington(?) for _____. I then went to Stewart College at Clarksville.
8. I never graduated. I attended Kentucky University at Lexington (see Covington above; Lexington is probably correct) in 1869-1870 and then Steward(Stewart) college, (Clarksville?), Tennessee.
9. At Cumberland University at Lebanon with a degree of B.L. - graduated in May 1872.
10. I began practicing law at Clarksville in June 1872, moved to Dover in June 1874 and opened partnership with Col. N. Brandan- since then I have practiced alone.
11. I was Justice of the Peace for 6 years; Chairman of the County Court of Stewart County, Tennessee; was Democratic Presidential Elector for the 6th Congressional District in 1896 and again in 1916; Was a member of the House of Representatives in 1899 and a member of the Senate in 1919.
12. None
13. Democratic Presidential Elector in 1896 and 1916. Member of the House of Representatives in 1899; member of Senate in 1919.
14. Christian Church
15. Masons, Knights of Pythias, Odd Fellows and Oriental Order of Humility.
16. I assisted Judge Quarles in writing "Quarles Digest of the Criminal Laws of Tennessee" (this not clear - Ed.)

17. 1st wife: Ellen D. (Blye) Quarles, December 17, 1871. 2nd Wife: Annie Hobing, November 15, 1893; daughter of Judge James M. Quarles and Mary Walker Thomas; Clarksville, Tennessee; 2nd wife was daughter of John Hobing and Eliza Hobing; Dover, Tennessee; My first wifes ancestors were on the Quarles side - Hugenots, came from a distinguished family in Virginia and on her mothers side from Gov. Walker of Virginia. My second wifes father came from Prussia and his wife was of Welsh ancestry.
18. I have no military record
19. Wert(?) Quarles Rice, married to Antonia Hester, P. O. - San Bernadino, California
Robt. Mainworth Rice, married to Alma N. Frey, Clarksville, Tenn.
Wm. Leopold Rice, married to Lelia Groves, Evansville, Indiana
Jas. Wm. Rice, Jr., Nashville, Tenn.
Mary Walker Rice, married to E. L. Gregery, Tullahoma, Tennessee

ROWSEY, JOHN EMMETT (1871-1953)
Henderson, Tennessee
Dec. 26, 1922

1. Dr. John Emmett Rowsey
2. Henderson, Tennessee
3. August 17, 1871, Montezuma(?), Chester county, Tennessee
4. William Franklin Rowsey; Camden, McNairy county, Tennessee; Montezuma, Tennessee - was a merchant; was a Confederate soldier and a lieutenant; ____________
5. Sallie Francis Rowsey; William Talliferro and _________; Water Valley, Mississippi.
6. My parents were of Scotch-Irish descent.
7. At Jackson district high school at Montezuma, Tennessee, Rev. B. F. Blackman and H. S. Taylor.
8. Henderson Male and Female College; graduated 1890 with B.A. degree.
9. Vanderbilt University in 1901 - D.D.S.
10. Dentistry; began practice in May of 1901 in Henderson, Tennessee and practiced there until August 1919.
11. City Council, member of the County Board of Education of Chester co. and member of the General Assembly in 1923.
12. ...
13. Democrat
14. Methodist Episcopal Church, South; member of the Board of Stewards and Trustee.
15. Knights of Pythias.
16. ...
17. ...
18. ...
19. ...

SIMMONS, JAMES THOMAS (1861-1939)
Whiteville, Tennessee
Feb. 5, 1922

1. James Thomas Simmons
2. Whiteville, Tenn.
3. Nov. 5, 1861, Bolivar, Hardeman county, Tennessee
4. Benjamin Allen Simmons, Halifax, Edgecomb county, North Carolina; he moved to Hardeman county, Tenn. in 1854, settling near Whiteville, Tenn. For several years he taught school but gave it up to become a southern planter. Served four years in the Confederate army; James Boyd Simmons and Sallie Anne Worrell, Halifax, North Carolina.
5. Martha Ophelia Harriss; Thomas Henry Harriss and Martha Ophelia Willoughby; Hardeman county, near Bolivar, Tennessee.
6. James Boyd Simmons was a typical souther planter, being very wealthy. So was Benjamin Allen Simmons, but he gave up all and followed the Confederate army for four years. We are all of Scotch-Irish descent and true to the Democratic party. James Boyd Simmons was a Justice of the Peace for many years in Edgecomb county, North Carolina.

7. Received early education at Simmons Academy near Whiteville, Tenn.; reaching to about the 10th grade. H. C. Rosemon was my most popular teacher.
8. None
9. None
10. Have been a planter all my life.
11. Member of the County Court of Hardeman county for past 5 years - at present am member of the 62nd General Assembly from Hardeman county, Tennessee.
12. When I was in the Legislature, I introduced 14 bills and 12 of them passed by a big majority; the bill that I fought for the hardest when I was in the Legislature was an educational bill to put girls and boys in school by law up to 17 years of age.
13. Democrat
14. Baptist
15. None
16. ...
17. Mary Eliza Sammons, Jan. 6, 1886, near Whiteville, Tenn.; Elder Wiley Washington Sammons and Martha Frances Wilkes; Bolivar, Tenn.; they descended from Scotch-Irish from near Raleigh, N. C.
18. During the recent war with Germany, I gave to the government about one hundred acres of my land (the Fair Grounds at Whiteville, Tennessee) free of charge.
19. Eugene Simmons
Horace Simmons
Opal Simmons
Walter Simmons
Millard Simmons
Benjamin Simmons
Vera Simmons, married Hiram Walter Evans, 1138 S. Quaker St., Tulsa, Oklahoma.

SLOAN, WARREN HASTINGS (1894-)
Savannah, Tennessee
Dec. 7, 1922

1. Warren Hastings Sloan
2. Savannah, Tenn.
3. Aug. 16, 1894, near Saltillo, Hardin county, Tennessee
4. Danny Sloan; near Saltillo, Hardin county, Tennessee; lived near Saltillo; Alex Sloan and Nancy Sloan; near Saltillo, Tenn.
5. Nancy Lee Owen; John D. Owen and Polly Hill, near Saltillo, Tenn.
6. Father's grandfather came from Ireland along with two bachelor brothers.
7. Rural schools for elementary; Savannah Institute for high school; W. E. Rogers, Principal of high school.
8. West Tennessee State Normal; no degree
9. ...
10. High school teacher 1914-1922
11. ...
12. ...
13. Republican
14. Methodist
15. Mason - F. & A. M.
16. ...
17. not married
18. Apprentice Seaman, U. S. Navy, December 15, 1917 to June 17, 1918; Private U. S. Army, AEF, August 6, 1918 to February 15, 1919.
19. ...

SMITH, CHARLES LOGAN (1892 -)
Maryville, Tennessee
May 9, 1922

1. Charles Logan Smith

(C. L. Smith cont'd):

2. Maryville, Tennessee
3. July 18, 1892, Harlan, Harlan county, Kentucky
4. Elisha E. Smith; Harlan county, Kentucky; in Harlan county and adjoining counties in the mountains of Eastern Kentucky during his entire lifetime; Jonathan P. Smith and Martha ________; Harlan co., Ky.
5. Leah Ritter Lewis; Jarrett J. Lewis and Nancy ________; Harlan co. Kentucky
6. No family history has ever been given me and I cannot give dates and names, however, (was) reliably informed that my great great grandfather came to America from Ireland and settled in Virginia; My grandfather, Jonathan P. Smith came from Virginia and settled in the upper waters of the Cumberland river in Harlan county, Kentucky. My father, Elisha E. Smith, was one of twelve (12) children, all of whom were born and reared in Harlan county, Kentucky. My mothers people came from Wales and settled first in Virginia and then in Kentucky. My grandfather, Jarrett J. Lewis was a soldier in the Civil War.
7. In an old log school house in the back woods of Harlan county, Kentucky; after I was 13 years old, I started in the second grade at a Presbyterian Mission School; finishing the grades in this Mission School at Harlan, Kentucky.
8. In 1910, I started in the 1st year of the preparatory department of Maryville College, Maryville, Tennessee and finished the preparatory department in 1913; finished two years of College at Maryville College, Maryville, Tenn.
9. Finished one semester of Law at the University of Chicago in 1916 just before I enlisted in the World War army.
10. January 1, 1919, I entered the real estate business in Maryville, Blount county, Tennessee and have been in the same profession since that date.
11. Was elected to the General Assembly of the State of Tennessee for 1921-1922.
12. I have been connected with the Civic Organizations of Maryville, Tenn. - President of the Local Chapter of the American Red Cross.
13. Republican - ancestors on both sides as far back as I can find out have been Republicans.
14. Presbyterian
15. Masons, K of P
16. ...
17. Nellie Edith Wilson, married September 29, 1917 at Louisville, Ky.; Edward Fife Wilson and Lucy May Tilden; Estherville, Iowa; she is a member of the D.A.R. and her ancestors on her mothers side came over on the "Mayflower".
18. Volunteered and went to the officers training camp at Fort Benjamin, Harrison, Indiana, from Harlan, Kentucky, May 29th, 1917. Was commissioned 2nd Lieutenant in the Infantry, August 15th, 1917. Transfered to Camp Zachary Taylor, Louisville, Kentucky, August 29th, 1917. Served in the 159th Depot Brigade, Camp Zachary Taylor, Louisville, Kentucky until discharged Dec. 3rd, 1918.
19. Charles Logan Smith, Jr., born June 7, 1918
Leah Lucile Smith, born March 8, 1920.
(The both live with their father and mother at Maryville, Blount co., Tennessee.)

STALCUP, CHRISTOPHER COLUMBUS (1849 -)
(Veterans form #2)
Pioneer marked through for Veteran

1. Christopher Columbus Stalcup
2. 73 years
3. McMinn co., Tenn.
4. no
5. ...
6. Farmer
7. Moses Stalcup; .....Virginia (nothing else noted)
8. Nancy Black; Joseph Black and ________; Green co., Tenn.

9. My father settled in this county when it was first settled; came from Virginia to Kentucky, married Annie Heard and settled here; after death of first wife, he married my mother, Nancy Black of Green county, Tennessee.
10. ...
11. no
12. 300 acres
13. $5500.00
14. log house - 3 rooms
15. I plowed - hoed - grubbed - chopped wood - made rails and fence - harvested and did anything in a general farming line.
16. Father did general farming work; mother cooked, carded, spun and wove all kinds of cloth and knit for a family of 12 boys and 2 girls.
17. no
18. yes, very much so
19. yes
20. very few of such men in my community
21. they did not, very few aristocrats in the county
22. yes
23. the feeling was always sociable and friendly
24. it did not
25. fairly good
26. they were never discouraged
27. public and private
28. about 3 yrs. I presume
29. 1/2 mile
30. we have quite a number of fine public schools in our county
31. we had both
32. 9 months
33. most (of) them fairly so
34. man
35. I was not in the service, being too young.
36. ...
37. ...
38. ...
39. ...
40. ...
41. ...
42. ...
43. I married at 23 and spent several years in Middle Tennessee, Texas, Arkansas and Indian Territory (now Oklahoma) - while in Arkansas I was Deputy Circuit Court Clerk for 6 years; returned to this county 25 yrs ago and have lived where I am now living for 22 years.
44. ...
45. While not having been in the service, I had 10 brothers that saw more or less service in the Confederate Army; One brother - in - law; four of them with my brother-in-law were in it up to the surrender of Vicksburg where the oldest was killed the night before the surrender and the youngest died soon after capture. There is only one of them living at this time and one younger boy.
46. L. H. Stalcup, Vernon, Texas
T. H. Chamlee, Athens, Tenn.
John Wilkins, Athens, Tenn.

Those old heros are nearly all gone ......"Peace to their ashes".

STEWART, HOYTE TATUM (1880-1926)
Murfreesbor, Tenn.
June 13, 1922

1. Hoyte Tatum Stewart
2. Murfreesboro, Tenn.
3. Jan. 20, 1880, Woodbury, Cannon county, Tenn.
4. Robert Cliffton Stewart; Woodbury, Cannon co., Tenn.; lived at Woodbury, Tenn., Ocalo, Florida and Gadsden, Alabama; Larkin Stewart and Mary Howard; Woodbury, Tenn.
5. Eliza Hatton Tatum; Alfred C. Tatum and Ann E. Tatum; Woodbury,Tenn.
6. ...

7. Woodbury College....teacher: E. J. Lehman
8. Woodbury, Tenn.
9. ...
10. Lawyer since June 1902, admitted to the Bar at Woodbury, Tennessee
11. Tennessee House of Representatives in 1909, 1922; State Senate in 1913; House in 1915; Delegate to Democratic National Convention, Baltimore in 1912; have been since September 1918, Attorney General of the 8th Judicial Circuit, Tennessee.
12. ...
13. Democrat; was chairman of the Democratic Executive Committee of Cannon county for 15 years.
14. Baptist
15. Masons, Odd Fellows, Kinght of Pythias, Elks, Modern Woodmen, Eagles
16. ...
17. Almeda Cummings, married at Woodbury, Tenn. on Oct. 30, 1898; James Harvey Cummings and Elizabeth Higgins; Woodbury, Tenn.
18. ...
19. Ruth Christine Stewart, Murfreesboro, Tenn.
    Walter Faulkner Stewart, ditto
    Hoyte Tatum Stewart, Jr., ditto
    Robert Clifton Stewart, ditto
    John Thomason Stewart, ditto
    Jean Elizabeth Stewart, ditto

SWANN, ROBERT EMMETT (1886 -)
Watertown, Tenn.
Dec. 7(?), 1922

1. Robert Emmett Swan
2. Watertown
3. Feb. 5, 1886, Commerce, Wilson co., Tenn.
4. Thomas Franklin Swann; Saulsbury, Wilson co., Tenn.; Commerce - was a farmer, served four years in the Confederate army as a private; Wiliam Swann and Susan Swann; Saulsbury, Tenn.
5. Sarah Johnson; Duncan Johnson and Betsy Johnson; Commerce, Tenn.
6. ...
7. Commerce and Watertown, Limited
8. none
9. none
10. farming, from boyhood
11. Justice of the Peace since Sept. 1, 1898 (this date was typed over-may be 1908)
12. ...
13. Democrat
14. Cumberland Presbyterian, Elder
15. Mason and Modern Woodmen of America
16. ...
17. Lurley McClanahan, Dec. 14, 1910, Grant, Tenn.; David McClanahan and Eliza McClanahan; Grant, Tenn.
18. none
19. Ray Thomas Swan, age 11
    Ralph David Swann, age 7
    Robert Hayden Swann, age 5

SWEET, MARK WHEELER (1874 -)
Memphis, Tenn., Route 3, Box 91
Mar. 6, 1922

1. Mark Wheeler Sweet
2. Memphis, Tenn.
3. Jan. 10, 1874, Sloansville, Schoharie (co.), New York
4. John Spencer Sweet; Sloansville, Schoharie, N. Y.; lived at Sloansville until death. Served in the 46th N. Y. State Vol. during Civil War as Pvt.; was elected, and served for 30 years as Constable in Esperance Township; John Sweet and Rachel Robins, Sloansville, Schoharie co.,N.Y.

5. Mary Elizabeth Sweet; George D. Estes and Ellanore Moyer; Sloansville, Schoharie co., N. Y.
6. My grandfathers father was Jessie Sweet, who was the son of Benjamin Sweet, who served under Gen. Jackson in the Battle of New Orleans. He was the son of Benjamin Sweet who was born in the state of Rhode Island. His father, John Sweet, was sent out of Scotland, a bondman, and bound out by England in the English colonies. After serving his time, he married and was the father of 14 sons.
7. Country schools near Sloansville. First teacher was my aunt, Ida Estes. Then Charley Schuyler, a Miss Monk, Mr. Van Vorhees, Mr. S. Carker, Mr. Halleck and C. W. Manchester.
8. none
9. none
10. Wheelwright (in) 1886 - at 12 years of age learning. Soldier, Nov. 9, 1891 at 17 9/12 (does he mean 9 months and 17 years?). Millwright in 1903 at 29 years of age. Followed millwright trade to date.
11. none
12. none
13. Radical Democrat and Independent of Party. Always for the most good to the most people.
14. none
15. none
16. none
17. Rosa Lena Gather, May 17, 1904 at Columbia, Tenn.; William Gather and Margaret Griggs; near Hopkinsville, Ky.
18. Enlisted Nov. 9, 1891 at Albany, N. Y.; was sent to David's Island (now Fort Slocum) for training; after three months training was sent to join the 11th U. S. Infantry Co. D, then stationed at Madison ___ks in Northern part of N. Y. state on the shores of Lake Ontario. Was there only two months when the 11th Infantry was sent to Prescott, Ariz. Territory to relieve the 9th U. S. Infantry. Was stationed at Prescott only one year when Companies D and A were marched overland to San Carlos, Arizona to relieve a Company of the 9th U. S. Infantry. San Carlos was then part of the Apache Indian Reservation and was about 120 miles from the nearest railroad. We were stationed at San Carlos for one year. That being the limit of time any company or troop was allowed to stay there on account of the great hear. (Cont'd at end of Questionnaire)
19. Mary Elizabeth Sweet, born Feb. 9, 1905, Chattanooga, Tenn.
Pleasant G. Sweet, born Feb. 26, 1907, Nashville, Tenn.
Clarabelle Sweet, born Mar. 28, 1909, New Market, Ala.
Viola May Sweet, born May 10, 1911, Nashville, Tenn.; died Nov. 30, 1915 at Springfield, Mo.
Mark Wheeler Sweet, Jr., born Jan. 6, 1914, Nashville, Tenn.
Bessie Sweet, born Nov. 29, 1917, Oklahoma City, Okla.
Kate Sweet, born May 4, 1921, Memphis, Tenn.

(Continuation of Q. #18 - Military record).... I have seen 128° in the shade for two weeks at a time in the month of August. At this time the Apaches were quiet most of the time and caused but very little trouble as a tribe. But there was one disquieting element which caused both the soldier and the U. S. Government a lot of trouble, that was the "Apache Kid". The Kid was an educated Indian. Schooled at Carlisle, Penn. in the Indian College there, he not only spoke English well, but was well versed in Spanish as well as his native tongue. The Kid's "grouch" did not seem to be against the whites so much as it was directed against his own people. Many a hot, sultry night, troubled sleep was broken by the Cavalry Bugles shrill notes sounding "Boots and Saddles". The Kid had made another raid on his own people, perhaps, he had murdered a whole family, while they slept, or he had carried off two or three of the virgin maidens to add to his wives. At such times, the warning was signaled to the Post Guards by means of a fire (if at night) or the looking glass on sunny days. The Kid was never caught. The Apache Scouts would follow his trail for days, leading one of the U. S. Troops of Cavalry, then suddenly loose all traces of the trail. It was often thought that the Scouts were getting too close, and the fear of the Kid was the cause of the lost trail. These same Scouts could follow the trail of a "wanted" white man and never make a failure. It is said that the Kid died in Old Mexico about 1896 or 7, but there was never anything but hearsay to verify the report. I finished up my enlistment, and was discharged in Apache, Arizona after a service of three years and three mos.

being discharged on Jan. 15, 1895 as a Private. Re-enlisted May 2, 1895 at Apache, for Co. G, 16th U. S. Infantry then stationed at Salt Lake City, Utah. After one year and six months in Salt Lake the 16th was sent to Fort Sherman, Idaho on Coeur D'Alene Lake near Coeur D'Alene City. Coeur D'Alene was then but a small town of about 3000. The country around was one vast forest of mighty trees. A few had sought and found a home on a Government Homestead among the foothills of Northern Idaho. Game was plentiful at this time. Deer, bear, cougar, lynx, snowshoe rabbits, blue grouse and rough grouse, elk were often seen in the forest and now and then a moose would find his way down from near the Canadian line. I was stationed at Fort Sherman when the battleship "Maine" was blown up in Havana Harbor and war was declared. I was then a Corporal in Co. G, 16th Infantry. My time of service had nearly expired and when the 16th left for Florida, I was left behind with some 15 or 20 other soldiers to look after the Fort and the Government property left there, also to pack and ship the necessaries to the ones who had left. My ambitions were to get up a Company of my own, and I made application to Gov. Stenenberger, then Governor of Idaho, but I did not have any political influence and my application was "placed in file". Thus, I missed the War with Spain. I would have liked nothing better than to have helped whip Spain, but I did not want to serve in the Army all my life as an enlisted man. I had a "grouch" about the way my application was treated and after a rest from the Army, I served the State of Idaho in the Coeur D'Alene Mine Strike of 1898. After two years of civil life, I became dissatisfied with the tameness of my life and went to Seattle, Washington, there I re-enlisted for service in the Philipines. Served with the 16th U. S. Infantry Co. K in the northern part of Luzon. The few skirmishes we had with the natives are not worthy of mention, but the place, should credit any man with, at least being lucky, to get away retaining any semblance of his former health. Was discharged as a Sergeant. The many places and different adventures and mis-adventures which I have been in during my service with the army would fill a good sized book and although some of them would prove interesting reading, if produced by a good writer, they would sound too much like fiction and some people would be inclined to doubt my truthfulness, so we will let the record go as it looks.

Letter addressed to Mr. Moore from Mr. Sweet: Memphis, Tenn. May 27, 1922....at the time (of receiving the questionnaire), I did not have at hand a record of my family, so I wrote to one of my sisters who resides in Schnectady, N. Y. and she refered me to the Newberry Library, 60 W. Walton Place, Chicago, Ill. I am sending you a copy of a letter I received in reply. This letter and the record it contains, I feel sure are correct in names and dates. This is the genealogy of my mother who was Mary Elizabeth Estes, daughter of George Dorris Estes and Mary Moyer.

(Newberry Library, Apr. 4, 1922)...Dear Sir, in response to your inquiry of Mar. 31, an investigation has been made by one of our assistants who submits the report noted on the enclosed sheet.....Geo. Blevley,Lib. Estes Genealogies by Charles Estes of Warren, Rhode Island -pub. at Salem, Mass. 1894. The author intimates, agreeing with your family tradition, that Robert Estes, father of Richard Estes 1647 - emigrant to Lynn, Mass. was of the famous House of Este by way of England. If this be true, your line runs directly from Adelberto, Duke of Tuscany, Italy 884 A.D. to Albert Azo of Esto, who died 1097. He married Cunegunda, descended from Charlemagne. Their son, Foulkes, remained in Italy and from him descended the famous Italian House of Este. Another son, Melf or Guelf, 1st, was ancestor of the four Georges of England, and of Queen Victoria. From Robert Estes of Dover, England, your line descends as follows: Richard Estes 1647, son of Robert of Dover, England, emigrated 1684 from Newington, East Kent county, England to Lynn, Mass. He married in 1687 Elizabeth Beck. Their son, Robert 1694, born in Salem, Mass., married in 1715, Ann Durfee, 1694-1734, daughter of Thomas Durfee and Ann Freeborn. Their son, Richard Estes, 1717-1793, married Mary Pearce, 1724-1792, a daughter of Philip Pearce. This Richard was a large landowner in Rhode Island. His son, R. Philip Estes, 1749, born at Warwick, Rhode Island, married a Miss Gage. Their son, Thomas P. Estes, 1778-1845, married in 1801, Mary Burlingham, daughter of Philip Burlingham, a Quaker. Their son, George Dorris Estes, 1827-married 1851, Mary E. Moyer, a daughter of John Moyer and wife, whose surname was Root. They lived in Charleston and Fonda, New York. They had seven children:

1. Mary Elizabeth, Oct. 9, 1852; married John S. Sweet

2. Philip, born 1855, married Sarah A. Meyers
3. Ida, born 1856, married Silas Nostrant(?)
4. Ophelia, 1858-1862
5. Ellen, 1860; married Jacob I. Dorn
6. John Moyer, 1861; married Ida Vandeveer
7. Kate O., 1865; married Robert Vanderworken

(Letter from Mr. Sweet to Mr. Moore):...I am after the record from my fathers side of the house and if I can get it I promise you a very interesting record.

SWINK, ROBERT BURLE (1873-1933)
Medan(?), Tenn. 3/21/1923

1. Robert Burle Swink
2. Medan(?)
3. Dec. 6, 1873, Medan(?), Madison co., Tenn.
4. Henry Morrison Swink; Medan, Madison co., Tenn.; lived at Medan; mercantile business; served with Forrest-wounded Yazo City, Miss.; Peter Swink and Matilda ____; Medan.
5. Sallie Williams; George Williams and Martha _____; Medan
6. ...
7. Miss Ivie Duke, W. M. Yorrell of Clarksville, W. D. Mooney (teachers)
8. South Western Baptist University, Jackson, Tenn., the Sewanee.
9. ...
10. Lumber, logs, ___ and farmer
11. J. P. for 12 years, Madison co., Lower House 1919 and Extra Session 1920.
12. 19th Amendment
13. Democrat
14. Presbyterian
15. Royal Arch Mason, Elk, Moose & Stags
16. ...
17. Myrtle May House, married Dec. 26, 1907; Albert House and Callie House, Medan.
18. ...
19. Burle Swink; Harry Swink; Bertie May Swink; and Dorothy Vanden Swink

TERRY, JOHN MARION (1868-1952)
Oneida, Tenn.

1. John Marion Terry
2. Oneida, Tenn.
3. Oct. 25, 1868, Oneida, Scott co., Tenn.
4. Milton Terry; then Campbell, now Scott co., Tenn.; Oneida, Tenn.; he was a private and a volunteer in the War of '61 to '65 and belonged to Capt. Joe New___ Co.; was elected Sheriff of Scott co., Tenn. ab. 1868 served one term, was Justice of Peace 18 yrs.; Josiah Terry and Nancy Stephens, in then Campbell co., now Scott co., Tenn.
5. Jane Thomas; Abner Thomas and Rebecca Thomas; near Oneida, Scott co.
6. My grandfather, Josiah Terry came from what then was Witt(?) co. Va. Abner Thomas came from North Carolina. Have no record farther back, but my father said he was of Irish descent. I have no record of any military record of my ancestors.
7. In common schools of Scott co., Tenn. and one term in a school at Mouth of Wolf River, Clay co., Tenn. a Mr. Henry was Principal of Huntsville school.
8. Never attended a college.
9. Civil Engineer; not graduate of any school.
10. Civil Engineer began his work 1892; taken up and learned profession myself, am now engaged in this work and farming; taught school in Scott co., Tenn. from 1888 to 1896; farmed 1912 to 1915, Grady(?) co., Okla.
11. Magistrate 6 years 1896;Postmaster at Oneida Tenn. 1898 to 1912.; Town Shop Board, Grady co., Oklahoma;Elected Representative for Scott, Cambell and Union co., Tenn.
12. Better schools for Tenn. For good roads; abolish saloons in Tenn.
13. Republican
14. Southern Baptist, Deacon
15. Mason
16. ...

17. Elizabeth Brown, October 12, 1889, Oneida, Tennessee; Hamilton Brown and Sally Brown, Oneida, Tenn.; her mothers maiden name was Phillips; Hamilton Brown was the son of John Brown who came from North Carolina to Tennessee.
18. I have no military record.
19. David(?) Sebastian Terry, married Bessie Lewis, Danville, Ky.
Edna May Terry, married D. D. Litton, Evansville, Tenn.
Janice Edith Dorothy Victory Terry, married James R. Davis, Ralston, Okla.(?)
Maudie Esther Terry, married Charles E. Chitwood, New River, Tenn.
Lela Agnes Terry, Oneida, Tenn.
Ruth Avo Terry, Oneida, Tenn.
John Milton Terry, Paris Island, S. C.
Caldwell Brown Terry, Oneida, Tenn.
William Howard Terry, Oneida, Tenn.

TESTERMAN, WILLIAM TECUMSEH (1862-1940)
327 - 7th Ave. __, Nashville, Tenn.
Jan. 31, 1922

1. William Tecumseh Testerman
2. Mooresburg, Tenn.
3. April 18, 1862, Kyles Ford, Hancock co., Tenn.
4. James Testerman, near Kyles (Ford), Hancock co., Tenn.; Kyles Ford, Tenn. all of his life. He was a farmer. Held no official position; Abraham Testerman and __________; Kyles Ford, Hancock co., Tenn.
5. Sarah Ann Baker; John Wallen Baker and Mary Anderson; Kyles Ford, Tennessee.
6. Abraham Testerman, my paternal grandfather came to Tennessee from Ashe county, N. C.; my paternal(?) great grandfather from Illinois to Tennessee; my maternal grandfather was reared in Hancock co., East Tenn.
7. Public schools of Hancock co., Tenn.; my first teacher was W. J. Livesay, then Will Chestnur , McMinn Academy, Rogersville, Tenn. 1878-79, under Prof. A. W. Maine; McKinney High School, Sneedville, Tenn. 1881, L. L. Livesay, teacher.
8. No college education
9. No professional education
10. Teacher in public schools of Hancock co. for five years. Mercantile business for 20 yrs.; Clerk and Master of Chancery Court, Hancock co. 8 yrs. 1895-1903. Seven yrs. in the Government service under Internal Revenue Dept. 1903-1911. On farm in Hancock co. from July 1, 1911 to Sept. 1, 1917; on farm in Hawkins co. (my present home) Sept. 1917. On Tenn. Highway Commission May 7, 1919, appt'd. for 2 yrs., re-elected for full term of 6 years.
11. 58th Gen. Assembly 1913; was delegate to Nat'l. Conv. Chicago 1912- and 1920.
12. While a member of the Gen. Assembly of 1913 gave full support to every measure to banish the saloon from Tenn.; have been interested in church for thirty-seven years, not only giving moral support but financial support.
13. Republican in politics; served as chairman of the Hancock county Comm. for many years and member of the Congressional Exec. Comm., First Congress for 8 years.
14. Baptist - Deacon for many years; also Church Clerk.
15. Odd Fellow
16. None
17. Julia Ann Livesay, married Dec. 23, 1883, Kyles Ford, Hancock co., Tenn.; Andrew Jackson Livesay and Mary Stafford Davis, Kyles Ford, Hancock co., Tenn.; her grandfather on her fathers side was Peter Livesay, on her mothers side, Milam Davis, pioneers in that section of East Tennessee, both accumulating considerable estates.
18. None
19. Frederick Jackson Testerman, wife: Nell Murrell
James Atwood Testerman, wife: Carrie Jarvis
Thomas Lloyd Testerman, wife: Elsie Baker
Winnie Parlee Testerman, husband: Murat Halstead Young
Mary Ella Testerman, husband: Marion Testerman Livesay
Kate Testerman
Nora Testerman
John Wesley Testerman, Jr.

TILLMAN, GEORGE N. (1851-)
(Veterans form #2)

1. George N. Tillman
2. 71
3. Bedford county, Tennessee
4. Neither, I was in my 10th year at the beginning of the war.
5. _________; (B) My brother, James D. Tillman enlisted in Confederate Army at the age of 19 as a 2nd Lt.; rose to the command of the 41st Tenn. _____ and was commanding regiments by the close of the war.
6. Farmer
7. Lewis Tillman; near Fairfield, Bedford co., Tenn.; near Shelbyville, Tenn.; he was in the Seminole Indian Campaign; he was Colonel of Bedford County Militia under three Governors; he held the office of Circuit Crt. Clerk of Bedford co. several terms and was also Clerk and Master; one of my uncles, A. M. Tillman, died in the Confederate army.
8. Mary Catherine Davidson; James Davidson and Harriet Hord(?); near Wartrace, Bedford co. (Tenn.)
9. The mother of my father was Rachel P. Martin, daughter of Matt Martin, who was Capt. in the Revolutionary War and who received a pension as such until his death in 1846. His wife was Sallie Clay of Charlotte co., Va. a cousin of the statesman, Henry Clay. My mothers people, the Davidsons of N. C., served in the Rev. War. Gen. Wm. Davidson was killed at the Battle of Cowpens, as I remember.
10. My father owned a farm and live stock and negroes worth I suppose about $20,000.
11. My parents owned I think not over 15 slaves.
12. 400 acres
13. $20,000
14. A two and a half story brick - 10 rooms and 4 rooms in basement
15. I did - during the war, all kinds of farm work. I began plowing at the age of 10.
16. My father did not do manuel labor in the farm, in my time; he did when he began life and for many years; my mother superintended everything about the house and did much work, but our servants were fairly good until freed.
17. Of the slaves, we had a cook and house servants, etc.
18. Certainly
19. Yes
20. Very few
21. O - no
22. Yes
23. No
24. No
25. Yes
26. Encouraged
27. Private
28. About six years
29. Mile and half
30. X
31. Private
32. Six
33. No
34. Men
35. - 44. ...
45. - 46. ...

WARREN, IRA MAURICE (1892 -)

1. Ira Maurice Warren
2. Dyersburg, Tenn.
3. July 9, 1892, Friendship, Crockett co., Tenn.
4. William Rome Warren, Friendship, Crockett co., Tenn.; lived at Friendship, Tenn.; I. M. Warren and Caline ___, Friendship, Tennessee
5. Barbara Ray, daughter of Dr. Joseph Ray and Marinie _______; lived at Crockett's Mills, Tennessee
6. ...

7. Perry School House, Elizabeth High School and Kenton, Tenn.
8. Union Univ., Southern Presbyterian Univ.
9. Cumberland Univ., 1919, LL.B, O.B.
10. Att'y. at Law, Sept. 1919, Dyersburg, Tenn.
11. No
12. ...
13. Democratic Executive Committee
14. Baptist- teacher
15. McCabees, Kappa Sigma, member of Lions Club
16. ...
17. ...
18. ...
19. ...

WEEMS, GEORGE HATTON (1891-1975)

1. George Hatton Weems
2. % Adj. Gen., U. S. Army
3. Sept. 27, 1891, Southside, Montgomery county, Tenn.
4. Joseph Burch Weems; Hickman co., Tenn.; served as scout under Gen. N. B. Forrest during the Civil War; settled on Braton(?) Creek near Southside, Tenn.; Nathaniel Weems and ________; Hickman co., Tenn.
5. Elizabeth Rye; Dr. T. H. Rye and Mattie Hegewood, Southside, Tenn.
6. The Wemyss (later changed to Weems) came from Scotland to Baltimore, (Maryland), one of the brothers coming to this country was Rev. Mason Lock Weems, who was the minister of Mount Vernon Church; Mason Lock Weems is commonly referred to as "Parsons Weems"; he was the originator of the cherry tree story of Washington's childhood; he was the author of several books: "Life of Washington", "Life of Marion", etc.
7. Country school at Ryes Chapel (Montgomery co.) High school at Waverly, Tenn.
8. One year at So. Western Univ., Clarksville; graduated from U. S. Military Academy, West Point, N. Y. and appointed 2nd Lt. Inf., Apr. 20,1917
9. (See above), graduate U. S. Inf. School, Ft. Benning, Ga.
10. Officer, U. S. Army (Regular) since Apr. 20, 1917
11. ...
12. ...
13. Democrat
14. Methodist
15. Masonic; Alpha Tau Omega (college fraternity)
16. ...
17. Not married
18. Assigned to 9th U. S. Inf. Apr. 1917; overseas with 2nd (Reg.) Div. Sept. 1917; commanded M. A.(?) Co., 9th Inf. throughout training period and in several actions; commanded M. G. Co. 9th Inf. at Paris-Metz Road near Chateau Thierry (near Bellauwoods) and at the battle of Vaux; ordered to army school center at Langres, France as Instructor of candidates for commissions; commissioned the first negro officers to win commissions in France; rejoined the Second Division, Dec. 1918; crossed the Rhine with the 9th Infantry on Dec. 13, 1918; served eight months with the Army of Occupation on the Rhine, promoted to Major of Infantry in 1919 and given command of the 4th Machine Gun Battalion; three times cited in orders for gallantry in action; awarded the Croix de Guerre by France and the Ordine della Corona d'Tealie (Order of the Crown) of Italy; returned to the United States, August 1919 and ordered to Camp Travis, Texas with my battalion (the 4th M. G. Bn.); ordered to U. S. Infantry School as instructor in September 1920; ordered to Davidson College, North Carolina as instructor in the Military Department in Jun. 1923, which is my present assignment.
19. None

The above form and documentation was sent from:
Geo. H. Weems, Capt.
Inf. U. S. A.
Davidson, N. C.
% Adj. Gen. U. S. Army
Date: Dec. 21, 1922

WEEMS, PHILIP VAN HORN (1889 -)
(Veterans form #2)

1. Philip Van Horn Weems, 9 Southgate Ave., Annapolis, Maryland
2. 35 - born March 29, 1889
3. Montgomery co., Tenn.; P. O. -Turbine, now closed.
4. Father was a Confederate soldier; I was in the World War.
5. U. S. S. Georgia; U. S. S. Orizaba; U. S. S. Murry - Lt. Commander U. S. Navy.
6. Farmer
7. Joseph Burch Weems; McEwen Place, Duck River, Hickman co., Tenn.; lived at place of birth and at Turbine, Montgomery co., Tenn. (corner of Dickson, Cheatham and Montgomery co.'s.); was a successful farmer; active Mason; steward in Methodist Church, South.
9. May Elizabeth Rye; Dr. Thomas Heartwell Rye and Martha Ellington Hagewood; Ryes Chapel Church.
10. Dr. Thomas Heartwell Rye was born 1832, was of the pioneer type and made at least one trip to New Orleans from Tennessee in a flatboat; he cut cord-wood to raise funds to go to college; was known throughout his community as a man of outstanding character, intelligence and professional ability; his wife, Martha Ellington Hagewood, was the mother of nine children, yet she found time to accompany her husband over rough country roads to give her assistance in serious cases.
10. Father, Joseph Burch Weems, had difficulty in saving his share of his father's land after the Civil War, but by good judgement and management, was the owner of about 600 acres of good land when he died in 1896.
11. Grandparents did; owned several, but the exact number is not known.
12. Between six and seven hundred acres.
13. Grandfather was estimated to be worth $125,000; this man, Nathaniel Chapman Weems, was an exceptionally successful farmer, lost most of his property during and following the war and settled in Montgomery county.
14. Grandfather's house in Hickman county, still standing, is a handsome frame home of large dimensions and well located; Father's house in Montgomery co. is a typical country house, originally a double log house, later weatherboarded and added to.
15. Father did what he could, but was slightly crippled; due to fact that father died when I was 9, I had to work pretty hard till I was grown up; I took place of a farm hand from the age of about 12 till I went to Branham and Hughes School in 1906 and to the U. S. Naval Academy in 1908; my father, grandfather and uncles, were in good financial circumstances til after the Civil War, but I never gathered the idea that they had an aversion to hard work; on the contrary, all of them apparently hard workers; Joseph Burch Weems, my father, was one of the first in neighborhood to use corn planter, mower, rake, cultivators and reapers.
16. Father did any kind of work which came to hand, but the extent of his land, more than 600 acres, called for most of his time as a manager; also, as he was slightly crippled, he assumed more the role of the "gentleman farmer"; as I remember him, he rode about his place on the famous old family horse "George", which horse lived well on toward forty years, and usually operated the cultivators, and other machinery; Mother did most of the housework but had help.
17. Mother usually kept one girl, but it is a marvel how she looked after eight children and did as much as she did; Father had plenty of help to feed, etc.
18. Although father did less of the hard work than the others in the neighborhood, yet all the landowners were "dirt farmers"; this was necessarily so when I came along toward manhood; I write about the years from 1892 to 1907, at which time I left the farm; not only did the best citizens in my community work, but I believe they have worked too hard.
19. They show the effects of this hard work, by stooped shoulders, etc. I cannot speak from first hand knowledge about the Civil War and reconstruction days.
20. (Q. #19 cont'd):....but it is my impression that all except a few exceptionally prosperous citizens in my section of the state, were honest, hardworking, and God-fearing people. more of the pioneer type than of the idle type.
21. I understand that the society was most democratic.
22. Yes, as far as I know.
23. Not qualified to state.

24. Don't know personally about this.
25. Opportunities were only fair; a good manager could make a success of it, but an average man had a hard row to hoe; for instance, about the only crop of tobacco I raised for myself, I sold for about four cents a pound; this was about 1906, when the cost of producing tobacco was at least as much as the sale price.
26. Have an idea they were encouraged.
27. Typical country school where the teacher did not spare the rod. I have been told that the reason my ears are so large is because Proffessor Billy Wyatt so frequently lifted me back to my seat by the ears!
28. Each winter till I went away to boarding school then full terms till I graduated from Annapolis in 1912.
29. A little more than a mile.
30. Fairly good country schools; the teachers as a rule were exceptionally good; they ruled with a firm hand but were usually capable.
31. Public
32. 7 or 8 months
33. The ones who went to all were usually regular and good students.
34. Both; when very young most of the teachers were men, later mostly women or a man and a woman.
35. Entered Naval Academy June 29, 1908.
36. Various assignements as a regular line officer in the Navy - two years duty in the vicinity of Panama.
37. World War was first active duty and that was mostly anti-submarine warfare where we dropped depth bombs, etc. without knowing the results.
38. No engagements other than with submarines; was on the Orizaba transport 1918, when the depth charge exploded killing Commander Williamson and several others and wounding about twenty.
39. Was with the fleet at Guantanamo when diplomatic relations were severed with Germany and was with one of the first picket boat patrols sent from the Nevada to guard the entrance to Guantanamo Bay - during the first part of the winter of 1917, I fought the "Battle of Yorktown" as we called it when we had to remain in York River behind nets and drill dun crews, without getting a smell of active overseas duty - early part of 1918, joined the Orizaba and in Oct. (5th) joined the destroyer Murray.
40. Not discharged after the war as I am in the regular Navy.
41. Just after the Armistice went to England to let all hands relax - navigation lights turned on, etc. - on return to Brest, France the destroyer Conner, leader and Murray, my destroyer, ran on the rocks - I was the Engineer Officer at the time - after about 36 hours we finally got the boat to Brest and in dry dock.
42. Usual Navy work - was a member of the Olympic Wrestling team which represented America at Antwerp in 1920.
43. Have undertaken some writing with fair success - won first prize for the outline for a book entitled "Naval Leadership", with twenty officers competing - hold Masters and Chief Engineers license for merchant service; in 1915 I married Margaret Thackray of Johnstown, Pa., daughter of George E. Thackray, Special Engineer for Bethlehem Steel Co.; I have children as follows: Phillip Van Horn Weems, born 21 July 1916; Margaret Thackray Weems, 2nd, born 27 Jan. 1919; George Thackray Weems, born 5 Jan. 1921.
44. Served more than a year under Admiral Wm. S. Simms on the battleship Nevada - I consider Admiral Simms the greatest character with whom I have come in contact - the motto of the ship was "Cooperation, concentration and cheerfulness" and the ships company lived up to this motto.
45. Have no access to Civil War records - would like to obtain the war record of my father, Joseph Burch Weems, who joined so am told, Forrests command when he was 16 years of age. It is possible that he did not enlist regularly due to his age, but he had active service under Anderson, a scout commander under Forrest so I am told - after the Civil War my father returned home without parole - there was a rumor that members of Forrest's command would not be paroled and that some of these troops attempted to go to Mexico after the surrender of Lee; my father got as far as the Mississippi river where some of his companions drowned attempting to cross the river; it was at this point that my father and a companion turned their poor horses toward home in Tennessee - after various exciting escapes from Irregulars, they reached home, settled down without a parole, and one of my recollections of about 1896 was of an ex-union soldier who was a tenant on my father's place, telling how he served 4

years in the Union army without firing a shot, drawing $15 per month for the service, and a generous pension in later life - apparently there was no feeling about the war between my father and this former Union soldier - I would like very much to verify the details of my father's Civil War experiences and would appreciate any light on it.
46. My service in the Navy keeps me out of touch with my people - with the result that I have very little data to fill in at this place.

WEST, OLIN (1874 -) Dr. Olin West
3-31-1922

1. Olin West
2. Nashville
3. July 12, 1874, Gadsden, Etowah co., Alabama
4. Anson West, D. D.; Robertson co., North Carolina; various places in Alabama; for 51 years a preacher in the Methodist Episcopal Church, So.; for many years a presiding Elder in North Alabama Conference; member of the most of General Conferences during last 40 yrs. of his life; years a member of Board of Trust of Vanderbilt University; once President of Birmingham College; author of "History of Methodism in Alabama", "The Old and the New Man", "The State of the Dead: and other books on religious topics; died at Athens, Ga., July 3, 1906; son of Andrew West and ______, Robertson co., N. C. - until about 1833 or 1834, then in Alabama
5. Sarah Bryan Kittrell; _______;_______
6. ...
7. Private schools in Alabama; Howard College at East Lake, Ala.
8. Howard College, Alabama; Ph. C. Vanderbilt University, 1895; M. D. Vanderbilt University, 1898.
9. M. D. - Vanderbilt University 1898
10. Physician in Nashville, 1899-1910; Director for Rockefeller Sanitary Commission (with Tennessee State Board of Health) 1910-16; Director of Rural Sanitation, Tenn. State Board of Health, 1916-1918; Sec'y. and Exec. Officer , Tenn. State Board of Health, 1918-1922; Sec'y. Tenn. State Medical Assoc. and Editor of its Journal 1912-22.
11. See above
12. ...
13. Democratic
14. Methodist Episcopal Church, South
15. Mason
16. Editor, Journal of Tennessee State Medical Association, 1912-1922
17. Susie Pinckney Hunter, married July 25, 1906 at Nashville; Robert Pinckney Hunter and Anna Green, Nashville; grand-daughter of Dr. A. L. P. Green.
18. None - rejected for service after volunteering in 1917.
19. (1) Robert Hunter West, born at Nashville, May 20, 1907
    (2) Olin West, Jr., born at Nashville, June 28, 1909.

WHITE, CLARA L. (1833 -)
(Veterans form #1)

1. Mrs. Clara L. White, 21 Vauxhall Apts., Nashville, Tenn.
2. 89 years
3. Lawrence co., Alabama
4. ...
5. Housejeeper
6. Cumberland Presbyterian Minister
7. Having married about 8 years previous to the opening of the war, my grandmother gave me 5 or 6 slaves; my husband, Albert Buford (White) owned 84 slaves and about 1500 acres of land.
8. My grandmother, Mrs. N. Johnson, together with my father, Carson P. Reed, owned many slaves.
9. Parents owned about 600 acres
10. ...
11. ten room frame house
12. ...
13. My father was a minister and employed a governess for the children; my grandmother superintended the house work; the cooking, spinning, and weaving, in fact all the sewing for the negroes was done by slaves.
14. ...

15. Such work was considered honorable and the workers were respected.
16. The majority of the community owned slaves.
17. While the majority owned slaves, they did work themselves too, and few if any led idle lives.
18. Slave holders mingled freely with those who did not own slaves.
19. ...
20. ...
21. No
22. In the majority of families the young men had interest in the home until of age, when parents would give them farms; the opportunities for a poor young man was rather slim.
23. They were encouraged in every instance I can recall.
24. We had a governess in our home after which I went to Greensboro, N. C. with my older sister, going through in private carriage; the younger sisters graduated in Nashville at Dr. Elliotts and Wards.
25. ...
26. The community school was two miles.
27. Pulaski, Tenn. was the nearest school center.
28. Private
29. Ten
30. Yes
31. Sometimes one, sometimes the other.
32. ...
33. ...
34. (Note: This was a form intended for women, but no complete form is shown on the microfilm)..As a girl I was trained to keep house, carry the keys, give out the rations to slaves, etc. Did some of my own sewing; in our community, most of the girls did.
35. No
36. I did not teach, but my sisters did.
37. Parties were the joy of our lives, where big suppers were served on the "groaning tables". Games were indulged in.
38. A church going people but took no other part in religious or political affairs; women were wakening and becoming interested in educational affairs.
39. Living on the Pulaski and Columbia Pike, we were on the line of the march of the two armies and our home was used often by the Yankees and the Rebels.
40. At one time during the war, I feared I would lose my silver, so decided to hide it in the strawberry patch. Some time after, when the berries were ripe, quite a Squad of Yankees came and spied the berries and went in - even lay down on the ground - and ate their fill. I sat on the side veranda and didn't take my eyes off of them until the last one disappeared and I knew my silver was safe. All the men excepting one and most of the women left after the war. Some begged to come back.

WHITE, LOONEY BETHEL (1871-1924)

1. Looney Bethel White
2. Lawrenceburg, Tenn.
3. Dec. 17, 1871, Fall River, Lawrence co., Tenn.
4. John Franklin White; Fall River, Lawrence co., Tenn.; Appleton, Tenn. and West Point, Tenn.; was a private soldier in Capt. Frank Matthews Co. -captured at Ft. Donelson, exchanged with Bragg on his campaign -wounded at Chickamauga - was with Jas. F. Johnson at Atlanta, Hood on his campaign into Tenn.; son of John White and ____; Fall River, Lawrence co. Tenn.
5. Cinthia Caroline Shelton; Mark Shelton and ___; Scott's Hill, Giles co., Tenn.
6. John White, my grandfather, came to Lawrence co., Tenn. from Virginia. The Shelton's were of Irish lineage and came from East Tenn. They were old hard shell Baptist and boasted of many preachers among them. They were of that old type who carried the Bible in one side of the saddle bag and something to cheer the inner man in the other. No officers of the law was needed to enforce order, it was said of them that they stood ready to enforce good order and did so by means of personal force when necessary.
7. In a private school which my father maintained at Appleton for some ten years; Frank James was the only teacher. He taught through the ele-

mentary and some high school branches - stressed spelling, reading, public speaking, languages and math.
8. Attended a local normal school at Bodinham in Giles co. under R. E. Dotson, now a Pulaski lawyer; got an inscription from him for self education.
9. Studied law under Judge Jno. F. Morrison now County Judge of Lawrence Co., while teaching in Wayne co. in 1898 and 1899.
10. Lawyer - began practice in Lawrenceburg in 1900; had been a teacher for 11 years having begum in public schools of Lawrence co. when only a 14 year old; was a merchant part of the time before began law practice.
11. Was elected to Senate 1903; Co. Supt. of Education, Lawrence co. for some 8 years ; took office at salary of $250.00 which the County raised in recognition of my work to nearly $100.00 per year (increase?) in the middle of my 1st term; was elected Att'y. Gen. of 11th Judicial, 1918.
12. Not a reformer; consider reforms of doubtful value; think a return to the old and substantial principles given us by the fathers more important than so called reforms.
13. Democrat; was chairman of Co. Exec. Comm.; managed Gov. Taylor's campaign for Senate in Primary in county; also, Cox for Governor and Patterson (Pollison?) for Governor; always carried the county in all contests; member of Ex. Comm. Co. nearly all time since old enough to vote.
14. M. E. Church, South; believe in the plain religion taught by the Bible.
15. Knight of Pythias; Master of Exchequer of Lawrenceburg Lodge (Lodge dead)
16. None
17. Virginia Florence Simms; Judge James Abram Simms and Katrina Abigail Simms; Lawrenceburg, Tenn.; she was the daughter of Joel B. Drake, pioneer citizen of Lawrence co., Tenn.; of Irish extraction.
18. I volunteered to go to Ft. Oglethorpe to train as an officer in the World War; Lt. L. O. Crane and I were examined in Nashville at the same time; he was accepted - I was never called owing to Lawrence county's quota being taken up.
19. Job Garner White and Margaret Simms White, twins born May 10, 1902; both live with their parents in Lawrenceburg, Tenn.

WILLETT, CHARLES (1886 -)

1. Charles Willett
2. Springfield, Tenn.
3. Apr. 27, 1886, Springfield, Robertson co., Tenn.
4. Wm. H. Willett, Mechanicsburg, ___ co., Ohio; lived at Adams, Robertson co., Tenn.; was veteran of the Civil War and a practicing physician
5. Sarah Bell; Joel Bell and Laura Bell; Adams, Tenn.
6. ...
7. Red River High School, Adams, Tenn.
8. None
9. None - in college
10. Lawyer, admitted to the bar in 1911, practiced since at Springfield and Adams, Tenn.
11. Mayor of Adams, Tenn. 1917-1922
12. ...
13. Democrat
14. ...
15. Mason
16. ...
17. Single
18. Up for service when World War closed.
19. ....
(Signed: "myself", Dec. 7, 1922)

WILLIAMSON, JENNIE (1837-)
208 Foster St., N.E., Nashville, Tenn.
Jan. 28, 1922

1. Miss Jennie Williamson
2. Nashville, Tenn.
3. Nov. 18, 1837, Hartsville, Trousdale co., Tenn.
4. John Newton Williamson; Granville, Jackson co., Tenn.; Granville, Hartsville and Nashville, Tenn.; he was employed in the construction of

the State Capital and was one of the pallbearers at the funeral of Mr. Strickland (architect) of the building; son of Michael Williamson and Sallie Roper, Hartsville, Tenn. having come from North Carolina.
5. Sarah Pleas Fentress; James Fentress and Cynthia Lewis Walker, Gallatin, Tenn. where they moved from Richmond, Va.
6. My grandfather, the said James Fentress, was a soldier in the War of 1812 and was on Gen. Andrew Jackson's staff and with him at the Battle of New Orleans. I have heard my grandfather Fentress say he was also at Gen. Jackson's side and heard the General say "Don't fire until you can see the whites of their eyes", then he said, "Fight on my brave boys - in fifteen minutes the battle will be ours, all hell can't stop us." In 1844, Gen. Jackson gave a dinner at the Hermitage, and my grandfather Fentress was a guest. He took with him my father, the said John Newton Williamson, who said the house was open and settees on display;among other things that attracted my father's attention was a pistol with a cross mark on it - when questioned about it, the guard said it was the pistol which Gen. Jackson used in the duel with Dickerson (Dickinson?) and that he had marked it so he could tell it as he never wanted to use it again. My grandfather Fentress family came from France and settled in Virginia. He was American born. It is a matter of record that some of his descendants have been in every war since 1812. My grandfather named his youngest son for Gen. Jackson - Andrew Jackson Fentress...he is dead.
7. ...
8. ...
9. ...
10. ...
11. ...
12. ...
(Note: the answer to Q. #6 is written in these spaces)
13. Democrat
14. Member of the Christian Church, Foster St.
15. ...
16. ...
17. ...
18. ...
19. ...
(Note appended: "This Q. contains special verification of the language used by General Jackson at the Battle of New Orleans regarding his famour order to "wait until you see the whites of their eyes, etc.")

WILSON, BENJAMIN FRANKLIN (1876-1952)
Dec. 6, 1922

1. Benjamin Franklin Wilson
2. Clinton, Tenn.
3. July 31, 1876, Crooked Fork, Morgan co., Tenn.
4. Henry Campbell Wilson, Huntsville, Scott co., Tenn.; Robertsville, Tenn.; Baptist minister; Charles Wilson and Abba (Williams) Wilson, near Wartburg, Tenn.
5. Charlotte (Jones) Wilson; Samuel Jones and Sallie (Stonecipher) Jon s; Crooked Fork, Morgan co., Tenn.
6. All of Scotch-Irish descent
7. Common schools of Roane county, Tenn.
8. ...
9. ...
10. Life Insurance, New York Life, since 1918, prior occupation - Rural Letter Carrier for 14 years, began teaching the common schools at the age of 18. Taught for 8 years.
11. Member of Anderson County School Board 1907-1910; member Anderson co. Court 1912-1916; member next General Assembly.
12. ...
13. Elected Nov. 7, 1922 as joint representative from the counties of Anderson and Morgan without opposition.
14. Member Baptist church.
15. Mason, Odd Fellow, Jr. O. U. A. M. - at present Master Alpha Lodge F. & A. M., Clinton, Tenn.
16. ...
17. Dora K. Pyatt, married at Robertsville, Tenn., Dec. 1, 1898; Joseph

L. Pyatt and Amanda Peak, Robertsville, Tenn.; an old established family of Anderson county.
18. ...
19. Bernard A. Wilson (son), age 23, Check Clerk, Magnet Knitting Mills, Clinton, Tenn. Not married.
Joseph H. Wilson (son), age 20, student Knoxville Business College
Vola Grave Wilson (daughter), age 17, student Clinton High School

WINSOR, HENRY MORTIMER (fl. 1865-1922)
Box 159, Wayne, Michigan
March 21, 1923

1. Henry Mortimer Winsor
2. Wayne, Michigan, P. O. Box 159
3. March 21, ___, Dearborn, Wayne co., Michigan
4. Mortimer Dellville Winsor, state of Massachusetts; (on data on his grandparents and father, who lived somewhere near Bershirehills, Mass.)
5. Polly Secord; Henry Secord and Lydia Harris Secord; Van Buren township, Wayne co., Michigan
6. ...
7. In common schools (district)
8. ...
9. ...
10. ...
11. ...
12. ...
13. Democratic
14. Baptist
15. Odd Fellows, Past Grand Noble
16. ...
17. Anice French, married Jan. 1(?), 1869 in Nanking township, Wayne co. in Michigan; Montgomery Nichols French and Tirza Convis(?) French; Van-Buren, Wayne co., Michigan.
18. Private Co. D, 9th Mich. Cavalry, who were in 96 battles and skirmishes during the war, in which I was in the most of them, was guarding Ford on Okmulgee river when Jeff Davis was captured by the 4th Michigan Cavalry.
19. Minnie Frances Winsor, only child. Address - P. O. Box 159, Wayne, Michigan.

WISEMAN, JOHN DITCHLER (1892-1968)
Murfreesboro, Tenn.
Mar. 21, 1923

1. John Ditchler Wiseman
2. Murfreesboro, Tenn.
3. 9th day of Jan. 1892, near Lynchburg, Moore co., Tennessee
4. Wilburn Thomas Wiseman; near Scivally(?), Tenn.; Franklin co., Tenn. has lived near place of birth all his life.
5. Sarah Bean; Ezekiel Bean and ________; near Scivally, Tenn.
6. Both grandparents served in Confederate Army during the Civil War. Grandfather Wiseman was wounded in battle of Chickamauga or Missionary Ridge, as soon as war was over, prepared to return home, but blood poison developed from old wound and he died without returning home. Both grandparents farmers; grandmother Bean, who is near 90 years old, still living in Moore county. She was mother of 15 children.
7. In public schools of Moore co., Middle Tenn.; State Normal (School) at Murfreesboro; University of Chicago.
8. ...
9. ...
10. Att'y. at Law at Murfreesboro in 1919 after returning from army
11. No other office.
12. ...
13. Democrat - member of the 63rd General Assembly in Upper House, representing Rutherford, Cannon and DeKalb counties. Chairman of Committee on Public Utilities; on committees on education; enrolled Bills; Federal Relations; Finance; Way and Means; Judiciary; Privilages and Elections; Public Grounds and Buildings; Railroads and Redistricting.

14. Christian church
15. Fellowcraft Mason - preparing lecture for third degree.
16. ...
17. Sarah Moon Wiseman, married at Eagleville, Tenn., Mar. 19, 1920;dau. of Dr. J. R. Moon, Eagleville, Tenn.
18. Private in Co. A, 34th Engineers, Volunteered for service. Physically disqualified for overseas work and transfered out of Co. shortly before company sailed for France. Assigned to domestic duties. Regained health in army and offered Commission as First Lieutenant, but declined in order to remain a private.
19. Jno. D. Wiseman, Jr., born Jan. 21, 1923.

YOAKLEY, JESSE MAT (1871 -)
Jan. 8, 1923

1. Jessee Mat Yoakley
2. Blountville
3. Dec. 6, 1871, Blountville, Sullivan co., Tenn.
4. William Frederick Yoakley; Blountville, Sullivan co., Tenn.; Blountville, Tenn.; Pres. of Farmers Mutual Insurance of Sullivan County; Confederate soldier; Jessee C. Yoakley and Mary A. Hull; Blountville.
5. Elizabeth Bowman; Madison Bowman and Ibby Campbell; Blountville.
6. ...
7. Holston Institute High School
8. ...
9. ...
10. Farming
11. 1923, House of Representatives
12. ...
13. Democrat
14. Methodist South
15. F & A. M.; I.O.O.F.
16. ...
17. Virgie Kate King; married at Bristol, Tenn., Aug. 9, 1899; Edward Rutledge King and Mary Pauline Gross; Piney Flats, Tenn.
18. ...
19. Mary Eva Yoakley, Blountville, Tenn.
Nellie Kate Yoakley, Blountville, Tenn.
King Frederick Yoakley (King Frederick Yoakley died Jan. 13, 1923, age 17 years and 3 months.)

YORK, LAFAYETTE (1872 -)
Jan. 16, 1922

1. Lafayette York
2. Grimsley
3. Dec. 25, 1872, Somerset, Ky., Pulaski co., Kentucky
4. ....
5. Margret Price; Nathaniel Price and Nancy Price; Somerset, Ky.
6. Nathaniel Price died during the Civil War; rank - Sergeant
7. Common school education obtained at Beatland, Tenn.; teachers - Greena Hudleston, E. J. Wright.
8. ...
9. ...
10. ...
11. Was County Road Commissioner in 1907-1908; was constable in 1917-1918
12. ...
13. Republican
14. ...
15. ...
16. ...
17. Etta Beaty, married at Bannersprings, Tenn., Aug. 13, 1899; Jesse Beaty and Jane Richards; Grimsley, Tenn.; grandparents - Flem Beaty and Sarah Cod(?) Beaty; John and Nancy Franklin Richards.
18. Private; Captain John W. Staples; I was enrolled July 7th, 1898 and stationed at Camp Bob Taylor at Knoxville, Tenn. and went from Knoxville to Savannah, Ga. and from there to Cuba.
19. Nora York — Anabelle York
Arnold York — Rosaline York

INDEX
PROMINENT TENNESSEANS

Colleen Morse Elliott
Fort Worth, Texas